Of Conflict and Concealment

 McMaster Divinity College Press
**McMaster Biblical Studies Series,
Volume 5**

Of Conflict and Concealment
The Gospel of Mark as Tragedy

ADAM Z. WRIGHT

☙PICKWICK *Publications* • Eugene, Oregon

OF CONFLICT AND CONCEALMENT
The Gospel of Mark as Tragedy

McMaster Biblical Studies Series, Volume 5
McMaster Divinity College Press

Copyright © 2020 Adam Z. Wright. All rights reserved. Except for brief quotations in critical publications or reviews, no part of this book may be reproduced in any manner without prior written permission from the publisher. Write: Permissions, Wipf and Stock Publishers, 199 W. 8th Ave., Suite 3, Eugene, OR 97401.

Pickwick Publications
An Imprint of Wipf and Stock Publishers
199 W. 8th Ave., Suite 3
Eugene, OR 97401

McMaster Divinity College Press
1280 Main Street West
Hamilton, Ontario, Canada
L8S 4K1

www.wipfandstock.com

PAPERBACK ISBN: 978-1-7252-5722-1
HARDCOVER ISBN: 978-1-7252-5723-8
EBOOK ISBN: 978-1-7252-5724-5

Cataloguing-in-Publication data:

Names: Wright, Adam Z, author.

Title: Of conflict and concealment : the Gospel of Mark as tragedy / Adam Z. Wright.

Description: Eugene, OR: Pickwick Publications, 2020. | McMaster Biblical Studies Series 5. | Includes bibliographical references and indexes.

Identifiers: ISBN 978-1-7252-5722-1 (paperback). | ISBN 978-1-7252-5723-8 (hardcover). | ISBN 978-1-7252-5724-5 (ebook).

Subjects: LCSH: Bible.—Mark—Criticism, interpretation, etc. | Greek drama (Tragedy)—Criticism, interpretation, etc.

Classification: BS2585.52 W75 2020 (print). | BS2585.52 (ebook).

10/23/20

Contents

Acknowledgements / vii

Abbreviations / viii

Introduction / 1

1 How Tragic has Jesus Been? A Summary of Scholarly Opinion / 12

2 The Prevalence of Tragedy: From Ancient Greece to the Twentieth Century / 42

3 The Elements of Tragedy / 76

4 Hiddenness and Recognition / 111

5 Miracles and Tragedy / 148

6 The Tragic Son of Man / 180

7 Final Conclusions Concerning Mark's Genre: The Tragic Christ / 206

Bibliography / 211

Index of Modern Authors / 225

Index of Ancient Sources / 229

Acknowledgements

THERE ARE A LARGE number of people to whom I am very thankful for their support and encouragement. First and foremost, I would like to thank my family: Mom and Dad, Jarrett and Desmond, Melissa, Abram, and Hudson—it is because of you that I have accomplished anything in this life. I would also like to thank the faculty and staff at McMaster Divinity College, and my esteemed colleagues Hughson Ong, David Yoon, Josh Walker, and Jamie Robertson for their friendship and continual support. I want to especially thank Stanley E. Porter and Christopher D. Land for their guidance and support throughout this process. The lessons that each of you have taught me are of the highest value.

Abbreviations

AB	Anchor Bible
ANRW	Temporini, Hildegard, and Wolfgang Haase, eds. *Aufstieg und Niedergang der römischen Welt: Geschichte und Kultur Roms im Spiegel der neueren Forschung*. Part 2, Principat. Berlin: de Gruyter, 1972–.
APATS	American Philological Association Textbook Series
BBR	*Bulletin for Biblical Research*
Bib	*Biblica*
BibInt	*Biblical Interpretation*
BSGRT	Bibliotheca Scriptorum Graecorum et Romanorum Teubneriana
CBQ	*Catholic Biblical Quarterly*
CE	*College English*
ChrCent	*Christian Century*
EB	Encyclopedia Britannica
For	Forum
HSCP	*Harvard Studies in Classical Philology*
HTR	*Harvard Theological Review*
HTS	Harvard Theological Studies
HUCA	*Hebrew Union College Annual*
HUT	Hermeneutische Untersuchungen zur Theologie
HvTSt	*Hervormde teologiese studies*

Abbreviations

IGR	*Inscriptiones Graecae ad res Romanas pertinentes*. Vols. 1, 4. Paris: Leroux, 1906–1927.
ILS	Dessau, Hermann, ed. *Inscriptiones Latinae Selectae*. 3 vols. Berlin: Apud Weidmannos, 1892–1916.
Int	*Interpretation*
JAAR	*Journal of the American Academy of Religion*
JBL	*Journal of Biblical Literature*
JGRChJ	*Journal of Greco-Roman Christianity and Judaism*
JJS	*Journal for Jewish Studies*
JR	*Journal of Religion*
JRH	*Journal of Religious History*
JSNT	*Journal for the Study of the New Testament*
JSNTSup	Journal for the Study of the New Testament Supplement Series
Lat	*Latomus*
LCL	Loeb Classical Library
LNTS	The Library of New Testament Studies
NovT	*Novum Testamentum*
NovTSup	Supplements to Novum Testamentum
ResQ	*Restoration Quarterly*
PRSt	*Perspectives in Religious Studies*
RL	*Religion & Literature*
RevExp	*Review and Expositor*
SBLDS	Society of Biblical Literature Dissertation Series
SBLMS	Society of Biblical Literature Monograph Series
SBT	Studies in Biblical Theology
SJLA	Studies in Judaism in Late Antiquity
SNTSMS	Society of New Testament Studies Monograph Series
Sound	*Soundings*
StPB	Studia Post-biblica
TBT	*The Bible Today*
TynBul	*Tyndale Bulletin*

Abbreviations

Via	*Viator*
WBC	Word Biblical Commentary
WCB	World Christian Books
WUNT	Wissenschaftliche Untersuchungen zum Neuen Testament
WW	*Word and World*
ZNW	*Zeitschrift für die neutestamentliche Wissenschaft und die Kunde der älteren Kirche*
ZTK	*Zeitschrift für Theologie und Kirche*

Introduction

AN INTRODUCTION TO THE CONCEPT OF TRAGEDY: IS MARK'S GOSPEL A TRAGEDY?

THE WORD *TRAGEDY* CAN be attributed to a large number of things and circumstances. We currently live in a world that seems infused with tragedy, a world in which the radical group ISIS is waging a war of religious terror through murder and threats of violence. It is a world in which many people continue to be subjugated and marginalized because of the color of their skin, their gender, and even their birthplace. Economic depression forces many to choose between buying food for their families or paying for the home in which they live. We live in a time of great uncertainty, a time when things may not be as they seem due to constant warnings of "fake news." We live in a tragic time, a time when one is confronted by the burden of their anxieties.

One of the most fundamental questions that humanity strives to answer is why we suffer.[1] This is a question that has demanded an unfathomable amount of attention and has garnered a large number of answers. But regardless of whatever answer one may come up with, the

1. Even throughout the Enlightenment, a large number of literary critics began to revisit fundamental questions about the ways that humanity coped despite their inevitable suffering, and many philosophers—not least of these being Nietzsche, Hegel, Kierkegaard, Freud, Jung, Heidegger, Frye, and Gadamer—began to turn to the tragedies for answers. There were also many attempts to emulate the Greek tragedians, with more modern versions of tragedy being penned by Shakespeare, Goethe, Brontë, Tolstoy, Nabokov, Dostoevsky, and Miller, to name a few. Tragedy has been at the forefront of both philosophy and literary theory for nearly two and a half millenia, a duration of time that tells us that there is something extremely valuable within it.

truth is that life is difficult and it is full of suffering, and it will *continue* to be difficult and full of suffering.

The ancients created an interesting way of examining life's suffering through the written and spoken word in the genre of tragedy. The Greek lexeme τραγῳδία (tragedy) originally meant "goat song," and it referred to the activities that occurred during certain religious festivals that celebrated the Greek god Dionysus through a goat sacrifice, a series of dances, and the drinking of wine. The death of the goat was meant to symbolize the death of one's trouble, and the dancing and drinking of wine symbolized the joy of rebirth from said trouble. At some point later on, this goat song evolved into what we might imagine when we think of "staged tragedy": a drama acted on stage by various actors which depicts a series of unfortunate events. These staged tragedies were performed at certain religious festivals and eventually achieved such eminence that competitions were created in order to judge the best tragic performance, giving rise to some of the most prominent names in Greek literature: Aeschylus, Sophocles, and Euripides. Of the surviving tragedies from the ancient world, most belong to these three significant writers. In fact, these writers were so prominent that they are featured in Aristotle's famous description of Attic tragedy entitled *Poetics*.

But just how does the study of tragedy relate to the study of the Gospels? I believe that the answer to this question can be found in what the ancients understood tragedy to be. An ancient tragedy is not simply a description of an occurrence that leads to the protagonist's downfall. Tragedy is an expression of overcoming life's suffering by engaging with and succumbing to it. Said another way, tragedy teaches us that suffering might be a useful tool to bring about a greater good. It is therefore a lesson that a life without progress can be harmful and one must continually progress in order to live a satisfying life. This is often why we find a tragic hero in conflict with some authority, be it an established religious institution, a government, or even the hero's own belief system or actions. The audience is then forced to contemplate the conflict between these two positions: one that has traditionally been accepted as ethically and morally viable, and one that contains within it the potential for a greater good. This is why, historically speaking,

Introduction

tragedies are written during a time of great social transition such as the Athenian democratic revolution or the destruction of the temple in Jerusalem. The story of Jesus in Mark is therefore not simply a biographical notation, as some have suggested[2]—this is not enough to explain the elements found within. It is instead an account of the triumph of a tragic hero that challenges a religious, political, and social system by introducing new potential, the kingdom of God.

The religious system that had governed the Jews since the time of Moses had failed, and Israel awaited its messiah to correct that which had gone wrong. Failure to maintain its rigorous laws had left Jerusalem a slave to Rome, its people bound by demonic forces and subject to sickness and impurity. However, with every healing miracle and exorcism, Jesus begins to establish a new kingdom by freeing Israel's people from the laws that divided and marginalized them. He taught a new way of thinking that confounded the religious elite and weakened Rome's grip, all while maintaining peace and solidarity amongst his followers. His was not an insurrection through violence, but the command to love one another issued an incredible violence to those who would rule by the sword. Jesus presented an ideal that no government or religious institution had been able to achieve. And, as tragedies often go, Jesus is killed because of what he did and said. However, proof that the new kingdom had been established was given when God fled the temple, giving way to the resurrection of Jesus.[3]

The resurrection of Jesus communicates two incredible truths that Aeschylus, Sophocles, and Euripides also sought to illustrate: that suffering the loss of a way of life is sometimes essential to the betterment of an individual and of society; and that potential is often obscured by traditional ways of thinking that make it unrecognizable. This is why Jesus remains mostly unrecognizable throughout the narrative, and it

---

2. More will be said below, but I direct the reader's attention to a number of more recent sources. See Burridge, *Gospels*; Licona, *Why are There Differences in the Gospels?*; Talbert, *What is a Gospel?*; Kennedy, "Classical," 125–55; Shuler, *A Genre*; Frickenschmidt, *Evangelism als Biographie*; Keener, "Targeted Comparison," 331–56.

3. This is often referred to as the "hero's boon," a concept that was popularized through the work of Joseph Campbell. One can find a discussion of this concept in Campbell, *The Hero*, 148–65.

creates an incredible amount of irony when the people who need to recognize the potential of the kingdom do not.

TRAGIC PLOT AND ITS THREE ELEMENTS

Since tragedy embodies the spirit of social, political, and religious change, the next question is how tragedy expresses these changes through plot. As mentioned, Mark's Gospel is not simply a recounting of the biographical events that occurred during a single year of Jesus' life—such a view is far too simplistic. Instead, Mark's Gospel is rife with tragic elements that are carefully and thoughtfully employed. This study advances the discussion of genre by arguing that Mark contains three specific tragic elements that have not been explicitly examined, and these include: suffering, conflict, and the elevated character-type of the tragic protagonist.

Each of these elements is critical to the plot because they are abstractions of things we find in reality. It has already been mentioned that life is full of suffering, and tragedy teaches a person how to think about it. Conflict with others is also a part of reality but, more importantly, tragic conflict embodies the internal, heart-breaking choices that one faces during a time of great change. The elevated protagonist, what Aristotle calls a *spoudean* character type,[4] exceeds the status of everyone else in the story. This is important because the members of the audience associate themselves with the protagonist, and it is from this position that the protagonist teaches the audience how to think about the conflict and suffering that they encounter in reality.

Plot as Related to Catharsis

This gives rise to the concept of *catharsis*. Since the elements of tragic plot are considered abstractions, the question then becomes how such abstractions are supposed to affect the audience. According to Aristotle, viewing a tragedy produces a purging, or *catharsis*, of the emotions pity and fear.[5] The problem with consulting Aristotle on this question

---

4. *Spoudean* is an adjective based on the Greek word σπουδαῖος found in *Poet.* 1448b.

5. Aristotle, *Poet.* 1449b.23–28. Pity is an appropriate emotional response to watching a hero suffer as a result of a virtuous cause, and fear follows because the

Introduction

is that he never explains exactly what he means. However, when one considers how the elements of tragedy are abstractions for reality, *catharsis* is then defined as the process by which a person confronts the realities of suffering—as the hero—with the hope of transcending it.[6] Therefore, by recognizing suffering as the first step towards bettering oneself and society, one is more readily able to descend into the belly of the whale, so to speak.[7] The underlying principle is that a person must perform a kind of self-annihilation (depicted by being swallowed) in order to solve the problem or to save others.[8] Tragedy functions exactly this way: a person must confront their own suffering in a heroic way in order to discover the cause of the suffering and alleviate its symptoms. Tragedy is therefore not simply a viewing of tragic circumstances in which people suffer, it is instead a means by which the audience learns to confront their own suffering. This is a complex task and the process by which one does this can be extremely painful, especially if one discovers that they, much like Jonah, are the cause of the tragic circumstance. This is precisely what Aristotle meant when he spoke of pity and fear as the proper emotions that a person ought to experience while viewing a tragedy. Through the experience described above, a person is able to purge such emotions as pity and fear by applying the abstracted truths found within tragedy to their own lives.[9]

---

same could happen to *me*. However, both of these emotions are purged when one considers how suffering can lead to potential through truthful speech. On an individual level, suffering and death are then abstracted as doing away with some part of the self, while resurrection is abstracted as the process of retooling some part of the self into something more productive and beneficial than the last.

6. In this sense, Christ is then abstracted as the part of the self that remains constant throughout the various changes since he is the embodiment of the eternal.

7. Campbell, *The Hero*, 74. This process is illustrated countless times within the stories of heroes in what Campbell calls descending into the "belly of the whale." Each hero must confront some form of suffering, either within him- or herself or on behalf of their community, and this process is depicted as entering into the mouth of a horrendous beast, such as in the case of Herakles entering the mouth of the sea monster to save Hesione, or Jonah who literally enters the mouth of a whale before he saves Nineveh.

8. Campbell, *The Hero*, 77.

9. As will be discussed below, Aristotle does not go into much detail about what this means, and he promises to return to it though he never does. This gives rise to a number of questions as to whether we have lost some of Aristotle's work, or whether

This leads to another important aspect of how these emotions can be purged, and this is through truthful speech or thinking truthfully. When Oedipus discovers that Thebes is suffering because of some treachery, Oedipus strives to discover what the cause of the suffering is. However, he is unwilling to face the truth of the matter even though he is confronted with it. Once he learns the truth, namely that he is the problem, he takes lethal action against himself and cures the plague. In Mark, Jesus is portrayed as a great teacher who has amazing powers, and the thrust of his potency as a speaker and miracle worker is related to his ability to tell the truth. To understand the kingdom of God is no simple task and not everyone will understand the means by which one can attain it, nor might they be willing to do the necessary actions to achieve it. Though on the surface Jesus and Oedipus may have little in common, each purges the problems that face their societies by telling the truth, which leads to conflict, suffering, and death.

TRAGEDY AS GENRE

Tragic Genre versus Tragic Mode

In this study, I argue that Mark exclusively belongs to the tragic genre. This rejects the notion that Mark contains within it simply a *mode* of tragedy; that is to say, Mark is not an amalgam of different genres. In addition to what has been mentioned above, my argument centers around how the motif of hiddenness is utilized throughout the entire narrative. As will be discussed, this has been a question that has been debated throughout the twentieth century with no consensus. The hiddenness motif raises a number of questions regarding why Jesus' identity is not recognized by those he preaches to and why he consistently commands that his identity remain a secret. I think there are two main reasons for a hiddenness motif. The first is that potential solutions to problems are not obvious and are often overlooked, meaning that a lack of recognition in the Gospel is a keen abstraction for not recognizing the solution to one's own problems. The second relates to how Jesus' identity *must* remain a secret until his death and resurrection which, referring again

---

he simply forgot to return to this important subject. It is also possible that he did not know the answer to the question of how *catharsis* occurs. Regardless of the answer, it is reasonable to suggest that *catharsis* refers to what I have described here.

Introduction

to Campbell's analogy of the whale, signifies the end of the suffering, death, resurrection cycle that the tragic hero must traverse. If Jesus is truly recognized as the Messiah and Son of God, then his death and resurrection might not have been achieved.

Tragedy versus Biography

I mentioned above that many scholars regard the Gospels as ancient forms of biography. Indeed, these theories have garnered much support and produced many fascinating studies that elucidate the ancient genre of biography and apply it to the Gospels. Many of these studies appeal to Plutarch's *Lives*, most likely because he was a contemporary to the Gospel writers. However, I remain unconvinced that these theories apply to Mark and, in this brief section, I aim to explain why Mark has more in common with the genre of tragedy than Plutarch's biographies.

The primary reason for why Mark ought to be considered a tragedy instead of a biography is that Mark's Gospel is not actually concerned with the life of Jesus. It is, instead, primarily concerned with the conflict that arises as a result of his ministry. When one reads Plutarch's *Life of Caesar*, more attention is paid to the intimate details of Caesar's life—much more than Jesus in Mark. For example, in the third section of *Life of Caesar*, we learn many things with regard to his life and accomplishments:

> ἐκ δὲ τούτου τῆς Σύλλα δυνάμεως ἤδη μαραινομένης καὶ τῶν οἴκοι καλούντων αὐτὸν ἔπλευσεν εἰς Ῥόδον ἐπὶ σχολὴν πρὸς Ἀπολλώνιον τὸν τοῦ Μόλωνος, οὗ καὶ Κικέρων ἠκρόατο, σοφιστεύοντος ἐπιφανῶς καὶ τὸν τρόπον ἐπιεικοῦς εἶναι δοκοῦντος, λέγεται δὲ καὶ φῦναι πρὸς λόγους πολιτικοὺς ὁ Καῖσαρ ἄριστα, καὶ διαπονῆσαι φιλοτιμότατα τὴν φύσιν, ὡς τὰ δευτερεῖα μὲν ἀδηρίτως ἔχειν, τὸ δὲ πρωτεῖον, ὅπως τῇ δυνάμει καὶ τοῖς ὅπλοις πρῶτος εἴη μᾶλλον ἀσχοληθείς, ἀφεῖναι, πρὸς ὅπερ ἡ φύσις ὑφηγεῖτο τῆς ἐν τῷ λέγειν δεινότητος, ὑπὸ στρατειῶν καὶ πολιτείας, ᾗ κατεκτήσατο τὴν ἡγεμονίαν, οὐκ ἐξικόμενος. αὐτὸς δ᾽ οὖν ὕστερον ἐν τῇ πρὸς Κικέρωνα περὶ Κάτωνος ἀντιγραφῇ παραιτεῖται μὴ στρατιωτικὸν λόγον ἀνδρὸς ἀντεξετάζειν πρὸς δεινότητα ῥήτορος εὐφυοῦς καὶ σχολὴν ἐπὶ τοῦτο πολλὴν ἄγοντος.

Of Conflict and Concealment

After this, Sulla's power being now on the wane, and Caesar's friends at home inviting him to return, Caesar sailed to Rhodes to study under Apollonius the son of Molon, an illustrious rhetorician with the reputation of a worthy character, of whom Cicero also was a pupil. It is said, too, that Caesar had the greatest natural talent for political oratory, and cultivated his talent most ambitiously, so that he had an undisputed second rank; the first rank, however, he renounced, because he devoted his efforts to being first as a statesman and commander rather, and did not achieve that effectiveness in oratory to which his natural talent directed him, in consequence of his campaigns and of his political activities, by means of which he acquired the supremacy. And so it was that, at a later time, in his reply to Cicero's "Cato," he himself deprecated comparison between the diction of a soldier and the eloquence of an orator who was gifted by nature and had plenty of leisure to pursue his studies (3.1–4).

From this, we learn that Caesar studied rhetoric with Apollonius at Rhodes, became himself a master of oratory, earned a second rank in rhetorical ability, preferred the status of a statesman and commander, and had interactions with Cicero. Mark's author does not do this, and he gives us no information about his birth, his upbringing, those people he surrounded himself with, his genealogy, nor his habits. Mark simply introduces his audience to Jesus as the Messiah and Son of God, after which he adds little to no biographical information. This may be a result of Plutarch's motives which he describes in his *Life of Theseus*:

> εἴη μὲν οὖν ἡμῖν ἐκκαθαιρόμενον λόγῳ τὸ μυθῶδες ὑπακοῦσαι καὶ λαβεῖν ἱστορίας ὄψιν, ὅπου δ᾽ ἂν αὐθαδῶς τοῦ πιθανοῦ περιφρονῇ καὶ μὴ δέχηται τὴν πρὸς τὸ εἰκὸς μῖξιν, εὐγνωμόνων ἀκροατῶν δεησόμεθα καὶ πρᾴως τὴν ἀρχαιολογίαν προσδεχομένων.

> May I therefore succeed in purifying Fable, making her submit to reason and take on the semblance of History. But where she obstinately disdains to make herself credible, and refuses to admit any element of probability, I shall pray for kindly

Introduction

readers, and such as receive with indulgence the tales of antiquity (1.3).

It is clear that Plutarch is interested in separating historical fact from mythology (fable) and aims to present the life of Theseus along the vein of history. Again, the author of Mark makes no introductory remarks concerning his motive and simply tells the story of Jesus and his conflict with the religious elite.

The open lines of Mark (1:1–15) read more like the introduction to a drama, an example being the opening lines of the *Bacchae*:

ἥκω Διὸς παῖς τήνδε Θηβαίων χθόνα
Διόνυσος, ὃν τίκτει ποθ᾽ ἡ Κάδμου κόρη
Σεμέλη λοχευθεῖσ᾽ ἀστραπηφόρῳ πυρί:
μορφὴν δ᾽ ἀμείψας ἐκ θεοῦ βροτησίαν
πάρειμι Δίρκης νάματ᾽ Ἰσμηνοῦ θ᾽ ὕδωρ.

Behold, God's Son is come unto this land
Of Thebes, even I, Dionysus, whom the brand
Of heaven's hot splendor lit to life, when she
Who bore me, Cadmus' daughter Semelê,
Died here. So, changed in shape from God to man,
I walk again by Dirce's streams and scan Ismenus' shore (1–6).

Here Dionysus is introduced as one who has come to the city of Thebes and, having taken the shape of a human rather than that of a god, aims to reestablish his rites. These lines are essential for understanding the actions of Dionysus that result in the eventual conflict with the antagonist. In much the same way, Mark introduces Jesus as the Son of God and Messiah (v. 1) who is recognized by God (v. 11) as one who will establish his kingdom (v. 15) and, much like the *Bacchae*, it is the conflict between Jesus as his opponents that is of central importance.

The purpose of these comparisons has been to highlight some fundamental differences between ancient biography and tragedy. These are by no means exhaustive, but they serve to highlight some of the fundamental differences that concern content: biographies are primarily concerned with the intimate details about a person that leads to their actions, whereas tragedy is primarily concerned with the conflict that their protagonists endure.[10] While the genre of ancient biography might well describe what is found within other Gospels,[11] it is more plausible that Mark wanted to highlight the conflict that arose between Jesus and his opponents.[12]

The Structure of Argument

In what follows, I will elucidate some of the points made in this brief introduction. The first chapter begins with a summary of the various articles and books which have also argued that Mark's Gospel belongs to the tragic genre. This will help orient the reader and will make clear how my research pushes the discussion forward.

The second chapter includes a summary of the various scholars, both ancient and modern, who have discussed tragic theory. This is important because it illustrates just how prevalent tragedy is, in addition to why certain authors choose to write about certain topics in the tragic genre. This summary will also touch on a number of crucial points with regard to the essential elements discussed on the third chapter. If we are to regard Mark as a tragedy, chapters 2 and 3 argue why.

The fourth chapter goes into detail about how Mark's plot incorporates conflict, which is one of the essential elements of tragedy. More

---

10. In fact, Plutarch emphasizes this point in his *Life of Alexander* when he says, "For it is not Histories that I am writing, but Lives; and in the most illustrious deeds there is not always a manifestation of virtue or vice, nay, a slight thing like a phrase or a jest often makes a greater revelation of character than battles when thousands fall, or the greatest armaments, or sieges of cities" (1.2). As mentioned, Mark's Gospel is not concerned with the intricate details of Jesus' life, only those that are essential to the plot.

11. The introduction of Plutarch's *Lives* strikes one as having more in common with the opening remarks of Luke–Acts, which begins with a footnote from the author that describes his intentions.

12. One may also note that Mark does not provide any form of lineage from which we can garner any perspective on Jesus' life. This appears contrary to Matthew and Luke's Gospels, which each provide a lineage that places Jesus within a rich history of important Jewish figures—even John's Gospel provides some context for Jesus' preexistent nature. Mark, on the other hand, introduces Jesus at some point during his life with no other explanation other than he is the Christ, the Son of God (1:1). Again, this is quite similar to how we are introduced to other tragic protagonists where are not given much context unless those characters have appeared in previous myths or tragedies, such as the *Bacchae*, *Oedipus the King*, and *Oedipus at Colonus*.

Introduction

specifically, Jesus enters into conflict with the temple establishment, which incorporates its representatives, rules and regulations, and the temple itself as the center of the worship and sacrifice.

The fifth chapter illustrates how the performance of miracles is essential to how Jesus engages with the temple establishment in conflict. The miracles, particularly the healing miracles, serve as a means to further establish Jesus' position against the temple, as well as serve to antagonize the religious leaders which leads to Jesus' arrest.

The sixth chapter aims to elucidate the motif of secrecy and recognition in the narrative. Jesus conducts a number of miracles and exorcisms, as well as a large number of speeches, but goes largely unrecognized by the general populace as the Christ, the Son of God. Instead, the reader becomes puzzled by the irony of the key recognition points: Jesus is recognized by demons and a Centurion but not by the people of Israel. This places special emphasis on Peter's recognition of Jesus as the Christ, but such recognition signals the opposite of what Peter expects of Israel's messiah.

It is reasonable to conclude that previous research into Mark's Gospel has not satisfactorily addressed the question of genre. It is much more plausible that Mark's genre is that of tragedy, and tragedy is an appropriate genre because it addresses the fundamental nature of life itself. Not only this, it will be shown that tragedy embodies a philosophy about the nature of life itself, a topic that Jesus addresses throughout Mark's Gospel. Because of this, I am arguing that Mark's Gospel has most in common with the ancient genre of tragedy. Though this is not necessarily a new theory, this study advances the discussion in a number of ways. In what follows, it becomes clear that the Gospel of Mark portrays the Jewish Messiah and Son of God issuing in the kingdom of God through the most important processes that humanity can fathom as a solution to a life that Thomas Hobbes once so eloquently called: "solitary, nasty, brutish, and short."[13]

---

13. Hobbes, *Leviathan*, 13.9.

1

How Tragic has Jesus Been?

A Summary of Scholarly Opinion

INTRODUCTION

THERE ARE A NUMBER of studies that have compared Mark with ancient tragedy and each of these studies provides an insightful description of Mark's plot.[1] This was an important achievement in the study of Mark because it showcases that Mark's Gospel is not simply a collection of stories about Jesus arbitrarily fitted together. Instead, Mark's plot is discernible and each of the authors in this section argue that the plot has most in common with ancient forms of tragedy. I mention these studies here because they provide the state of play with regard to how and why many scholars view Mark as belonging to the genre of ancient tragedy.

In what follows, I provide a detailed analysis of each study. If it is accepted that a structured plot is present in Mark's Gospel, criteria must be established by which we can make accurate comparisons with Greek tragedy. This is why most studies that have compared Mark's Gospel with Greek tragedy appeal directly to Aristotle's *Poetics*, which

---

1. See Burch, "Tragic Action," 346–58; Beach, *Gospel of Mark*, 48–51; Moser, "Mark's Gospel," 528–33; Lang, "Kompositionsanalyse," 1–24; Standaert, *L'Evangile*; Smith, "Divine Tragedy," 209–31; Bilezikian, *Liberated Gospel*; Stone, "Mark and Oedipus," 55–69; Schwartz, "Christian Tragedy," 208–13; Cherbonnier, "Idea of Tragedy," 23–55; Sorrentino, "God's Cosmic Drama," 432–50; Jay, *Tragic*.

provides the most comprehensive description of fifth-century Attic tragedy. At this point, scholars are able to compare and contrast Mark and tragedy by way of the *Poetics*, and draw conclusions based on their observations.

Another important feature found within these studies is the comparison of Jesus and the tragic hero. Much like an analysis of plot, a comparison of tragic protagonists requires criteria by which we can compare Jesus with other tragic heroes. This is more difficult than an analysis of plot, however, because the poets do not say much with regard to the character of their tragic heroes, and we are left to discern their character only from within the context of plot. Yet, Aristotle's *Poetics* continues to play a large part in this aspect of comparing Mark with tragedy.

THE GOSPEL OF MARK AND GREEK TRAGEDY

The first study that I will consider is Ernest Burch's 1931 essay entitled "Tragic Action in the Second Gospel: A Study in the Narrative of Mark." In it, he concludes that "the Man of Nazareth is to be classed among the outstanding tragic figures of the race, an accompanying conclusion being that the Second Gospel comes under the classification of Greek tragedy."[2]

He begins by centering his study around the plot of Mark's Gospel as well as Jesus' correspondence to the ideal tragic hero, and he does so by appealing to Aristotle's *Poetics*. One of the problems that Burch addresses is why Mark's Gospel appears to have a different form from that used in Greek tragedy. For example, Burch notes that the Gospel "is not divided into acts and scenes, consists only in part of dialogue, has no stage directions, and lacks the 'embellishment of song,' unless, with some, a kind of Hebrew parallelism be discovered in certain verses."[3] Burch avoids this problem by calling Mark's Gospel a "closet drama"—that is, "a drama whose power is felt by the reader without stage presentation."[4]

---

2. Burch, "Tragic Action," 346.
3. Burch, "Tragic Action," 346.
4. Burch, "Tragic Action," 346.

Burch divides the contents of Mark's plot into two halves. The first half (1:1—8:30) consists of the Galilean ministry and it presents the action of the tragedy of Jesus. The hero's fortune, however, changes with his words in 8:31, where Jesus announces to his disciples that he must be rejected and killed. This announcement contrasts sharply with the messianic expectation that Burch ascribes to the disciples and Peter's recognition provides the opportunity for Jesus to expound on the meaning of his messianism.

The second half (8:31—16:8) is quite different from the first. Burch describes this section as containing "murky and shadowy premonitions, skulking figures, treachery within the band, double-edged questions from inquiring scribes and at last definite conspiracy on the part of the hierarchy."[5] This leads to what Burch calls the tragic incident, which includes the trial, condemnation, and crucifixion.[6] Both halves of the Gospel contain a number of bystanders which Burch likens to a chorus. These can include the crowds who comment upon the action, or even the disciples who offer "Chorus-like" comments.[7] The chorus in Mark's Gospel thus serves to add prominence to a particular scene. For example, the disciples verbally ponder the character of Jesus after he calms the storm by saying, "Who, then, is this, whom even the winds and the sea obey?" (4:41). This question heightens the dramatic effect of the scene similarly to how the chorus in Greek tragedy operates.[8] Burch then highlights several other examples (1:27; 2:12b; 7:37; 8:27–30; 9:5–7) during which the crowds attempt to connect Jesus' actions with his character.

Next, Burch discusses Jesus as a tragic protagonist and asks whether Jesus meets the requirements of the ideal tragic hero. To do so, Burch consults Aristotle, who lays out the characteristics of the tragic hero in the thirteenth chapter of his *Poetics*. "The ideal hero is neither extremely good nor utterly bad," says Burch, "but rather inclines toward the

---

5. Burch, "Tragic Action," 350.

6. Burch ("Tragic Action," 351) suggests that these categories are analogous to Aristotle's definitions found in *Poet.* 6.6.

7. Burch, "Tragic Action," 352.

8. Burch ("Tragic Action," 252) notes the *Antigone*, in which the chorus comments on how the body of Polyneices had been improperly buried: "I had misgivings from the first, my liege, of Something more than natural at work" (2.278).

good and is preferably of exalted station in life."[9] This equally excludes a blameless or bad person from a proper tragic plot because neither provoke the kinds of emotions typical of tragedy. Thus, a proper tragic hero—according to Burch—is a human being of elevated social status. The hero "must be human, like the spectators or readers of the tragedy, else he cannot inspire in them the appropriate emotions."[10] This means the hero must meet his or her fate through some type of error in judgment and "not through sin."[11]

This forces one to reconsider what it means for Jesus to be "sinless." In response, Burch points out that Jesus' sinlessness is never mentioned in Mark's Gospel. Instead, Jesus' genuine humanity is stressed so that it may be possible to identify a tragic error.[12] It is also true that certain tragic heroes—namely Antigone—serve admirably as fully human and blameless protagonists.

Burch continues his analysis of the tragic nature of Mark's Gospel by suggesting that the resurrection could also be seen as something which could obscure the tragic nature of Mark. He says this for two reasons. The first reason is that the resurrection forms the beginning of a new story, and the second reason is that the resurrection offers an "anticlimax" to the tragic story that Mark offers.[13] With regard to both reasons, Burch appeals to Aristotle's eighth chapter in the *Poetics* and suggests that a tragedy cannot end happily.[14] If the resurrection offers a "new story," as Burch suggests, then Mark's Gospel has no definitive end.

Does Jesus fit the mold of the tragic hero? The blameless Jesus proceeds to accomplish his mission despite the throes of death in much the same way that Antigone challenges the established order to accomplish her ends. It is the *persistence* of each hero that causes their downfall and this persistence can thus be identified as their flaw. This may be the most likely identification of a tragic "flaw" in Mark, and it

9. Burch, "Tragic Action," 353.
10. Burch, "Tragic Action," 353.
11. Burch, "Tragic Action," 353.
12. Burch, "Tragic Action," 353.
13. Burch, "Tragic Action," 355.
14. Burch, "Tragic Action," 355.

is highlighted in the many controversy sections throughout the Gospel (2:1—3:6; 11:27–33; 12:13–40).[15] With regards to these, Burch is satisfied with the suggestion that Jesus fulfills—at least in part—the classic requirements for a tragic protagonist.

The final question is whether the action in Mark functions like that of tragedy. As I mentioned above, the tragic hero must be a believable one in that the audience has to be able to relate. When the hero passes from life to death or from prosperity to adversity, the audience ought to be moved to pity or fear. It is the contact between the hero and his audience that indicates that tragedy is actually a universal human experience. Burch suggests as much when he says that "pity in a real sense is felt not for the man hanging on the cross so much as for the man who prophesies his own fate yet continues resolutely upon the fateful path."[16]

I think Burch has an excellent point here because this type of pity is much more than just empty sentiment. It strikes the spectator at a level much deeper than simply viewing someone's death. This is what Burch would label as *catharsis*; that is, the feeling one has when they view a tragic situation that leads to a deeper insight into themselves and into life. I think we often label this kind of experience as something that "puts things into perspective" in that we are faced with the possibility that pursuing truth costs us our comfort and perhaps even our lives.

Burch concludes his study by stating that Mark's Gospel belongs "among the ranking tragedies of world-literature."[17] He argues that, though Mark may not have been familiar with Aristotle, his work corresponds to Aristotle's principles in many ways. Mark therefore is not a biography of Jesus but "a portrayal of the meaning and the power of his self-sacrificing ministry."[18]

The second study that compares Mark's Gospel with Greek tragedy is Gilbert Bilezikian's *The Liberated Gospel*, written in 1977. It arose

---

15. Burch ("Tragic Action," 356–57) continues to refer to Aristotle at times while departing from him at others. But, in accordance with Aristotle's theory of the tragic "flaw," Burch suggests that the flaw for seemingly blameless characters like Jesus and Antigone is their rigid adherence to their program.

16. Burch, "Tragic Action," 357.

17. Burch, "Tragic Action," 358.

18. Burch, "Tragic Action," 358.

out of a dissatisfaction with the source and redaction criticisms that dominated Gospel studies beginning in the mid-fifties.[19] In it, Bilezikian attempts to rescue the "plain-looking maiden" from its mysterious "wall flower status," and to reveal the secret of its purpose through a literary approach.[20]

Bilezikian points out that Mark lived in a time and place in which various forms of literature were made available to him. Greek education was such that students studied and imitated the masters of literary composition, thus making the case that Mark's audience—if not Mark himself—was both familiar with and educated by these various forms of literature.[21] It was an age of imitation, perhaps one dominated by an obsession with rhetorical and stylistic refinements,[22] and it was in this age that Christianity penned its Gospels. For these reasons, Bilezikian argues that Mark was fashioned in the form of tragedy, and there are a number of plausible reasons for this. The first reason is that tragedy originated as an essentially religious art form, written and performed in honor of Dionysius. The word *tragedy* is traditionally understood to mean "goat-song," and reflects the practice of a ritual goat sacrifice as a prize.[23]

The second reason would be the aesthetic needs that tragedy evolved to serve. Poets began to borrow from mythology and tragedy and this material became a reenactment of a mythico-historical event—known as the *Aition*—that had an "etiological and kerygmatic" effect.[24] The *Aition* often included the veneration of a tomb that was dedicated to the memory of a deified hero who had died in unusual circumstances.[25] The hero was often divine—or at least at a level beyond human capacity—who would suffer on behalf of his or her people. This suffering often took the form of a sacrificial death as the *Pharmikos*—the

19. Bilezikian, *Liberated Gospel*, 12.
20. Bilezikian, *Liberated Gospel*, 13.
21. Bilezikian, *Liberated Gospel*, 17.
22. Bilezikian, *Liberated Gospel*, 18. See also Duff, *Literary History*.
23. Bilezikian, *Liberated Gospel*, 24. Bilezikian also notes that the designation may also be derived from the choric dancers who were dressed in goatskins or even acted like goats. See also Lucas, *Tragedy*.
24. Bilezikian, *Liberated Gospel*, 25.
25. Bilezikian, *Liberated Gospel*, 25.

cure—for some type of pollution that was affecting others. These kinds of tragedies were performed in the Spring since they contained some type of resurrection-ritual that celebrated the resurgence of life after the winter. This is perhaps best stated by George G. Murray, who writes that the "most influential of all the ritual types is the *Pharmikos*, the old polluted year, the sin-bearer, who has to be stoned or cast out, to suffer for his people. Oedipus and Orestes are typical; but almost every tragic hero has the traces of the *Pharmikos* in him—he bears some pollution and he dies for the sins of others."[26]

It can certainly be said that these beliefs and practices depict humanity's quest for an explanation of a merciless and baffling universe. It also helps to identify humanity's place within the universe, and gives a reason for its constricting existence and yearning for ultimate reality.[27] It also reveals that early Greek poets were theologians; their inquiries led to a greater understanding of God—or the gods—and how humanity relates to God or vice versa.[28]

After establishing a logical basis for why Mark chose Greek tragic form, Bilezikian devotes several chapters to a discussion of Mark's plot. He identifies—under the influence of Aristotle—Mark's structural development of plot, character, message, diction, melody, and spectacle.[29] He also notes that a tragic drama's primary concern is that of action and not of character. This means that Bilezikian's analysis has everything to do with the actions of Jesus and not the development of Jesus' character within the story.[30]

---

26. Murray, "Greek Drama," 7:582; Bilezikian, *Liberated Gospel*, 25.

27. Bilezikian, *Liberated Gospel*, 25.

28. Oates and O'Neill, *Complete Greek Drama*, 1:xxiii.

29. Bilezikian, *Liberated Gospel*, 51; *Poet*. 1450a 6.9–14.

30. Bilezikian (*Liberated Gospel*) suggests that the modern fascination with biography and character development is due, in part, to "modern man's loss of identity" (51) and that this may impede a full appreciation of Aristotle's emphasis. While it is impossible to separate a study of Gospel structure from its protagonist Jesus, both Bilezikian and—I think—Aristotle want to emphasize that the characters in Mark do not change. According to Aristotle, agents must necessarily have distinctive qualities of character and thought, since it is from these that we ascribe their actions as good or bad, as successful or as failure. Bilezikian stresses this point when he says that the "New Testament emphasizes the events of Christ's ministry rather than the development of His own consciousness and character" (53). Bilezikian is right to

How Tragic has Jesus Been?

"The action in Mark follows a course identical to the one recommended by Aristotle for Greek tragedies."[31] This statement refers to Aristotle's tripartite categorization of Complication, Crisis, and Dénouement. Bilezikian separates Mark into three stages: the events in the first half of the Gospel constitute the Complication (1:1—8:26); the recognition at Caesarea Philippi is the Crisis (8:27–30); and the remainder of the Gospel of the Dénouement (8:31—16:8).[32]

The Complication is developed early in the Gospel as Jesus begins his ministry. Despite many miracles and struggles with demonic powers, the dumbfounded crowds fail to draw the appropriate conclusions regarding the identity of Jesus. Instead, they continually ask who Jesus is and ponder the authority by which he conducts his ministry (1:27). Here Bilezikian keeps in close connection with Aristotle, who suggests that the Complication consists of a developing anticipation which culminates in the Crisis. He delves more deeply than Burch, however, by noting the occasions when the disciples and followers fail to recognize Jesus though demons do.[33] All of this serves to create the Complication: why do those closest to Jesus not recognize him? This, according to Bilezikian, pertains to the very essence of tragedy.[34]

But what of the crowds? Bilezikian notes that the crowds respond to Jesus—albeit favorably—without faith.[35] The same can be said of the teachers of the law who are juxtaposed to Jesus by the crowds (1:22), the result of which leads to Jesus' ultimate demise. But it is this demise that characterizes the Messiah and the secret to the kingdom of God.

Jesus' demise is part of the Dénouement, but Mark cannot fully develop it until the Crisis has been established. Bilezikian, like Smith,

---

point out that the Gospels are more interested in the work of Jesus rather than his feelings. I will, however, talk more about this in subsequent chapters. See also *Poet.* 1449b–1450a.

31. Bilezikian, *Liberated Gospel*, 55.

32. Bilezikian, *Liberated Gospel*, 55, 79. Unlike Smith ("Divine Tragedy," 203–31; see discussion below), Bilezikian includes the prologue within the category of Complication (1:1—8:26), the Crisis is all of four verses (8:27–30) and the Dénouement as (8:31—16:8).

33. Bilezikian, *Liberated Gospel*, 60.

34. Bilezikian, *Liberated Gospel*, 62.

35. Bilezikian, *Liberated Gospel*, 63.

identifies the Crisis to be Peter's recognition because it "constitutes the turning point in the action."[36] This moment creates a sense of relief since, until this scene, no one seems to be able to grasp Jesus' identity. Any sense of relief that one may have, however, is quickly turned on its head; though Peter recognizes Jesus as the Christ, the true Crisis lies in the fact that he misunderstands the implications of the role.

The misunderstanding of who exactly Jesus is continues into the Dénouement. One of Jesus' central aims within this section is to train the disciples for the demands of following Him, but their failure to grasp his teaching is rather shocking.[37] By portraying the disciples' repeated failures to meet the challenges for which Jesus has prepared them, Mark is able to highlight just how tragic Jesus' fate is.

The tensions between Jesus and the so-called chief priests and teachers of the law are also heightened in this section. The struggle culminates when Jesus predicts the destruction of the temple (11:15–19), leading the priests to challenge Jesus' authority (11:27–33), which leads to their plot to murder him (11:18). To do so, they intend to trap him in his talk (12:13, 18–27), but Jesus uses these occasions to point out their wicked motives—an example of which can be found in the parable of the vineyard (12:1–12). Both parties engage in a number of ripostes until Jesus is finally arrested and tried for his actions.

There is great irony in the fact that Jesus dies accused of the very position that he has so strenuously avoided.[38] He is given the title "the king of the Jews," a title that lends itself to the tragic irony (15:2, 9, 12, 18, 26, 32). The tearing of the curtain (15:39) signals the abolishment of the corrupt establishment that the priests had established, along with their petty accusations now rendered obsolete by the transaction of the cross. Mark adds a final ironic twist by noting how a centurion—not a Jew—finally recognizes Jesus for who he really is (15:39).

But what of the disciples? Bilezikian notes that, despite a large number of occasions during which Jesus predicted his resurrection (8:31; 9:9, 31; 10:34; 14:28), the disciples are nowhere to be found

---

36. Bilezikian, *Liberated Gospel*, 77.
37. Bilezikian, *Liberated Gospel*, 83, 85.
38. Bilezikian, *Liberated Gospel*, 95.

How Tragic has Jesus Been?

during the crucifixion.[39] Their absence at his burial may also suggest their feelings of finality with regard to the death of Jesus. And again, even though Jesus highlights his resurrection after three days, no disciple approaches the tomb.

But the three women present at the crucifixion do. To their surprise, they see the very large stone rolled away and a young man dressed in dazzling clothes waiting for them. The young man's ringing announcement that Jesus has risen generates an extremely dramatic reaction: silence and fear. It is on this note that Mark chooses to end his Gospel, and thus the Dénouement.

Mark's tripartite development of plot is flawless according to Bilezikian.[40] In addition, Bilezikian notes that Mark artistically makes use of three other Aristotelian categories: recognition, reversal, and suffering.[41] This leads to perhaps the most intriguing aspect of Bilezikian's study. He suggests that "the plot of the Gospel resides in the failure of men to recognize in Jesus their spiritual Messiah and the necessity that lays upon Jesus to fulfill His task in spite of their blindness."[42] He is right to note this, but he does not fully develop this train of thought. If Mark's plot is dependent upon recognition—or a lack of recognition in this case—then it follows that the crucifixion and subsequent resurrection are also dependent upon whether anyone recognizes Jesus. What makes this problem even more complex is that Jesus is presumably

---

39. Bilezikian, *Liberated Gospel*, 97.

40. Bilezikian, *Liberated Gospel*, 100. This point is contested by Robbins (Review of *The Liberated Gospel*, 480) who says that "we must not imagine that they (the Gospels) approximate literary perfection." This is not even close to what Bilezikian is suggesting, however. It is clear that Bilezikian's comments are referring to Mark's careful delineation of Complication, Crisis, and Dénouement. What Bilezikian is not suggesting is that Mark appears in perfect tragic form, but rather that Mark grants equal space to both Complication and Dénouement with crisis being the central turning point.

41. These categories are applied to Peter's recognition in 8:27–30, which also constitutes the crisis portion of plot. The recognition occurs when Peter identifies Jesus as Christ, and the reversal occurs when the recognition is followed by a somber prediction of catastrophe. This is a shock to Peter since he begins to rebuke Jesus, but this reversal marks a shift in subject matter within the Gospel. The suffering portion occurs in the tragic death of Jesus, and should be a natural outcome of the reversal. See Bilezikian, *Liberated Gospel*, 100–102; *Poet.* 1452a 10–11.

42. Bilezikian, *Liberated Gospel*, 104.

attempting to convince everyone of the good news of the kingdom of God. His crucifixion would then be the evidence that he has failed in his mission—assuming that if he was adequately convincing and correctly identified he would not have been put to death. It could therefore be argued that God, Satan, or "sin" provided a level of spiritual blindness that is so often alluded to in Mark.[43] But was Jesus aware of the source of this blindness? Jesus appears genuine with regard to his attempts to convince others of his message, but if his message was meant by God to fall on deaf ears—so to speak—then it would follow that Jesus is unaware of God's plan and his death comes as a surprise. This seems unlikely since Jesus alludes to his future death and resurrection a number of times. And so, we are left to ask why no one recognizes Jesus and whether Jesus is aware of God's willingness to purposefully deafen everyone in order to achieve Jesus' death and resurrection. These are certainly large questions with even larger implications, and I am not sure if it was for these reasons that Bilezikian avoided them completely. Regardless, these questions must be addressed, and I will do so in a subsequent chapter.

The third study that I will discuss here is Jerry Stone's "The Gospel of Mark and Oedipus the King: Two Tragic Visions," written in 1984.[44] In this work, Stone is careful to bifurcate Christian tragedy from certain catch phrases that unfairly dismiss the possibility that the Gospels might be tragic in form.[45] Mark certainly contains a number of tragic elements: misunderstanding, doubt, betrayal, denial, and desertion—to name a few—but can we really compare Mark and *Oedipus Rex*?

---

43. According to Oates and O'Neill, tragedy assumes a superhuman power or force that resides over humanity. Throughout the history of tragedy, this force has taken on a number of names and forms, even in Shakespeare's essentially secular tragedies. Whatever name or form it takes, tragedy always presents humanity as living under the authority of a divine reality which determines his actions. See Oates and O'Neill, *Complete Greek Drama*, 1.xxvii–viii.

44. Stone, "Mark and Oedipus," 55–69.

45. Stone notes in particular Laurence Michel, who states, "Christ was and is God: he became man, instituted the sacraments, died for our sins, rose from the dead, and reopened the gates of heaven." While I agree with Michel here—as does Stone—one cannot deny the tragic thread that runs through the Gospels. For Michel's full argument, see Michel, "Possibility," 233. See also Stone, "Mark and Oedipus," 56.

How Tragic has Jesus Been?

Certainly, Jesus and Oedipus share in what appears to be predetermined misfortune. However, Stone takes the comparison a step further and ascribes to both Jesus and Oedipus a level of ignorance—that is, a failure to recognize who they are and/or their circumstances.[46] This failure is what Stone calls the tragic hero's "error," which eventually leads to their ultimate misfortune.[47] Aristotle's examples of Oedipus and Thyestes are appropriate because both characters fail to recognize something crucial that eventually causes their downfall. The theme of non-recognition can be found in Mark as well. Peter is most like Oedipus who fails to recognize the identity of Jesus, and any number of allusions can be drawn between the healing of the blind man in Bethsaida and Oedipus's literal blindness.[48] But can Oedipus be compared to Jesus in this regard?

On first glance, Oedipus's ignorance cannot be compared to that of Jesus, who appears as all-knowing and who is aware of his identity. But Stone argues that Jesus possesses a bi-level consciousness. On the one hand, Jesus is aware that he must suffer, be rejected, die, and after three days rise again (8:31). Yet Stone notes that he is uncertain about identifying himself as the one to whom this must happen and he points to Jesus' prayer in Gethsemane, "Abba Father, all things are possible with you; remove this cup from me; yet not what I will, but what you will" (14:36). This glimpse of uncertainty may also inform the reading of 15:34, in which Jesus cries out that he has been forsaken by God. Whether or not Jesus actually said these things is not a concern for Stone; his concern rests in how Mark utilizes these statements. Taken at face value, they reflect a tragic plot in which Jesus fails to fully recognize himself as the suffering Messiah.[49]

---

46. Stone, "Mark and Oedipus," 57.

47. It should be noted at this point that Aristotle does not clearly define "mistake" (*hamartia*). Stone ("Mark and Oedipus," 57) notes this, and points out that Aristotle more clearly defines it in his *Nicomachean Ethics* as "the failure to recognize the identity of the injured party."

48. Stone, "Mark and Oedipus," 59.

49. Stone, "Mark and Oedipus," 60. Stone goes on to say that "they (Jesus and Oedipus) are tragic figures because of their failure to fully recognize their own circumstances in relation to God—and they come to their misfortune through that failure." I disagree with this conclusion on the basis of the fact that Jesus' crucifixion comes about not because of his own failure to recognize himself and his role, but

Of Conflict and Concealment

The strength of Stone's study is that he has highlighted a serious tension in Mark's Gospel. If Mark's plot is driven by non-recognition—that is, the failure of the authorities to recognize Jesus—then we are faced with two options with regard to Jesus' self-awareness. The first is that Jesus *is* fully aware of who he is and what the outcome of his ministry will be. There is certainly a lot of evidence for this, one example being found in 8:31 as I highlighted above. However, the second is that Jesus *is not* fully aware of who he is and what the outcome will be. This argument is logically made by asserting that, if Jesus knows that no one will truly recognize him, why does he become frustrated at the disciples for their ignorance (4:13, 40)?

Stone's observations reflect my earlier comments about Bilezikian's study. There is certainly a tension between whether Mark's Jesus is or is not fully aware of his identity and the outcome of his ministry. However, I depart from Stone's argument insofar as he allows Oedipus to guide his interpretation of Jesus. It can be argued that Oedipus is not aware of his true identity, and that this ignorance brings the drama to its tragic climax. I do not think we can compare Jesus and Oedipus in this regard because there are too many instances in which Jesus appears to fully know who he is. We may, however, be able to argue that Jesus is like Oedipus in that Jesus may not have been aware of the final outcome of his ministry until much later in the narrative. Jesus certainly *is* aware of what will happen by 8:31 but we cannot be certain of whether he foresaw this outcome at an earlier point.

Stone also uses the wrong passages to state his argument. It is true that Jesus' words in Gethsemane could reflect a moment of self-doubt. It is also true that Jesus' quotation of Ps 22 from the cross could reveal the emotion of feeling abandoned by God. But a counterargument could easily be made for each instance. For example, Jesus' words in Gethsemane may not actually portray a self-doubting Jesus but could portray an honest Jesus who is submitting to the terror that lies ahead. Likewise, Jesus' quotation of Ps 22 may not actually reflect a feeling

---

because of everyone else's failure to recognize who he is and his role. Stone admits as much when he suggests that non-recognition is central to the plot of Mark, but I think he stretches plausibility of the evidence by suggesting that Jesus was unaware in the same way as Oedipus.

How Tragic has Jesus Been?

of abandonment but could be foreshadowing the vindication of the lamenter. Stone may have been better off highlighting each instance of recognition and non-recognition in the Gospel.

One of the most intriguing parts of Stone's study is his discussion of what I call the "point of view." If Mark's plot is driven by non-recognition as Stone suggests, what purpose do the miracles serve? Certainly, one can argue that the miracles heighten Mark's ironic nature, but aside from the obvious practical outcomes—such as blind people being able to see—they do not serve to convince the disciples or the religious authorities. On this point, Stone suggests that Mark's Gospel is primarily about human relationships which are broken due to misunderstanding.[50] From this point of view, a miracle-performing "divine man" is unconvincing as a necessary part of the plot which moves the characters towards their ends, the miracles themselves being an extraneous feature of the plot.[51] Being unconvinced by the miracles, Jesus' followers abandon Jesus. Even the women who visit Jesus' tomb flee in such fear that they do not tell anyone what they have seen. This certainly generates a level of pity and fear in the audience—as prescribed by Aristotle.[52]

---

50. Stone, "Mark and Oedipus," 65.

51. Stone, "Mark and Oedipus," 65. Stone argues that this perception of Jesus only further confuses the disciples. Jesus is portrayed as a miracle-producing hero who is able to do amazing things. The disciples are so inspired by this hero that they themselves are able to drive out demons and cure the sick (6:12–13). Under this premise, it makes sense that James and John argue amongst themselves as to their place in glory with Jesus after their own miracle working episodes (10:35–36). This theory leads Stone to suggest that the miracle stories in Mark's Gospel deter the disciples from actually realizing who Jesus is.

52. It has been argued by Cherbonnier and Jaspers that Christianity and tragedy are not comparable on the basis of the resurrection. They suggest that the resurrection provides an outlook for the Christian that eliminates the sense of pity and fear that tragedy ought to produce. Schwartz responds by pointing out that tragedy has its origins in the religious festivals of Dionysus, in particular the death and resurrection of a hero whose resurrection symbolizes the cleansing of the worship community. I would also like to add to the argument that the resurrection of Christ and the promise of eternal life do not eliminate tragic possibility. In fact, one does not need to look very long at the history of the Church in order to discover that tragedy envelops everyone—even the Christian. For the full article, see Schwartz, "Christian Tragedy," 208–13; Cherbonnier, "Idea of Tragedy," 23–55; Jaspers, *Tragedy*, 38–40.

Stone concludes his article by asking how this vision of Mark's Gospel provides insight into the larger Christian vision. He answers this question by suggesting that this Gospel "presents us with flesh and blood characters who move through life experiences that resonate with modern sensibilities."[53] Stone goes on to suggest that "few twentieth century persons can identify with the New Testament miracle-filled world, but we can all understand broken relationships."[54] The result of viewing the Gospel from this perspective is that Jesus' divine authority emerges from his experiences with suffering and love rather than from his powers as a divine being—something that humans cannot equate themselves with. I think this is a fascinating response. The real tragedy in Mark—and the very essence of tragedy in general, I think—is that the hero constantly struggles against an established power of some type.[55] Tragedy then becomes tragic when this struggle confronts the audience and their preconceptions of this established power. Stone's article is important because it forces us to reevaluate whether Mark's focus is a wonder-working savior or the tragedy of the human condition.[56]

53. Stone, "Mark and Oedipus," 66.

54. Stone, "Mark and Oedipus," 66.

55. In an exposition on the tragic Puritan view of life, Sorrentino ("God's Cosmic Drama," 432–50) makes a similar observation. He points out that "human beings are faced with irreconcilable conflicts that result in their having to choose between two goods and to suffer the consequences of being unable to choose both" (434). The paradox of Christian tragedy then lies in the fact that humanity suffers while on earth but Christians transcend into a world of victory. Once again, Karl Jaspers (*Tragedy*, 38–39) argues that there can be no real Christian tragedy because the mystery of redemption is the basis of the plot. Sorrentino is critical of such assertions, maintaining that comments such as these oversimplify the Christian experience. The fact remains that humanity suffers the effects of original sin regardless of their faith.

56. In an interesting article on Christianity's attitude towards the theatre, Sticca ("Christian Drama," 1025–34) makes a number of comments about tragedy and the human condition. He likens the Christian person to the Aristotelian tragic actor in that both are "imperfect, born with original sin and because his salvation is truly dependent on the result of the struggle, within himself, of the forces of evil and good, which are not simple extension and projection of his interior tendencies but also forces which have an existence outside of him." Each person's tragic flaw then stems from his or her radical freedom to choose between good and evil. As for Jesus and tragedy, Sticca argues that Jesus transcends the rigid demands of the Aristotelian tragic hero. Sticca goes on to say that the audience of Christ's passion experiences catharsis because he or she feels "pity of the agonist and fear not only for His life but also of that very sin which made the sacrifice necessary" (1031). So it seems that,

How Tragic has Jesus Been?

The next study I will examine is Louis A. Ruprecht Jr.'s 1992 article "Mark's Tragic Vision: Gethsemane."[57] In it, Ruprecht argues that the Gospels are best understood as tragedies, and that "the misleading dichotomy between pagan and Christian, between Greek and Jew—with its profound roots in Pauline theology as well as in Nietzsche's anti-Christian polemics—has crippled the Church's ability to read its own canon well."[58]

After an explanation of why he believes Luke, Matthew, and John all fit within the tragic genre, Ruprecht turns to Mark and highlights the Gethsemane narrative found in ch. 14. He argues that tragedy is not necessarily defined by its happy or tragic ending, but by moral collision—an opinion he gleans from Hegel. Hegel delineates two dimensions on which collisions take place. The first is a *horizontal* dimension that can be best described as a tension between human institutions that govern law and justice. This type of collision can be found in the *Antigone*, in which Antigone is caught between the law and what she believes is right.[59]

The second type of collision is a *vertical* one, and it is concerned with multiple wills. Using the example of the *Oedipus Rex*, the will of the gods is juxtaposed with that of Oedipus, and from the clash of these wills a destiny is created. In other words, "Fate is what the gods will. Destiny is what we make of it."[60]

Though Hegel is skeptical that both kinds of collisions can successfully unite in a single tragedy, Ruprecht sees both illustrated in Mark. If Mark is to be read as a tragedy, then what kind of tragedy is it? Ruprecht appears frustrated by the lack of concise definitions in Markan scholarship, and I am in agreement. It can certainly be argued that Jesus is colliding with the religious authorities on a horizontal

---

though Sticca is hesitant to call the Gospels a tragedy, he admits that an essential level of catharsis occurs while viewing the Passion.

57. Ruprecht, "Tragic Vision," 1–25.

58. Ruprecht, "Tragic Vision," 2.

59. This sense of "rightness" is usually derived from some "unwritten laws" of heaven, as Ruprecht calls it, and is best exemplified by Antigone's speech to Creon. Ruprecht also observes this tension in the first-century debate concerning the "letter and spirit" of the Jewish law. See Ruprecht, "Tragic Vision," 9.

60. Ruprecht, "Tragic Vision," 9.

level—this much is obvious. But Ruprecht's handling of the vertical collision is what makes his study most intriguing. Is Mark simply about one person's encounter with religious authorities, or is this a story of "one man's encounter with a world he did not make, a Will not his own, and his anguished attempts to incorporate these things into his Destiny?"[61] Like Stone, Ruprecht appeals to Jesus' prayer in Gethsemane to emphasize the struggle between God's apparent will and his own destiny. This comes a little closer to discussing the concept of Jesus' consciousness that I mentioned above. However, I have a number of concerns with the evidence that Ruprecht uses to make his point.

While several scholars tend to emphasize only the horizontal relationship between Jesus and the temple, what is really at question in Mark's Gospel is Christ's destiny. Concerning this, Ruprecht notes that Mark tends towards a passive use of verbs when they relate to Jesus, insisting that this indicates that Jesus is most often being acted upon.[62] Ruprecht's argument is perhaps most clearly demonstrated by his analysis of Jesus' request to have the cup of suffering taken away from him. In Luke, it is clear that God did not want to take the cup away from Jesus. Ruprecht offers the following syllogisms:

1. "Father, *if you will*, take this cup away from me."
2. The cup is not taken away.
3. God did not wish to remove it.

It appears that God's will is otherwise, and that Jesus' will disappears completely. Matthew presents the prayer somewhat differently by suggesting that the cup cannot at all be avoided:

1. "My Father, *if it is possible*, take this cup from me."
2. The cup is not taken away.

---

61. Ruprecht, "Tragic Vision," 10.

62. Ruprecht, "Tragic Vision," 10–11. Ruprecht also notices that Matthew and Luke render the linguistic elements of the prayer quite differently. For example, Ruprecht argues that Matthew and Luke have Jesus addressing God directly in the vocative, whereas "John sees the union between Jesus and God as virtually complete." In Mark, however, Ruprecht argues that Jesus addresses God in a manner that appears distant: "Abba, *the* Father" (10–11).

How Tragic has Jesus Been?

3. It is not possible for God to remove it.

Matthew then tells us why it is impossible, and that is because it had been written long ago by the prophets (Matt 26:54). Mark, however, presents the prayer in stark contrast to both Luke and Matthew:

1. "Abba, the Father, *all things are possible for you.*"
2. The cup is not taken away as Jesus asks.
3. We are left to wonder why.[63]

God's silence is conspicuous, and Ruprecht notes that God's voice—though it seldom appears in Mark—appears at two major points in the narrative: the baptism and transfiguration. However, God's silence here is meant to draw out the anticipation in this moment of crisis.[64]

I find this analysis intriguing, but I am uncertain about Ruprecht's conclusions based on the evidence he presents. My first concern is in regard to his use of the passive voice as evidence for tension between God's will and Jesus' destiny. Such an argument lacks considerable linguistic sophistication, especially with regards to how the passive functions within discourse. This issue is beyond the scope of this chapter, but for now let it suffice to say that Mark's use of the passive voice may have other motivations that Ruprecht overlooks.

My second concern with Ruprecht's analysis involves the conclusions drawn from the syllogisms sketched above. Ruprecht makes interesting observations concerning the distinctions in Jesus' prayer. However, I am not sure that we are "left to wonder why" God is not able to remove the cup of suffering from Jesus in Mark's Gospel, especially since Jesus fully submits to God's will in the next verse. It seems more plausible to suggest that Jesus is showing some level of fear, but I am not certain that we can draw the theological conclusions that Ruprecht does here.

Ruprecht ends his study by describing Mark as a tragedy despite a very common consensus that it is not. The reason for the mistaken consensus, he argues, is that Christianity has been reading the Gospels through the theological lenses of Paul and John, who make the

---

63. See Ruprecht ("Tragic Vision," 11) for each of the examples.
64. Ruprecht, "Tragic Vision," 12.

Of Conflict and Concealment

resurrection the "paradigmatic happy ending." Mark stands in contrast to each of these because Mark appears "far from happy" about the resurrection.[65] "The Christian," he writes, "goes 'beyond tragedy' not when he or she believes in the resurrection but rather when he or she claims that this faith will take your pain away."[66]

The next study that I will examine is Stephen H. Smith's "A Divine Tragedy: Some Observations on the Dramatic Structure of Mark's Gospel" written in 1995.[67] In this study, Smith outlines several elements of Mark that correspond to Greek tragedy, and does so in correspondence with B. Standaert's book *L'Evangile selon Marc: Composition et genre littéraire*.[68] Each of these authors compare Mark with tragedy, and do so in conjunction with Aristotle's *Poetics*. However, Smith rightly notes that Aristotle can be "at best no more than a literary adjudicator or critic" with regard to the principles of tragedy that had been established in fifth-century Athens.[69] This point is well taken—as Standaert also observes—because Aristotle's assessment of the "ideal" play may only reflect the subtleties of his own thinking.[70]

Smith also observes a clear distinction between structure and plot in tragic drama. This is a point that Standaert fails to recognize, at least according to Smith, because he fails to understand Aristotle's distinctions. For example, Standaert "treats 'prologue,' 'recognition,' and 'epilogue' in direct sequence, as if they all operate at the same structural level."[71] Standaert does this by linking the prologue and epilogue via a recognition scene in Mark 8:27–30.[72] This is partly true, as Smith points out, since Aristotle does include prologue as a substance related to the epilogue, and these work in conjunction with the recognition scene found in 8:27–30. However, the problem for Standaert lies in his application of Aristotle's categories. It is true that Aristotle thinks that every

---

65. Ruprecht, "Tragic Vision," 20.
66. Ruprecht, "Tragic Vision," 21.
67. Smith, "Divine Tragedy," 209–31.
68. Standaert, *L'Evangile*.
69. Smith, "Divine Tragedy," 210.
70. Standaert, *L'Evangile*, 30–34, 82–108; Smith, "Divine Tragedy," 210.
71. Smith, "Divine Tragedy," 210.
72. Standaert, *L'Evangile*, 83–106.

literary whole must have a beginning, middle, and end,[73] but Standaert misunderstands how recognition fits into this scheme. Smith points out his error—and I agree with Smith on this point—that recognition is to be regarded as a part of the *plot* and not of *structure*.[74] Plot consists of complication, recognition, and Dénouement; structure, by contrast, consists of a prologue, an episode, an exode, a parody, and a stasimon.

This sets the stage for the rest of Smith's study, which attempts "to demonstrate how and why the structure of Mark's Gospel conforms to the principles of tragic drama."[75] In particular, he aims to show how Mark follows the tripartite nature of *plot*: complication (δέσις); recognition (ἀναγνώρισις); and Dénouement (λύσις). He chooses *Oedipus Rex* to illustrate his arguments both for the "sake of homogeneity" with Aristotle and because his was the "most striking of all Greek tragedy."[76]

According to Smith, the character and actions of Jesus and Oedipus can be both compared and contrasted. The Markan complication (δέσις), as with that of Oedipus, occurs as a result of Jesus' action: the more resolutely Jesus engages in his task, the nearer he draws to catastrophe (3:6). An observable difference occurs in the characterization of Jesus, who—unlike Oedipus—has no discernible "tragic flaw."[77]

A Recognition scene (ἀναγνώρισις) is an important aspect of plot, and Smith draws a number of parallels between those found in Mark and other Greek tragedies. Again noting *Oedipus Rex* and now also Euripides' *Electra*, Smith suggests that one of the more intriguing aspects of recognition occurs when an author postpones the actual moment of recognition.[78] For example, when Orestes and Electra first

---

73. Poet. 1450b 7.26.
74. Smith, "Divine Tragedy," 210.
75. Smith, "Divine Tragedy," 211.
76. Smith, "Divine Tragedy," 211.
77. Smith ("Divine Tragedy," 212n11) makes note of the name "Oedipus," which means "swell-foot." It is a derivative of a child's being discovered with his or her feet pinned together. "Oedipus" also can be understood as a pun on the Greek word οἶδα, which means "know." The irony occurs when Oedipus—the one who knows—strives to know what is causing the plague in Thebes. Little does he realize, however, that knowing will lead to his downfall. Comparing Jesus to Oedipus fails in this regard since Jesus is never portrayed in Mark as one who suffers from *hubris*.
78. Smith, "Divine Tragedy," 214.

meet, the audience is kept in eager anticipation as to whether Orestes will reveal his concealed identity. Euripides builds this anticipation by stressing the urgency with which so many desire his return; Orestes resides amongst the ones he has come to save, yet no one recognizes him. Finally, an old servant is introduced who recognizes Orestes by the scar above his eye. A similar thing happens in *Oedipus Rex*, in which the super-confident Oedipus strives to discover the origins of the plague in Thebes. After a series of interrogations, Oedipus learns that his foster father Polybus has died, and that Polybus reared him after an old shepherd saved him from exposure. Eventually the old shepherd arrives on the scene and reveals that Oedipus is responsible for both patricide and incest. In both dramas, the power of the recognition scene is dependent upon the gradual revelation of the truth.[79]

Smith suggests that the recognition scene in Mark 8:27–30 is delayed in the same way as those described above. Though Jesus is observed as being distinctive already in 1:27–28, his true identity is not recognized despite a large number of opportunities. Smith also argues that each recognition scene is preceded by some sort of preparatory scene, and the above described scenes in *Oedipus Rex* and the *Electra* are an example of this. Mark's Gospel is similar in that the recognition scene found in 8:27–30 is preceded by a preparatory episode, which is the healing of the blind man in 8:22–26.[80] This is contra Burch and Standaert, who argue that the preparatory episode is the discussion of Jesus' identity in 8:27–28.[81] Smith argues that the healing of the blind man better fits within Aristotle's definition of recognition accompanied by reversal.[82]

---

79. Smith, "Divine Tragedy," 213.

80. Smith ("Divine Tragedy," 215) argues that Peter's recognition scene is "imperfect" because, though he correctly recognizes Jesus as the Christ, he fails to understand what that means. This can be paralleled with the healing in 8:22–26. The once blinded man is now able "to see Jesus as the Messiah, but does not appreciate what messiahship entails."

81. Burch, "Tragic Action," 346–358; Standaert, *L'Evangile*, 93–94. Smith ("Divine Tragedy," 215) does admit that the conversation about Jesus' identity in 8:27–28 is a part of the recognition but argues that the healed man provides a better parallel with Peter's "imperfect recognition."

82. Smith, "Divine Tragedy," 215–16; *Poet.* 1452b 11.1.

How Tragic has Jesus Been?

The Dénouement (λύσις) is the part of the action that follows the recognition scene and leads to the resolution of the plot. Smith argues that the "extent of the Dénouement depends, of course, on the position of the recognition scene."[83] In *Oedipus Rex*, it occurs quite late (1223–1530), and we are told what happens as a result of the recognition. In other plays, such as Aeschylus' *Choephoroi*, the recognition happens early in the play (164-263), and the Dénouement is much longer. In Mark, Smith observes that the Complication (1:1—8:26) and the Dénouement (8:31—16:8) are given equal space.[84] The recognition scene also marks a shift in content, from miracles and healings to messianic teaching. It is also within the Dénouement that the elders, chief priests, and scribes are set up as opponents (8:31).

Smith then turns to the elements of structure, which are treated by Aristotle as different from those of the plot. These are categorized by Smith as Prologue, Epilogue, and Episode.[85] The Prologue serves to introduce one or more characters who are integral to the plot. This character can be either divine or mortal, the protagonist, or a minor character. This character often declares his or her own credentials before informing the audience of the setting and situation of the plot. This information is also used to foreshadow certain events or motifs which are likely to occur throughout the course of the plot. When this character has given all of the necessary information, he or she leaves the stage and does not return.

Smith designates 1:1–13 as the Markan prologue. It is at this point that Mark exploits his position as omniscient author who discloses information of which the readers and characters are unaware.[86] During the prologue, we are introduced to John the Baptist and to God, both of whom have something to say about Jesus. After the events of the prologue, John the Baptist never appears as a speaking character, though we are often told about him (1:14; 2:18; 6:14-29; 8:28; 9:11-13;

83. Smith, "Divine Tragedy," 217.

84. Smith, "Divine Tragedy," 217.

85. Aristotle (*Poet.* 1452b 12.14-20) divides the structure into four categories: Prologue, Episode, Exode, and a choral portion. The choral portions can be divided further into Parodes or Stasimons, and these two are common to all tragedies. There are occasions when songs can be sung from the stage, and these are called Commoe.

86. Smith, "Divine Tragedy," 219.

11:27–33;). Smith compares John's function to that of Hermes in the *Ion*, who appears as a messenger and informs the audience of the action against its background. The same thing occurs in Mark with a quotation of Isaiah, positioning the actions of Jesus against an Old Testament background. In addition, the messenger motif that begins Mark's Gospel also brings the Gospel to a close (16:5–7).[87]

The prologue of Mark also functions to foreshadow a number of occurrences. For example, Smith notes the use of the term ὁδός in the prologue and notes that it appears five times within the central section of the Gospel (8:27—10:52). John's appearance as a messenger in the likeness of Elijah (2 Kgs 1:8) may conform to Elijah's appearance in 9:11–13. In addition, God's voice in 1:11—though echoing Ps 2:7—serves to foreshadow the appearance of the same voice at the Transfiguration (9:7). It also seems that Jesus' encounter with Satan in 1:13 foreshadows his many encounters with the forces of evil (1:23–26, 34, 39; 3:11, 15, 22–27; 5:1–20; 6:13; 7:24–30; 8:31–33; 9:14–29, 38–39).[88]

The Epilogue is considered by Aristotle to be the final section of the play, and Smith treats 16:1–8 as such an epilogue. Smith notes the use of a *deus ex machina* device—the appearance of the young man at the tomb—to announce Jesus' resurrection. This he notes as an apparent violation of Aristotle's principle that such a device not be used to unravel the plot. Mark may have chosen to do this since there seems to be no other alternative for announcing Jesus' resurrection once he has been laid in the tomb. Smith reminds his readers at this point that Mark is not a professional playwright, and that Mark's Gospel is not a play and was not written for performance.[89] He does admit, however, that it is not unusual for Mark to use a messenger to deliver pertinent information (1:2–8).

But how are we to regard the ending of Mark? Smith suggests that our response to the ending—whether or not we accept the resurrection as external to the dramatic action[90]—is a tragic one and points to a life

---

87. Smith, "Divine Tragedy," 220.

88. Smith, "Divine Tragedy," 220; Robinson, *Problem of History*; Best, *The Temptation*; Danker, "Demonic Secret," 48–69.

89. Smith, "Divine Tragedy," 222.

90. This opinion is held by both Burch and Beach. See Burch, "Tragic Action,"

How Tragic has Jesus Been?

beyond itself.[91] This is, according to Smith, to the fact that all tragedies were written to be performed as a part of a tetralogy. The first two plays generally end in an open-ended way, allowing the events of the third play to reach a settled conclusion.[92] This was observed by Bilezikian who understands Mark's ending to be a happy one. Smith disagrees and points out that the "epilogue is not happy, but mysterious: the overriding mood is one of fear, in the sense of awe."[93]

A number of scholars, more notably F. G. Lang,[94] have noted that Mark can be divided into five episodes (1:1—3:6; 3:7—8:26; 8:27—10:52; 11:1—13:37; 14:1—16:8) and the first episode contains a prologue (1:1-13).[95] This proposed structure is based on the theory that most Greek tragedies were divided into five scenes. Smith, however, contests this point and suggests that a five-part structure was not always the norm. He notes that later Latin playwrights clearly adopted this structure, but the same cannot be said of Euripides or Sophocles, who structured their plays in a variety of ways.[96] As a result, it is difficult to say that Mark fits a "mould" of tragic episodic form, and Smith

---

355–56; Beach, *Gospel of Mark*, 50. This opinion is contra Dan Via (*Kerygma and Comedy*, 45–46, 98–101; *Middle of Time*), who suggests that the resurrection is integral to the plot though we never actually see it. Smith ("Divine Tragedy," 223) counters Via and suggests that what happens is appropriately understood as the *deus ex machina*. This means that the announcement found in 16:6 refers to something outside of the narrative and thus is not directly related to the material found in the narrative. Bilezikian (*Liberated Gospel*, 27) shares Via's opinion that Mark's ending is essentially a "happy" one but disagrees that Mark is better understood as a Tragicomedy since not all tragedy ends in doom.

91. Smith, "Divine Tragedy," 223.

92. This is suggested in our only surviving trilogy: Aeschylus' *Oresteia*. Smith notes that the ending of the first play, the *Eumenides*, is likely due to its position in the trilogy. Bilezikian also notes the *Philoctetes* of Sophocles and the *Elcestis* of Euripides. Smith, "Divine Tragedy," 223; Bilezikian, *Liberated Gospel*, 27n52.

93. Smith, "Divine Tragedy," 223–24; Bilezikian, *Liberated Gospel*, 27.

94. Lang, "Kompositionsanalyse," 1–24; See also Lausberg, *Handbuch*. Horace was also an advocate of a five-part structure, and suggested that any playwright who wanted their work to be taken seriously ought to adopt such a structure. See Horace, *Ars* 189.

95. Smith, "Divine Tragedy," 224. The five-part structure of Mark has also been noted by Standaert, *L'Evangile*, 106–8.

96. Smith, "Divine Tragedy," 224.

suggests that we should not feel obligated to "shackle Mark to a five-part dramatic structure."[97]

The chorus in Greek tragedy is understood by Smith to be used as a transitional segment, though he admits that it can be used in a variety of ways.[98] For example, the chorus can be used to anticipate the arrival of various characters and prompts dialogue between those characters. The chorus also acts to arouse emotions within the audience, specifically fear and pity. Though no chorus is used in Mark, a number of transitional passages serve the same purpose.[99] For example, minor characters comment on the action, thereby exciting the reader's emotions. Most often these comments include emotive words, such as θαμβέω (1:27); ἐξίστημι (2:12); φοβέω (4:41); ἐκπλήσσω (7:37). Smith is suggesting that the chorus serves to guide the audience in terms of their response. In this way, the transitional statements in Mark serve to draw attention to the action in Mark, responding appropriately to various questions concerning the identity of Jesus.[100]

In conclusion, Smith makes a number of observations concerning the popularity of tragic drama and the possible reasons why Mark may have written his Gospel in tragic form. The first observation is that Greek tragedy was "part of the staple diet of Greco-Roman education."[101] The second is that Mark would have been familiar with what Smith calls a "closet drama." These were works that were written in dramatic

---

97. Smith, "Divine Tragedy," 225. Here Smith suggests a seven-part structure (1:16—3:6; 3:13—6:6; 6:14—8:26; 8:31—10:45; 11:1—12:44; 13:3–37; 14:3—15:47) and includes a prologue (1:1–13) and an epilogue (16:1–8). Each of these episodes is separated by a transition (1:14, 15; 6:7–13; 8:27–30; 10:46–52; 13:1, 2; 14:1, 2). Smith offers no justification for his argument, though he points out that a similar structure is offered by Perrin. See Smith, "Divine Tragedy," 225–26; Perrin, *Pilgrimage*, 5; Hendrick, "Role," 289–311.

98. Smith, "Divine Tragedy," 226.

99. Smith, "Divine Tragedy," 226.

100. Smith, "Divine Tragedy," 227.

101. Smith, "Divine Tragedy," 228. On this point, Smith draws from Marrou, *History of Education*. Smith notes a two-stage system: textual criticism (διόρθωσις) and rhetoric. Smith argues that many of Mark's readers would not only have been familiar with the content of Greek tragedy but also with its literary analysis and presentation. As a result, Smith believes that the tragic form would have been an appropriate avenue by which the gospel message could have been communicated.

form but intended for private recitation rather than for public performance.[102] Smith is sure that Mark was not writing a history but rather using historical traditions in a dramatic way. This would have been a familiar method to Mark's audience and perfect for Mark's theological and ethical purposes.[103] This is evident by the fact that Mark is writing about a novel concept—the εὐαγγέλιον—which otherwise may have been unintelligible.

Smith's study is an important one because he presents a number of important facts about tragedy. However, his analysis of Mark's Gospel as a tragedy is lacking, and there are two reasons for this. The first reason regards Smith's treatment of recognition scenes. He rightly asserts that Peter's recognition in 8:27–30 fits within Aristotle's categories, but he does not mention a number of other recognition scenes in Mark. For example, there are several occasions when others recognize Jesus, such as demons and a centurion. Since Smith relies heavily upon Peter's recognition scene as the point when the narrative shifts focus, I am curious how the other recognition scenes may help to emphasize the one found in 8:27–30.

The second reason regards Smith's lack of attention to what constitutes tragic form. It is one thing to suggest that Mark has some type of form and to discuss whether or not that form coincides on some level with the tragic. It is quite another to show *how* Mark's form coincides with tragic form. Smith's study lacks a philosophical aspect, which is inseparable from the tragic. If Smith is going to assert that Mark's audience would have been familiar with tragic form and that tragic form would have deeply resounded in that audience, he ought to discuss why. If the tragic was so prevalent, why was it so prevalent? And to

---

102. Smith, "Divine Tragedy," 228. Smith notes those tragedies written by Seneca, and suggests that Mark may have been composed in a similar fashion. This practice may have begun with Seneca, and was rather wide-spread by the time of Mark's composition. See Tarrant, *Seneca's Thyestes*, 13–15; Watling, *Seneca*; Ahl, *Three Tragedies*. Each of these studies suggest that "closet dramas" were written and performed in private settings. There is evidence of such a practice in several of Ovid's works (*Tristia*, 5, 7, 27), Pliny the Younger, (*Ep.* 7.17), and Tacitus (*Dial.*, 2.1–3.3) and Suetonius (*Dom.* 7).

103. Smith, "Divine Tragedy," 230. See also Via, *Middle of Time*. Both Smith and Via stress the importance of narrative as the primary means of conveying an ethical message.

which aspect of human experience does it speak? What about Mark's Gospel resonates with the tragic form so that it becomes an appropriate vehicle through which the εὐαγγέλιον can be transmitted? However, regardless of these two reasons, Smith's study yields a number of important facts for our inquiry into Mark as tragic drama. I agree with Smith on a number of points, but as Smith himself observes, "further progress may yet be made."[104]

The final study that I will examine is Jeff Jay's 2014 book entitled *The Tragic in Mark: A Literary-Historical Interpretation*. In it, he seeks to examine the relationship of Mark's Gospel and Greek tragedy according to a theory of modes. By suggesting that Mark illustrates his story by using a tragic mode, Jay is able to avoid the criticism of certain scholars who observe that Mark does not appear in the same style as fifth-century Attic tragedy.[105] On mode, Jay defines it as "an evocation or distillation of a genre's internal repertoire."[106] He goes one step further by suggesting that construing the relationship between Mark and tragedy in terms of mode "reveals the relevance of motifs and moods that are not central to Aristotle's account, such as revenge, lamentation, general pathos (beyond pity and fear), the supernatural, and the oracle."[107] It is clear from this quote that Jay's adoption of the tragic mode as an interpretive lens for the Gospel is an attempt to demarcate Mark's Gospel from Aristotle. This is an appropriate step, since Aristotle ought to be seen as nothing more than an observer of tragedy, as Smith points out.[108]

But what is a tragic *mode*? Jay does not explicitly define what a tragic mode is other than to suggest that a it is an "evocation" or a "distillation" of a genre's repertoire. At several points, Jay seems to refer

---

104. Smith, "Divine Tragedy," 231.

105. Jay (*Tragic*, 18–19) notes Lang ("Kompositionsanalyse," 18–22), who calls Mark's presentation of the Gospel story as "in Analogie zu einem antiken Drama" ("in analogy with an ancient drama"). Lang prefers to understand Mark's "genre" as a type of epic which, according to Aristotle, is a mix of drama and narrative. For others who suggest that Mark contains modes of tragedy that are separate from its genre, see Burridge, *Gospels*, 239–40; Collins, *Mark*, 91–93.

106. Jay, *Tragic*, 21.

107. Jay, *Tragic*, 21.

108. Smith, "Divine Tragedy," 210.

to this phenomenon but does so by a different title. For example, he uses unexplained phrases such as "tragic type of narrative"[109] and tragic "motifs and moods" that appear in biographies, histories, and novels.[110] He then goes on to explain that his argument will demonstrate the value of the concept of "mode" as a lens for ascertaining the "inter-generic" evulsions of tragic drama.[111]

Jay then turns his attention to ancient biography and historiography, and suggests that the tragic mode can be discerned in the writings of such authors as Dionysius of Halicarnassus, Lucian of Samosata, and in various ancient novels.[112] He stresses that the identification of tragic typologies within the works of these authors ought not to be understood as genre-defining, but again as indication of the presence of a tragic mode. One is able to identify a tragic mode by its announcement through "tragic motifs, moods, values and attitudes."[113] Again, Jay does not offer any definitions or criteria by which one can discern such motifs, moods, values, or attitudes, though he does offer certain examples. One such example is found in a story by Xenophon (*The Ephesian Tale of Anthia and Habrocomes*), in which Hippothous warns Habrocomes that his narrative "is long and contains much tragedy."[114] This is problematic—especially since Jay's adoption of tragic modal articulation helps him avoid the rigid, genre-defining challenges that Aristotle presents—because Jay has to articulate a set of criteria by which to discern the presence of a "tragic mode." As a result, Jay runs the risk of being equally as dogmatic as Aristotle or of not being able to provide any sustainable criteria.

Jay then applies his theory of tragic modes to various other kinds of literature and authors such as Maccabean literature, Josephus, Philo, Mark's Gospel, and John's Gospel. With regard to Mark's Gospel, Jay devotes only 55 of 268 pages to an analysis of Markan material. Where he *does* apply his methodology to Mark's Gospel, he discusses such

109. Jay, *Tragic*, 27.
110. Jay, *Tragic*, 28.
111. Jay, *Tragic*, 28.
112. Jay, *Tragic*, 25–78.
113. Jay, *Tragic*, 76.
114. Xenophon of Ephesus, *Eph.*. 3.1–3. Jay, *Tragic*, 75.

topics such as reversal, oracular inexorability, recognition, revenge, *deus ex machina*, the ending of Mark's Gospel, lamentation, and the events of the Passion (mockery, procession, and crucifixion). While I appreciate the great effort that Jay has put into his research, I do not find his treatment of these subjects convincing. This is primarily because Jay does not establish how, and in what ways, a tragic mode can be readily identified.

This can be illustrated by examining what Jay says with regard to reversal. Jay argues that Jesus' true identity—known from the prologue (1:1–13)—constitutes "first-level" knowledge known only by the narrator and the audience. "Second-level" knowledge, on the other hand, is reserved for "the other characters, including Jesus, John the Baptist, the disciples, the Pharisees, Herod, Hernias, the chief priest, Pilate, and others."[115] Because Jesus' true identity is known as early as the prologue, the audience is able to fully appreciate how Jesus' identity fits into his ministry. In addition, the audience is able to appreciate the great number of plot reversals that occur throughout the narrative. For example, Jay argues that the power that is revealed through Jesus in the early chapters of the Gospel provides the basis for the greatest reversal as he hangs dying on the cross *deus absconditus*.[116] But this "suffering reversal" is not the only type of reversal in the Gospel. Jay points to the reversal of events in the life of the demoniac in ch. 5 as an example of a positive reversal: the man who once lived amongst tombs and cut himself now sits calmly with Jesus having a sound mind (5:15).[117] This treatment of reversal in Mark's Gospel is contrasted with that of Bilezikian and Smith, who argue that the narrative hinges on one key reversal, which occurs in 8:27–31.[118] Jay suggests that this interpretation is too closely linked to Aristotle, who asserts that reversal is best accompanied by recognition.[119] However, this is rather confusing, especially with regard to the suggested examples of Jesus' death and Legion's exorcism, because both instances of reversal occur in conjunction with

115. Jay, *Tragic*, 179.
116. Jay, *Tragic*, 183.
117. Jay, *Tragic*, 184.
118. Jay, *Tragic*, 185.
119. Jay, *Tragic*, 185.

recognition (5:7; 15:39). For this reason, I find Jay's treatment of reversal problematic for two reasons. The first reason is that Jay fails to convince as to why reversal is exclusively "tragic." It is plausible that reversal exists within tragic plots—or modes, as he suggests—but it is not plausible that a reversal of plot only occurs in tragedy or, when it does, that a tragic "mode" has been inserted. The second reason why this is problematic is because Jay never establishes a working set of criteria by which we can test the occurrence of a reversal. Bilezikian and Smith offer a better model by hinging reversal on recognition, whereas Jay's model appears rather subjective and is difficult to agree or disagree with as a result.

CONCLUSIONS

This chapter has summarized and evaluated the major works that compare Mark's Gospel with the genre of tragedy. Each of the authors mentioned above brings something unique to the discussion. Yet although each of these works is important and intriguing in many ways, I have highlighted a number of shortcomings with regard to each one. Each of these shortcomings is in need of reevaluation and reconsideration, which I will provide throughout the chapters to come.

2

The Prevalence of Tragedy

From Ancient Greece to the Twentieth Century

INTRODUCTION

THE FIRST CHAPTER OF this study focused on modern scholarly conceptions of Greek tragedy as it relates to the Gospel of Mark. This chapter will survey the legacy of Greek tragedy from Plato to the modern day. The purpose of this chapter, therefore, is to highlight the massive impact that Greek tragedy has made. It can be argued that tragedy has helped shape an enormous number of academic disciplines from ancient and modern philosophy to grammar—and certainly biblical studies. What I will demonstrate in this chapter is that the essence of tragedy goes beyond a classification of genre; it is something that pervades human existence. This is perhaps why tragedy is still regarded as a major focal point in philosophy: because tragedy provides a means by which we can begin to come to terms with things like suffering and mortality. It seems natural, therefore, to suggest that Mark would root his Gospel within the tragic tradition because suffering and death are prominent themes in the Gospel of Mark.

The Prevalence of Tragedy

ANCIENT GREEK TRAGIC THEORY

Plato (427–347 BCE)

Plato's attitude towards tragedy is mostly negative, though he does acknowledge that tragedy possesses a power that can influence an audience.[1] One must keep in mind that Plato's negative review of tragedy is tied to his larger concern for justice and for establishing an idealized, healthy state.[2] In many ways, tragedy is regarded as a threat to the stability of such a state, and has a quality that subverts the standards that Plato seeks to establish.[3] As Gellrich points out, the fact that Plato wants to discuss an ideal construct rather than the social reality of his time does not mitigate the force of his critiques, which reveal a disapproval of the poetic arts as they were and had been practiced in Greece.[4]

At the heart of Plato's attack on tragedy lies his concern for pedagogy and he asks what kinds of education will equip his people with the proper attitudes for guardianship of the state. Said another way, what kinds of restrictions ought to be placed on exposure to Homer, Hesiod, and the tragedians?[5] Plato's major problem with tragedy, as with all genres of poetry, is the level of discord that is produced within the individuals who hear it. He names Homer, whom he calls the "teacher of tragic poets,"[6] as being chiefly responsible for this discord since the epics are filled with quarrels, and quarrels are the basest of all things.[7] Citizens of the ideal state must, therefore, not be exposed to such quarrelsome fables—especially when gods are involved—or else they may find themselves imitating the actions of the characters depicted. Tragedy, then, has the power to engender certain negative passions within its audience and these passions are based on the lies that Homer and Hesiod tell about the strife between the gods and humanity.

---

1. Along with comedy, Plato (*Phileb.* 104–5) lists tragedy as one of the chief species of drama that mixes pain and pleasure.
2. Gellrich, *Tragedy and Theory*, 96.
3. Plato, *Gorg.* 502b.
4. Gellrich, *Tragedy and Theory*, 96.
5. Plato (*Leg.* 7.816b–817) later describes certain restrictions on viewing comedy and tragedy.
6. Plato, *Resp.* 606e.
7. Gellrich, *Tragedy and Theory*, 97.

Of Conflict and Concealment

In books 2 and 3 of the *Republic*, Plato differentiates three kinds of speech that appear in poetry: narrative, dramatic, and mimetic. Dramatic and mimetic speech are considered to be especially dangerous with regard to what was said above and are to be avoided. This is primarily because literature that employs dramatic and mimetic speech—the epic and tragic genres—are concerned with imitating the sublime, or what the poet falsely perceives to be the sublime. Here we notice a fundamental difference in the way that Plato conceptualizes the physical and metaphysical realms, which is quite different from how the poets conceptualize them. For the poets, the gods fight and scheme with and against one another, but for Plato, God is unable to commit such evil, nor is he quarrelsome. Plato seems to be charging the poets with the crime of falsely imitating the heavenly realm, and this crime deserves the highest penalty because audiences tend to imitate that which they see and hear in dramatic and mimetic speech—especially that of the sublime. Those who imitate others in such a way become "two or more" persons at once (διπλοῦς καὶ πολλαπλοῦς), a practice that will, in time, erode one's integrity.[8]

In book 10 of the *Republic*, tragedy is at the forefront of the discussion. Here Plato's Socrates epitomizes tragedy as embodying the worst dangers for society. Tragedy is entirely mimetic in nature, and its content is almost always morally and socially subversive.[9] Tragic characters embody a state of self-contradiction without rational control, making it more harmful for the audience who wants to enter into their plights and mourn for them. This emotive response to tragedy then encourages the audience to imitate the morally misdirected characters being represented. This is why Socrates says that, "few, I believe, are able to infer that enjoying another's feelings necessarily affects our own, for once pity has grown strong through others' sufferings, it is not easy to

---

8. Plato, *Resp.* 394a–395.

9. Gellrich, *Tragedy and Theory*, 99. Here Gellrich points out that the force that drives Plato's argument is gained from the discussion of the tripartite soul found in book 4 of the *Republic*. Mimetic art does not have its origin in, or appeal to, the highest part of the soul, the logical faculty. Instead, it draws its subject matter from an inferior type of person who does not have unity of mind. Such a person is at war within themselves. See Plato, *Resp.* 435c–442d.

restrain our own."[10] Thus tragedy breeds a level of conflict through pity that subverts a person's psychological, moral, and social mind. Such discord, contrary to what Plato calls *stasis*, leads only to chaos and anarchy.[11]

What must be noted in the above descriptions is that Plato admits to the powers of tragedy in much the same way that Aristotle and the other grammarians do (see below). Plato's major objections, however, are concerned with values and philosophical justification.[12]

Aristotle (384–322 BCE)

While Plato understood tragedy as tending to erode integrity and subvert the minds of its audiences, Aristotle offers a counter argument in favor of tragedy.[13] Like Plato, Aristotle understands poetry to be a mode of imitation. Beyond this point, however, we find little in common between Plato and Aristotle with regard to tragic theory. This lack of commonality can be accounted for, I think, as a result of the distinctly different philosophical bases upon which their theories are built. As mentioned, Plato asserted that the poet creates an imperfect copy of the actual, while the actual is an equally imperfect copy of the Ideal. As a result, a poet is twice removed from Truth, and is, therefore, superficial in his knowledge of the things he imitates. Yet imitation for Aristotle is something quite different. Poetic imitations of real life are not superficial renderings of twice-removed Truths, they are instead vehicles for understanding universal Truths. In other words, poetic imitations are replicas of things that happen in the real world, and these imitations represent lessons that Aristotle considered to be universally applicable.

All that we have left of Aristotle's teachings on tragedy are found in the *Poetics*. This is unfortunate because the *Poetics* appears to be

---

10. Plato, *Resp.* 606b; Gellrich, *Tragedy and Theory*, 101.

11. Plato speaks of such discord in other places as well. For example, Plato (*Leg.* 48a) suggests that the states of pain and pleasure originate in tragedy and comedy. He also sets out guidelines by which society ought to regulate the viewing of both tragedy and comedy (7.816b–817).

12. McMahon, "Seven Questions," 105.

13. I am indebted to the work of Sandys (*Classical Scholarship*, 62), who provides an excellent survey of ancient scholarship.

incomplete in many ways.[14] The first example of its apparent incompleteness is found in Aristotle's definition of tragedy itself. He defines tragedy as: "the mimesis of an action which is elevated, complete and of magnitude; in language embellished by distinct forms in its sections; employing the mode of enactment, not narrative; and through pity and fear accomplishing the catharsis of such emotions."[15] Perhaps the most famous point of debate with regard to this definition, and the *Poetics* in general, is the mention of *catharsis*. As we will see, scholarship has struggled to define exactly what Aristotle means by this, since Aristotle himself never tells us what he means. This is hugely problematic because Aristotle seems to correlate the degree to which a play is tragic and the degree to which the audience responds to it emotionally.

Another example of how the *Poetics* appears to be incomplete is in Aristotle's lack of attention to conflict. The *Poetics* does not mention anything about gods, fate, or ethics—all of which feature prominently in Greek tragedy. We cannot be sure why Aristotle left this out of his exposition of tragedy, though we might surmise, as Gellrich does, that Aristotle's lack of attention to these topics might well preclude his overall goal of creating a systematized, logical treatment of tragedy.[16] So, in one regard, we should praise Aristotle's attempt to arrange such an exposition, but, in another, we ought to be aware of its apparent shortcomings.

Such shortcomings, however, have not exempted Aristotle's *Poetics* from taking a prominent role in a large number of discussions regarding tragedy. This much is obvious from the previous chapter, which showed how prevalent the *Poetics* is in discussions of how Mark might relate to tragedy. But is this a valid representation of how the ancients regarded the *Poetics*? I think there are a number of good reasons

---

14. Sandys (*Classical Scholarship*) asserts that the *Poetics* is "a most suggestive work which has come down to us in an unsatisfactory condition, imperfect in some of its parts and interpolated in others" (73). Sandys sees the *Poetics* as "obviously incomplete" (74), with lyric poetry ignored and comedy noticed in a "slight sketch of its origin" (74). With regards to comedy, Aristotle sets out to explain comedy, but does not actually arrive at explaining it. With regards to *catharsis*, he tells us in the *Politics* that he will attempt to explain it more fully in his treatise on Poetry (ἐν τοῖς περὶ ποιητικῆς), but he does not do so in the text we have.

15. Aristotle, *Poet.* 1449b 23–28.

16. Gellrich, *Tragedy and Theory*, 11.

to suggest that Aristotle's *Poetics* became an obscure document shortly after his lifetime and that it was not regarded as an important document until the Middle Ages.[17] In fact, none of the theorists from either the Greek or Roman periods that I mention below ever cite the *Poetics*. Instead, they all refer to a definition of tragedy that cannot be found in the *Poetics*. This could mean that the *Poetics* was written in two or more parts, now lost, as Janko has argued at length,[18] or that Aristotle wrote a completely separate document. The latter view has been argued by McMahon,[19] who suggests that Aristotle wrote a second treatise on drama entitled *On Poets*[20] that is now mainly lost.[21] I do not intend to argue for either position here, but I do want to draw attention to the fact that the ancient Greek and Roman definitions of tragedy do not originate in the extant document we call the *Poetics*.

This creates a number of problems for those scholars who want to interpret Mark as a tragedy in light of the *Poetics*. While it is possible that Aristotle's *Poetics* existed and was influential during the first century, it becomes much less probable when we consider that none of the major tragic theorists mention it. I do, however, think that it is important to summarize Aristotle's description of tragedy found in the *Poetics*—however problematic it may be—because it does provide some insight into how he perceived fifth-century Attic drama.

This being said, it is important to note that Aristotle's description of tragedy is not prescriptive. What is more, a large number of the

---

17. The *Poetics* remained in obscurity until it was translated into Latin by William of Moerbeke in 1278. For a complete discussion, see Kelly, "Aristotle," 161–209. This particular translation survives in only two manuscripts and received almost no attention until the twentieth century.

18. Janko, *Aristotle on Comedy*.

19. For further discussion, see McMahon, "Seven Questions."

20. According to Rose (*Aristotelis*, 76), we have only eight fragments of this treatise, which provide evidence of a greater treatment on the subject of tragic and comedic poetry.

21. Halliwell ("Introduction," 17–18) suggests that a second book is not completely inconceivable, but that it is more likely that the *catharsis* clause is more fully explained in Aristotle's earlier work *On Poets*. Halliwell speculates that Aristotle's treatment of *catharsis* would have been introduced to block the Platonic charge that the arousal of emotion by tragedy was dangerous. See Ross, *Aristotelis Fragmenta Selecta*, 69, fr. 5.

extant tragedies diverge from his description, reducing his description to mere opinion. But it is an important opinion, nonetheless, since no one had ever attempted such a description until Aristotle.

Aristotle understood any dramatic performance to be an imitation of reality. He says, "epic poetry and tragedy, as also comedy, dithyrambic poetry, and most flute-playing and lyre-playing, are all, viewed as a whole, modes of imitation."[22] To create a tragic play, one must learn to imitate real-life situations and depict them on stage. Creating a tragic play, therefore, is no different than an artist who chooses the right colors and forms by which to imitate an object in a painting.

The dramatist imitates actions with characters who are either ethically good or bad. Aristotle divides the characters into two groups: the *spoudean*, who are of above average quality in character, and the *phaulic*, who are below average quality in character.[23] The differences in various types of drama—epic, tragic, and comedic—depend on what type of characters the dramatist chooses.

Aristotle defines tragedy as an imitation of an action that is essentially *spoudean*. He names Homer's *Iliad* as the epic model upon which tragedy is based: *spoudean* men engaged in actions in narrative form. The major difference between epic and tragedy, then, is that tragedy is explicitly written for the purpose of being performed on stage.

These acted, *spoudean* actions are portrayed in such a way as to promote *catharsis* in their audience. *Catharsis*, we may remember, is the release of emotion, particularly pity and fear.[24] We do not know exactly what Aristotle meant by this, but we can say that he believed that emotion ought to be a byproduct of viewing tragic drama.[25] *Catharsis* is realized by the unfolding of plot and Aristotle is careful to distinguish those things which make a good tragic plot from those things that do not. For example, a bad person going from bad to good fortune is the most "untragic," whereas moving from good to bad fortune is preferable. A wholly good and virtuous person suffering a tragic fate is also rejected by Aristotle, as well as the fall of a wholly evil person. The only

---

22. Aristotle, *Poet.* 1447a 14–19.
23. Aristotle, *Poet.* 1448a 1–20.
24. Aristotle, *Poet.* 1449b 27–28.
25. Kelly, *Ideas and Forms*, 2–3; McMahon, "Seven Questions," 98–118.

type of plot that works, then, is that of a person not thoroughly good, who falls because of some defect (*hamartia*). Of course, it is important to note that not all tragedies follow this plot structure; it is merely Aristotle's opinion that the best tragedies do so.[26]

At first, it appears as if Aristotle prefers that a tragedy end in an unhappy way, since he names Euripides as the most tragic of poets due to his unhappy endings. But Aristotle later declares that certain plays with happy endings are the best, and he outlines four possible plot trajectories:[27]

1. The protagonist intends to commit an evil deed and commits it
2. The protagonist commits an evil deed and only later realizes it to be evil
3. The protagonist intends to commit an evil deed but realizes it to be evil in time to stop
4. The protagonist intends to commit an evil deed, well aware of how evil it is, but stops

Aristotle prefers the third option and declares the fourth to be the worst. He cites Euripides' *Iphigenia Among the Taurians* as an example of the best, in which Iphigenia is about to sacrifice her brother Orestes but stops short when she realizes that he is her brother. The fourth option is the worst because it is not tragic in the sense that it contains no *pathos*, or tragic occurrence. There is an obvious contradiction between what Aristotle says here about happy endings and what he says earlier about unhappy endings.[28]

---

26. This is also noted by Kelly (*Ideas and Forms*, 3) who says that most modern, simplified reports of the *Poetics* do not make this distinction.

27. Aristotle, *Poet.* 1453b 26–43.

28. Kelly (*Ideas and Forms*, 4–5) argues the same, and points out that Aristotle could not avoid calling the works of Euripides "tragic" though more than a third of his plays ended happily. There is no doubt that Aristotle's ambivalence towards a happy ending was rooted in his devotion to Homer. At one point, he calls the *Odyssey* a comedy due to its outcome, but also praises the unity of both the *Iliad* and *Odyssey* by suggesting that tragedies can be derived from each (*Poet.* 1459b 3–5). This is because Aristotle believes the parts of epic to be similar to those of tragedy, and that Homer produced two kinds of tragic plots (*Poet.* 1459b 6–8).

OF CONFLICT AND CONCEALMENT

In conclusion, while Aristotle's description of tragedy in the *Poetics* is important for our overall discussion, it is a problematic text due to its apparent contradictions and lack of description of certain prevalent features of Greek tragedy. It is possible that Aristotle explained some of the missing features in another document, but such a document is lost and leaves us with, at times, a rather confusing exposition of tragic theory.

Theophrastus (371–287 BCE)

Theophrastus is important to this discussion because he succeeded Aristotle as the head of his school, called the Peripatos.[29] Cicero tells us that Theophrastus taught on the same topics that Aristotle did, and most likely taught the whole of Aristotelian philosophy as the head of the school.[30] Diogenes Laertius ascribes to him the authorship of at least ten works on rhetoric, one in particular entitled *On Style* (περὶ λέξεως) that was still existent at the time of Cicero.[31] Theophrastus is explicitly named in Cicero's *Orator* in connection to excellence in style, rhythm of prose, use of the paean, the effects of emotion, beauty of diction, and use of metaphor. Quotations of his work also appear in the Augustan age, in which traces of his work can be found in several passages of Dionysius of Halicarnassus.[32]

Theophrastus provides a link to the Latin world with regards to tragedy, as witnessed by the grammarian Diomedes.[33] We read Theophrastus' definition of tragedy in Diomedes: τραγῳδια ἐστὶν ἡρωϊκῆς τύχης περίστασις, which translated means, "tragedy is the encompassing

---

29. Kelly, *Ideas and Forms*, 1n2. Aristotle died in 322 BCE and was succeeded by Theophrastus, who named the school as such because of the covered walk in the buildings that he set up. He died in 287 BCE and was mostly known for his anti-matrimonial treatise called *Characters*. This treatise is preserved by St. Jerome (*Jov.* 1.47).

30. Cicero, *Fin.*, 1, 2, 6.

31. Diogenes Laertius, *Lives* 5, 36; McMahon, "Second Book," 43–44.

32. Sandys, *Classical Scholarship*, 99. Dionysius of Halicarnassus, *Comp.* 16; *Lys.* 14; *Dem.* 3; *Isocr.* 5.

33. Some of what Theophrastus wrote is preserved by fourth-century Latin grammarian Diomedes. I will discuss Diomedes and his contributions to tragedy in more detail below.

of heroic crisis."³⁴ Here we find traces of Aristotle's *spoudean* category, but worded much differently. As a result, there is some speculation, particularly by McMahon, as to where Theophrastus' definition of tragedy came from. It is possible that Theophrastus constructed his own definition quite apart from Aristotle, but it is also possible that he gleaned his definitions from another of Aristotle's works.³⁵ This may tell us that the *Poetics* had already begun to fall out of circulation as early as the time of Theophrastus.

Aristophanes of Byzantium (257–185 BCE)

Aristophanes of Byzantium is listed by Sandys as holding one of the foremost places in scholarship the ancient world.³⁶ He was the successor of Eratosthenes as head of the library in Alexandria during the second century BCE and was most known for his text-critical work on Homer. He also generated a number of *scholia* on the Greek poets—particularly on Euripides and Aristophanes—and edited the texts of a number of others, even writing introductions to each of the three tragic poets.³⁷ Pertinent to this discussion, however, is the lack of reference to the *Poetics* in his discussions of tragedy. Instead, we must surmise, Aristophanes derived his definitions and knowledge from another source(s).³⁸

---

34. Keil, *Grammatici Latini*, 1:487.

35. As mentioned above, McMahon ("Second Book," 46) argues that Theophrastus is drawing from a definition found in Aristotle's *On Poets*. He dismisses the idea of a second book of the *Poetics* on the basis that there is no reference to a second book on poetics in the Aristotelian corpus. Instead, he appeals to several bibliographic lists provided by later authors who mention a separate document entitled *On Poets*, which was split into three different books. At the end of his article, he says, "The Theophrastian definition (of tragedy) would then have been found in the third book of the dialogue *On Poets*."

36. Sandys, *Classical Scholarship*, 126.

37. Sandys, *Classical Scholarship*, 128–29.

38. McMahon, "Seven Questions," 106.

Dionysius Thrax (170–90 BCE)

Dionysius Thrax was a prominent grammarian during the Alexandrian age, authoring the earliest extant Greek grammar.[39] He also authored two or three works on rhetoric and a number of commentaries on Hesiod and Homer. He commented on tragedy in a number of places and defined it as, Ἵνα τὴν μὲν τραγῳδίαν ἡρωϊκῶς ἀναγνῶμεν ("so that we might know tragedy heroically").[40] We notice a convergence with Theophrastus' definition, particularly with the usage of ἡρωϊκῶς ("heroically"). Again, this may suggest that the definition of tragedy found in Theophrastus was being used more prominently than what is found in the *Poetics*.

A consideration of how viewing tragic drama influenced one's personal ethics was beginning to become a prominent theme amongst critics of this time, especially in Dionysius. McMahon has noted that later interpreters of Dionysius, such as Melampus and Diomedes, note the stress placed on ethics in Dionysius's writings. Tragedy was thought of as a warning to the audience against wrongdoing.[41]

ROMAN TRAGIC THEORY

Livius Andronicus (c. 290–200 BCE)

Boyle calls Livius the "father of Roman tragedy,"[42] even though he was Greek. He was born in southern Italy in the area called Magna Graecia and it is perhaps for this reason that Suetonius felt obliged to call him *semigraecus* (*Gram.* 1.2). His first work was perhaps the *Odusia*, which was a Latin adaptation of Homer's *Odyssey*. It is thought that this work preceded the rest of his dramas, though the *Odusia* constitutes the first attested literary translation of a literary work.[43]

In addition to translating the *Odyssey*, Livius began to translate a large number of Greek books into Latin, which helped foster a specifically Roman literary culture. He later began to write tragedies that were

---

39. Sandys, *Classical Scholarship*, 138; McMahon, "Seven Questions," 108.
40. Bekker, *Anecdota Graeca II*, 629.
41. McMahon, "Seven Questions," 110.
42. Boyle, *Roman Tragedy*, 27.
43. Boyle, *Roman Tragedy*, 27.

all Latin adaptations of the Greek originals. In doing so, he altered the verse to one more appropriate to a Roman audience and also adapted the story to fit with Rome's mythical Trojan origins.[44]

Livius seems to have preferred the works of Sophocles and Euripides, although he adapted their iambic and trochaic verses for more suitable cretic patterns. He also added more *cantina*, or sung monodies, to the originals, thereby increasing the musical emphasis in Roman theatre in contrast to Greek.

We have only fragments from eight of Livius's tragedies, and each deal with some aspect of Greek epic poetry: *Achilles*, *Ajax Mastigophrus*, and *Equos Troianus*, for example.[45] None of his plays were popular at the time of Cicero (*Ep. Brut.* 2.1.69–75), nor was Livius considered to be among the top ten Roman comic dramatists in a list compiled by Volcacius Sedigitus (*Gellius* 15.24).[46] He is, however, worth mentioning within this discussion because he provides a link between Greek and Roman tragic traditions.

Gnaeus Naevius (c. 280–201 BCE)

Naevius is also important to the founding of the Roman tragic genre because he was responsible for two major innovations. The first is that he established the practice of *contaminatio*, which is the fusion of two or more "source plays" into one.[47] The second is that he created a sub-species of tragedy called *fabula praetexta*, which is a type of historical play. Each of these innovations contextualized his plays within their culture, thus making them exceptionally relevant. For example, the practice of *contaminatio* allowed for ethnically diverse experiences to be culminated into what Boyle calls "single tokens of power."[48] His *praetexta*, on the other hand, allowed him to fuse foundational cultural myths to contemporary historical events. *Praetexta* is evident within

---

44. Boyle, *Roman Tragedy*, 28.
45. Boyle, *Roman Tragedy*, 29.
46. Boyle, *Roman Tragedy*, 36.
47. Boyle, *Roman Tragedy*, 37.
48. Boyle, *Roman Tragedy*, 37. This was particularly important since, as Rome expanded its territories, several different types of culture were being represented as "Roman."

his tragic plays, for example, in which several plots are derived from Trojan myth. Horace praises the *praetexta* (*Ars* 285–8), and Aelius Donatus likens them to tragedy (*De Com.* 6.1).[49] Diomedes also acknowledges the *praetexta*, and points out that, while the *praetexta* deal primarily with public affairs, they also incorporate Roman kings or generals in a way similar to tragedy (*Ars* 3; *GL* 1.489).[50]

The introduction of *fabula praetexta* also allowed dramatists to create a plot which embodied an ideological form of a chosen historical event. As Boyle points out, "The *praetexta* which directed itself to contemporary or recent historical events seems to have functioned in signal part as political laudation of a living or recently deceased member of the Roman elite."[51]

Lucius Accius (170–c. 86 BCE)

Lucius Accius was one of Rome's more active tragedians, writing nearly fifty plays in his lifetime. He covered a broad spectrum of topics, such as the house of Atreus, the Trojan war and its aftermath, the Theban cycle, the Argonautic expedition, the myths of Bacchus, of Hercules, of Theseus, of Perseus, of Prometheus, of Meleager, of Io, and a number of others. He thought highly of the famous Greek tragedies, though he seemed to favour Aeschylus and Sophocles over Euripides. He also imitated Homer and Hesiod and attempted to trace the mythic sagas throughout several generations.

His plays seem to favor a display of high spectacle in order to intrigue his audience. His *Phoenissae*, for example, opens with a spectacle of Jocasta's prayer to the sun; the *Medea* with a massively bewildered shepherd; and the *Decius* featuring ritualistic self-sacrifice. This tells us that tragedians like Accius very often attempted to evoke an emotive response—perhaps why Horace tells us that the mind is more affected by the eyes than ears (*Ars* 180–82; see below).[52]

---

49. Boyle, *Octavia*, xiv.

50. Boyle, *Roman Tragedy*, 49.

51. Boyle, *Roman Tragedy*, 49–50. For example, the performance of Gnaeus Naevius' *Clastidium* would have bolstered Marcellius' election to the plebeian tribunate (Livy 29.20.11).

52. See Boyle, *Roman Tragedy*, 109–42 for a full review of the fragments of

The Prevalence of Tragedy

Varro (116–27 BCE)

M. Terentius Varro is characterized by Cicero as *diligentissimus investigator antiquitatis* ("thorough investigator of history"),[53] by Quintilian as *vir Romanorum eruditissimus* ("the most educated man of the Romans" or "the most educated Roman man"),[54] and by Augustine as one who had done so much reading, that one wondered how he had any time left for writing.[55] Sandys tells us that his books numbered as many as 620, belonging to seventy-four separate works.[56] Of these books, he wrote a number on drama, on poetry, and on style.[57] He composed his own satirical poems, though they only survive in fragments.

McMahon argues that Varro's close connection to Dionysius Thrax and his pupils who edited the works of Aristotle and Theophrastus—especially Tyrannion—connects him to the Peripatetic tradition of tragedy.[58] Important to this discussion, however, is that Varro shows no knowledge or direction quotations of the *Poetics*, which may indicate that his conceptions of tragedy—derived from the Peripatetic school—were derived from a source other than the *Poetics*.

Cicero (106–43 BCE)

Cicero began his education by studying Greek philosophy under the Epicurean Phaedrus but soon averted his attention to the work of the Stoic Diodotus and to the Academic Philo, the student of Clitomachus. He studied in Athens (79–77) and at Rhodes. He had a keen interest in Greek literature and spent considerable time studying the works of Theophrastus.[59] As McMahon points out, Cicero complains at the beginning of the *Topics* that few philosophers at the time were familiar

---

Accius' surviving plays.
- 53. Cicero, *Brut.* 60.
- 54. Quintilian, *Inst.* x.1.
- 55. Augustine, *Civ.* vi .2.
- 56. Sandys, *Classical Scholarship*, 174.
- 57. Schanz, *Geschichte*, 433.
- 58. Fragments of his theory are preserved in Funaioli, *Grammaticae*, 209.
- 59. Sandys, *Classical Scholarship*, 182–84; Radford, *Cicero*, 18. Cicero mentions Theophrastus at several times throughout his works.

with the treatises of Aristotle.[60] Thus, while Cicero may provide little help in defining tragedy, he does tell us that Aristotle's treatises—and by extension, the *Poetics*—had little influence during Cicero's lifetime. It is more possible that this famous orator relied more heavily on the works of Theophrastus.

Horace (65–8 BCE)

The major work concerning tragedy in the ancient Roman world is the *Ars Poetica* (Art of Poetry) by Horace. It is a collection of observations on poetry with a major focus on tragedy, written to the Piso family, and published sometime towards the end of the first century BCE.[61] The *Ars Poetica* is written as a technical manual for poets in a way similar to the *Poetics*, with an aim similar to that of Aristotle.[62]

Horace does not give specific examples of how tragedy should be composed, though he contrasts the tragic with the comic and suggests that the two should never be mixed—except when contextually appropriate. Horace prefers that comedy, on the one hand, deal only with private people and their affairs, written in *priuata carmina* ("private songs"). Tragedy, on the other hand, ought to be concerned with public people, written in *sublimia carmina* ("lofty [public] songs"). Unlike Aristotle, Horace does not explicitly mention how or in what ways a good tragedy is written. Yet, like Aristotle, Horace seems to prefer the story of Thyestes as the exemplar of a well-written tragedy.

Though Horace does not offer examples of how a tragedy ought to be composed, he does give us a clue as to the purpose of tragedy. In line 98, Horace tells us that tragedy is meant to "touch the heart" of the audience in order that they might sympathize with the sufferings they witness (*Si curate cor spectantis tetigisse querela*, "If we take care to touch the heart"). This may reflect the attention being paid in the first century to rhetorical and literary theory that emphasized types of

---

60. McMahon, "Seven Questions," 121; Cicero, *Top.* section 1.

61. Kelly (*Ideas and Forms*, 5–8) dates the *Ars Poetica* to 13 BCE. He also notes that classical scholars frequently use the term "puzzling" when referring to this work. It is not certain exactly who the Piso family was, nor how original his ideas were, nor how accurately his opinions reflect the tragedy of his own day.

62. McMahon, "Seven Questions," 122–23.

speaking,⁶³ or it may reflect the *catharsis* clause that Aristotle mentions, but does not elaborate on, in the *Poetics*. On this point, Horace does not mention pity or fear as derivatives of good tragic form, yet there is attention paid to the emotive response of the audience. This tells us that Horace, like Aristotle, identified a common response to viewing tragedy, and it may suggest a link between Horace and the Peripatetic school. There is no evidence, however, that Horace was influenced by, or even aware of, the *Poetics*.

Another similarity between Horace and the Peripatetics is their shared respect for Homer. Horace thinks of Homer as the greatest writer for the stage, but, as noted by Kelly, we cannot be entirely sure what Horace thinks of epic and tragedy. It is probable that, like Aristotle, he viewed them as a similar prototype.⁶⁴

Ovid (43 BCE–18 CE)

The Roman poet Ovid is more explicit about his preference for tragedy over other forms of poetry. In his *Amores*, Ovid says that tragedy consists of *sublimia carmina* in contrast with elegy, which is a clear allusion to Horace.⁶⁵ He often attempted to imitate Homer and the Greek tragedians, even writing his own tragedies based on these authors.⁶⁶ In his *Tristia*, he states that tragedy surpasses all other kinds of writing in seriousness⁶⁷ and refers to his version of the *Medea*, which he calls "kingly writing."⁶⁸

---

63. Kelly (*Ideas and Forms*, 7) lists three types: grand, polished, and plain. He also argues that Horace thought of tragedy as an example of the highest rank. See also Brink, *Horace on Poetry* and the first-century anonymous treatise entitled *Rhetorical ad Herennium* (4.8.11).

64. Kelly, *Ideas and Forms*, 8.

65. Ovid, *Am*. 3.1.39–42.

66. Sandys, *Classical Scholarship*, 188.

67. Ovid, *Trist*. 2.381.

68. Ovid, *Med*. 2.553–54.

Of Conflict and Concealment
Lucius Annaeus Seneca (4–65 CE)

Of the many the Roman tragedies written during the early first century, Seneca's ten tragedies are some of the most prolific.[69] It is debated as to whether his tragedies were meant for the stage or to be read privately.[70] This is a difficult question to answer since a play could be brought to realization in a number of ways during this period. Boyle rejects the idea that the plays were written to be read privately, instead suggesting that the plays were meant to be performed to some audience, with more than one reader. This could happen, he says, "in the theatre or in a private house to a coterie audience (or both)."[71]

Seneca's plays dramatize a large number of themes and ideas: determinism of history; the genealogy and competitive cyclicality of evil; the fragility of social and religious forms; the fragility of epistemological formality and the failure of reason; civilization as moral contradiction; man as appetite, as beast, as existential victim; power, impotence, delusion, self-deception; the futility of compassion; the freedom, desirability, and value paradox of death; man, god, nature, guilt, unmerited suffering; the certainty of human pain, the terror of experienced evil; the perverse and paradoxical order of things; the triumph of evil; the possibility of human redemption; and the gap between language and the world.[72] It is clear from this long list that Seneca's tragedies represent an evolution, of sorts, in dramatic play writing.

The time during which Seneca wrote these plays was itself rather tragic. It was the end of Julio-Claudian Rome and was perhaps best characterized by the violence of Nero.[73] Seneca himself was affected by this violence, being forced to commit suicide because of Nero's suspicions. This is noteworthy because tragedies are often written within the

---

69. There is some debate as to whether all ten tragedies were written by Seneca. Boyle (*Roman Tragedy*, 189) lists *Hercules Furens*, *Troades*, *Medea*, *Phaedra*, *Oedipus*, *Agamemnon*, *Thyestes*, and *Phoenissae* as undisputed, and the *Hercules Oetaeus* and *Octavia* as uncertain.

70. Boyle, *Roman Tragedy*, 192.

71. Boyle, *Roman Tragedy*, 193.

72. Boyle, *Roman Tragedy*, 197–98.

73. Boyle (*Roman Tragedy*, 207) describes Nero as a fratricide, matricide, sororicide, uxoricide, and as a political murderer of children, and notes that he is often represented in Seneca's tragedies as a great source of evil.

context of great violence and political turmoil. In a way, the writing of tragedy—and this can be said of Seneca—is itself a type of *catharsis*. This is evidenced by Seneca's morbid glorification of death, the *libido moriendi* ("a lust for death"), which gave it a certain ascetic pleasure (Seneca the Younger, *Ep.* 24.25).

Dio Chrysostom (40–114 CE)

Dio Chrysostom was responsible for a revival of interest in Greek literature towards the end of the first century. He is said to have been a wandering poet, having been exiled from Italy sometime during the reign of Domitian (81–96 CE). He completed close to eighty discourses on various topics, including Homer and the three Greek tragic poets.

Regarding the three Greek tragedians, Dio notes how differently each spoke of the same subject. He suggests that the work of Aeschylus was "marked by customary grandeur, his antique simplicity, his audacity of thought and expression"; that of Euripides by "precision, acumen and rhetorical skill"; and Sophocles was in "the happy mean between the two, with its noble and elevated composition, and once tragic and harmonious, charming and sublime."[74] These quotations tell us that the Greek tragedies were still being studied and imitated in the first century.

Plutarch (40–125 CE)

Plutarch is considered by Sandys to be one of the most versatile and prolific literary critics of his time.[75] He went to Athens at the age of nineteen to study rhetoric, mathematics, and philosophy—especially that of Plato. He also appears to be influenced by Aristotle and Theophrastus on several points.[76]

With regard to tragedy—and poetry in general—Plutarch shows some reservation with regard to the older Greek poets and suggests

---

74. The original work is preserved by Arnim (*Leben und Werke*, 162). An English translation can be found in Sandys (*Classical Scholarship*, 299).

75. Sandys, *Classical Scholarship*, 302.

76. Hunter and Russell, *Plutarch*, 10. Plutarch engages in a familiar exegetical pattern of "problem" and "solution" which is observable in Aristotle's *Homeric Problems*.

that younger people should exercise great caution while reading them due to their primitive and undeveloped moral and religious thought.[77] It seems that Plutarch's concerns are primarily pedagogical, as he insists that teachers ought to be careful to administer pedagogical correctives where necessary. This also means that Plutarch is concerned with a tragedian's ability to inspire certain ethical standards—good or bad.[78]

Diomedes (c. 300–400 CE)

Diomedes was a fourth century Latin grammarian who appears to rely mostly on Theophrastus, Suetonius, and Varro as his main sources for discussing tragedy.[79] As we observed above, Diomedes credits Theophrastus for his definition: "Tragoedia set heroicae fortunae in adversis comprehensio ['Tragedy is a comprehension of heroes in adverse fortunes (scenarios)'];[80] a Theophrasto ita definita est: 'τραγῳδία ἐστὶν

---

77. This is found in a tractate entitled "How a young man should study poetry" (Plutarch, *Mor.* 14–37). Sandys (*Classical Scholarship*, 304) is unsure as to whether Plutarch himself wrote the tract but admits that the author is certainly influenced by Platonic thought concerning poetry. Poetry is dangerous in that it has the powerful ability to negatively influence its readers.

78. Hunter and Russell, *Plutarch*, 18–20. Plutarch urges his students to ask *why* a certain character chooses the course of action they do. By doing so, a student is able to judge what is ethical and what is not, hopefully avoiding the latter. Students should also be careful not to go too far in admiration of the poet, but instead learn to separate the imitation and the one doing the imitation. A student can therefore begin to judge poetry on the basis of the poetry itself.

79. Kelly, *Ideas and Forms*, 9.

80. I translate this word as "encompassing" or "arrangement." Latin writers, such as Cicero and Quintillian, also render this word to mean a collection of units (see Diomedes' *Ars Gramm.* 427, 465, 483–84). So, as Kelly (*Ideas and Forms*, 10) suggests, a syllable is a comprehension of letters; an epic is a comprehension of divine, heroic, and human matters. Another potential problem occurs when translating Theophrastus' περίστασις ("a standing around"). This could be confused with Aristotle's use of *peripateia*, which would then render the translation as "tragedy is the reversal of heroic fortune." This may link Theophrastus' definitions to Aristotle's *spoudean* category of tragedy, but I think, like Kelly, that this is a mistranslation. The word *peristasis* (literally "a standing around") is much broader than *peripateia* (literally "a falling around") and should be translated in a broad sense of "circumstance" or "situation." So, Theophrastus' definition has little to do with the *spoudean*: "tragedy is the encompassing of heroic fortune." The word *could* be translated as "crisis," in which case Theophrastus may be alluding to the effect of pity and fear. This is a reasonable conclusion and is most likely, given Diomedes' use of *in adversis*

ἡρωϊκῆς τύχης περίστασις' ['tragedy is the encompassing of heroic crisis']."⁸¹ He goes on to say that,

> Comedy differs from tragedy in that heroes, leaders, and kings are introduced into tragedy, but humble and private persons into comedy. In tragedy, there are lamentations, exiles, and slaughters, whereas in comedy we have stories of love and the abductions of virgins. Finally, tragedy frequently and almost always has sad outcomes to joyful affairs and the recognition that one's children and former good fortunes have taken a turn for the worse.⁸²

It appears that Diomedes prefers a tragedy whose characters are miserable, and a tragedy that ends badly. But what of the more cheerful Greek tragedies that ended well? Diomedes gives us no sign that he thought tragedies should embody anything other than sadness, perhaps best exemplified in the story he tells of Euripides' refusal to write a tragedy for Archelaus because Euripides hoped the king would experience nothing that is appropriate to tragedy.⁸³

As Kelly notes, Diomedes' definitions of tragedy are entirely descriptive and not prescriptive.⁸⁴ He does not provide as detailed a description as does Aristotle, nor is there any evidence that he consulted the *Poetics*. He does seem to allude to Horace in his descriptions of comedy and tragedy, in particular that comedies present only private persons whereas tragedies present more sublime content. It is also possible that his descriptions here allude to Aristotle's categories of *spoudean* and *phaulic* characterization. We do know that his direct quotation of Theophrastus links him to the Peripatetic school but we cannot be certain how aware Diomedes was of Aristotle's work.

("in contention with").
81. See n34 above.
82. Diomedes, *Ars Gramm.* 488.
83. Diomedes, *Ars Gramm.* 488.
84. Kelly, *Ideas and Forms*, 11.

Donatus (c. 300–400 CE)

Donatus, also writing in the fourth century CE, deals with tragedy in his commentary on the comedies of Terence.[85] Let us recall that for both Plato and Aristotle, Homer was the father of tragedy and comedy, though Aristotle thought that the *Odyssey* more resembled comedy.[86] Donatus also thought that Homer laid the foundations for what was to become tragedy and comedy. He says, "Homer, who is the most abundant source of nearly every kind of poetry, gave examples for these kinds of poems as well, and set down as it were a kind of law for them in his works. For one can see that he made his *Iliad* to be like a tragedy, and the *Odyssey* after the fashion of a comedy."[87] Drawing out the distinctions between the two genres, he later says,

> Many things distinguish comedy from tragedy, especially the fact that comedy involves characters with middling fortunes, dangers of small moment, and actions with happy endings, whereas in tragedy it is just the opposite: imposing persons, great fears, and disastrous endings. Furthermore, in comedy what is turbulent at first becomes tranquil at the end. In tragedy, the action is just the reverse. Then too, tragedy presents the sort of life that one seeks to escape from, whereas the life of comedy is portrayed as desirable. Finally, all comedy is based on invented stories, whereas tragedy is often derived from historical truth.[88]

---

85. Kelly (*Ideas and Forms*, 11–12) argues that much of what Donatus has to say about Terence and his comedies was taken from the work of Evanthius, another grammarian of the time. Evanthius' work is lost except for his introductory remarks which are preserved in Donatus' commentary. Donatus, who, according to Kelly, was one of St. Jerome's own teachers, flourished in the fourth century and was famous for his work entitled *Ars Grammatica Minor* and *Ars Grammatica Major*. See also McMahon, "Seven Questions," 126–28.

86. Bieber (*Greek and Roman Theater*, 2–3) tells us that Homer was considered to be the father of history, lyric poetry, tragedy, and comedy. She analyzes a relief from the second century BCE in which Homer is shown flanked on either side by a personification of comedy and tragedy. It seems that most of the ancient poets considered the *Iliad* to be the model for tragedy and the *Odyssey* the model for comedy.

87. Donatus, *Comm. Ter.* 1.5.

88. Donatus, *Comm. Ter.* 4.2.

The Prevalence of Tragedy

We can infer a number of things from this description. The first is that tragedy ought to begin well and end badly. This is different than comedy, which was to take the opposite trajectory of beginning badly and ending well.[89] However, this may be a distorted view, since the ten tragedies of Seneca—some of the only tragedies to have survived from the Roman period—do not begin pleasantly.[90] The second is that Donatus does not take into consideration the emotional effects of tragedy. This sets him apart from most other Roman commentators after Horace and his comments concerning the unhappy endings of tragedy link him to the Peripatetic school.

MEDIEVAL THEORY OF TRAGEDY

Ibn Rushd *aka* Averröes (1126–1198 CE)

Ibn Rushd—better known by his Latin name, Averröes—provides a link between the Aristotelian concept of tragedy found in the *Poetics* and the medieval world. As we have seen, the *Poetics* had been largely ignored until this time with the exception of an Arabic translation from Syriac, translated by Abu Bishr Matta sometime before 932.[91] A translation of Averröes' *Poetics Commentary* into Greek was conducted by Hermannus Alemannus in 1256, and a Latin version was later carried out by William of Moerbecke in 1278.[92]

Averröes' analysis of the *Poetics* deals largely with the effects of tragedy on its audience, in particular, the ways in which virtue and vice are communicated through the acts of either good or bad men. Tragedy, then, dealt with the works of virtuous men who are worthy of emulation, whereas comedy dealt with vicious men who ought to be condemned, categories which obviously correspond to Aristotle's categories of *spoudean* and *phaulic*.

---

89. Plautus, *Amphitruo*; McMahon, "Seven Questions," 119. Roman playwright Plautus attempted to write what he called a "tragico-comedy" in his *Amphitruo*. He classified it in this way because of the characters he introduced: gods and kings (tragedy) as well as slaves (comedy).

90. Kelly, *Ideas and Forms*, 14.

91. Kelly, "Aristotle," 163.

92. Gellrich, *Tragedy and Theory*, 165–66; Kelly, "Aristotle," 162–63.

OF CONFLICT AND CONCEALMENT

NINETEENTH-CENTURY THEORY OF TRAGEDY

Georg Wilhelm Friedrich Hegel (1770–1831 CE)

Hegel is one of the most important philosophers to discuss tragedy and this is largely due to the fact that he reconciles a number of lacunae that exist within Aristotle's *Poetics*. As was discussed in the section on Plato above, Plato's major critique of tragic drama was of its ability to conjure a level of *stasis* within its audience. Aristotle wrote his *Poetics* with this in mind, and the opinions of his predecessor no doubt influenced his approach of systemically analyzing fifth-century tragedy. However, while Aristotle certainly brought a level of rationalization to tragic drama contra his predecessor, the *Poetics* does not address some of the most important aspects of tragic drama—namely the concept of strife that produces *stasis*.[93]

Hegel attempts to answer questions that were left unaddressed by the *Poetics*, and this is precisely why Hegel is so important to our discussion of tragedy. Hegel's theory of tragedy is based on what he calls *Collision*,[94] a concept that he more or less adopts from the pre-Socratics.[95] Every tragedy contains some type of conflict or *Collision*: conflict of feelings, modes of thought, desires, wills, purposes, of persons with

---

93. This has been noted by Gellrich (*Tragedy and Theory*, 11), who says that "if conflict does not figure as an item in Aristotle's treatment of drama, it is because his insistence on the *logos* of tragedy precludes attention to precisely those elements that unsettle logical, ethical, and social order." The *Poetics* excludes any discussion of gods, necessity, and fate, as well as the issues of ethics that feature so prominently in the plays. Jones, *On Aristotle*, 11–62; Else, *Aristotle's Poetics*, 305–7.

94. Hegel (*The Philosophy of Fine Art*, 1:266) defines *Collision* as such: "The Collision arises, as we are now considering it, in an act of violation, which is unable to retain its character as such, but is compelled to find a new principle of unity; it is a change in the previous existent condition of harmony, a change which is still in process. The Collision, however, is not an action, and is to be taken as a stimulus to action to all that characterizes the situation . . . the Collision disturbs this harmony of what is truly real and ethical, and drives this concept of the Ideal into discord and opposition." See also Paolucci (*Hegel*, 113–14).

95. Since a discussion of pre-Socratic philosophy is beyond the aims of this chapter, I refer the reader to Gellrich, *Tragedy and Theory*, 23–93. However, let it suffice to say that strife was thought to be a force within the universe that brought about universal order. Hegel's theory disrupts the Platonic concept of strife insofar as it is understood negatively, thus giving it a regenerative quality.

The Prevalence of Tragedy

one another or themselves.[96] For Hegel, the essential element of tragedy is not whether it ends happily or unhappily, but in the purging effects of *Collision* on the audience who views the tragic drama. That a tragedy is a story about suffering is obvious and Hegel says almost nothing about it. Pity and fear understood in a traditional sense of empathy and shock do not suffice, either. Instead, the connection that each of us feels with tragedy lies much deeper within our sensibilities. *Collision* in tragedy is the portrayal of a conflict between two powers that the audience can relate to. Thus, the audience views one power, which is embodied by the hero, in conflict with another power that tests the hero's ethical substance. These conflicts can be between family and state, parent and child, brother and sister, husband and wife, citizen and ruler, or citizen and citizen with all the obligations and feelings appropriate to these bonds.[97]

Every audience member is therefore familiar with these powers of influence, which tragedy displays in *Collision*. Often, these conflicts are not between something good and something evil—this is uninteresting in tragedy. Instead, as audience members, we encounter a conflict between two good things that make incompatible demands.[98] For example, we can observe a tragedy that portrays a family demanding what the state forbids, or love demanding what honor forbids.[99] The solution comes at the cost of one power gaining precedence over the other and, therefore, the exclusive right of one power is denied. This is most clearly depicted in the story of Antigone, who is pressed between the tensions of duty to the state and duty to her family. The result is her death, which is her absolute assertion of the family against the state.[100]

---

96. Bradley, "Hegel's Theory," 55.

97. Bradley, "Hegel's Theory," 56.

98. Paolucci, *Hegel*, 117. Hegel gives a number of examples in which this type of conflict occurs. For example, he notes a number of instances in literature in which brothers are at odds with one another for certain rights. His primary example is that of Eteocles and Polynices, who, having been left to rule Thebes in alternating yearly successions, end up fighting one another for absolute control. We find this concept of Collision in a number of other sources as well, such as in the conflict between Cain and Abel, in the tale of Shah-Rameh, and in MacBeth.

99. Bradley, "Hegel's Theory," 56.

100. Bradley, "Hegel's Theory," 57.

The level to which we feel its power depends on how highly we value the two things in contention. By implication, then, one would not understand the tragic nature of Antigone's choice if great value was not ascribed to both family and to the state.

Once the common characteristic of *Collision* has been established, one can begin to appreciate how each tragic drama forms the conflict. For example, we can distinguish one tragedy from another in terms of the nature of the conflicts or the forces that move the characters within the drama, et cetera.[101] Conflict, therefore, can be identified as the *logos* of drama that provides unity to the shape of dramatic events.[102] Tragedy displays this conflict and thus provides a means for bringing order to an otherwise unexplainable tragic event.[103]

Søren Kierkegaard (1813–1855 CE)

Kierkegaard represents a continuation of Aristotelian analysis of tragedy in the nineteenth century. His pseudonyms mention tragedy in a number of places, but I will discuss those sections found in his *Either/Or* and *Fear and Trembling*. Each of these works feature an analysis of Aristotle's *Poetics* that, in particular, focuses on Aristotle's lack of attention to both κάθαρσις ("catharsis") and ἁμαρτία ("flaw"). Kierkegaard also applies his interpretation of the *Poetics* to a polemical reading of

---

101. Hegel (*Lectures on the Philosophy of History*, 31) mentions the concept of *Geist* as the force which moves the individual towards certain actions. The concept of *Geist* is fairly obscure, but he does seem to regard *Geist* as a rational substance that periodically immerses itself into the lives of nations and of individuals. Hegel understands world history to be the representation of *Geist* as it reveals itself to humanity and absolute knowledge can be apprehended when an individual apprehends him or herself as identical with the *Geist*. This grants to the concept of *Geist* a teleological end, and provides a sense that humanity is guided by a rational force despite being able to think and act for itself. *Geist* can manifest itself in a number of ways. One way is through human action, which according to Hegel is the actuality of a person's innermost being. Another way, closely related to the first, is through art—especially tragic drama.

102. Gellrich, *Tragedy and Theory*, 41–42, 94. Hegel's theory is comparative with Aristotle's in this regard, since both believe that there is a set of ordering principles that structure drama into a unified, contained whole.

103. Concerning this, Hegel (cited in Zerba, *Tragedy and Theory*, 40) states, "for ordinary sight only obscurity, accident, and confusion seem to have control, for him is revealed the real self-fulfillment of that which is in and for itself rational and true."

The Prevalence of Tragedy

Hegel's moralizing interpretation of Greek tragedy, an interpretation which greatly influenced classical scholarship during his lifetime.[104]

In his *Either/Or*,[105] the author—named "A"[106]—seeks to establish the differences and similarities between ancient and modern tragedy.[107] If we are to speak in generalities, tragedy remains the same: sad occurrences make people feel sadness just like funny occurrences make people laugh. But when we examine how different the things are that make people feel sad or laugh, we begin to realize that what is essentially "tragic" or "comic" is different depending on the generation, life situation, et cetera.[108] A attempts, then, to discern the special characteristic within ancient tragedy that still exists in modern tragedy.[109]

Modern tragedy differs from ancient in terms of its focal point. In modern tragedy, character and situation are predominant.[110] This leads to a modification of the Aristotelian notion of guilt, which in modern tragedy becomes highly ethical due to its focus on the hero.[111] A applies this observation to the age as a whole and suggests that individual choice and subjective reasoning governs its ethos. This fools everyone

---

104. Greenspan, "Poetics," 60.

105. The translation of Kierkegaard's *Either/Or* that I will be using is that of Victor Eremita.

106. According to Stendahl (*Søren Kierkegaard*, 83), "A" belongs to a club where elected and selected members come together to read papers to each other on aesthetic subjects. They call themselves the "Symparanekromenoi," which can be loosely translated as "the fellowship of those who live buried lives."

107. For a complete discussion, see Kierkegaard's words in the section entitled, "The Ancient Tragical Motif as Reflected in the Modern" (*Either/Or*, 139–61).

108. Kierkegaard, *Either/Or*, 140.

109. Kierkegaard, *Either/Or*, 140.

110. Here Kierkegaard (*Either/Or*, 143) distinguishes modern tragedy from how Aristotle characterizes the ancient. In ancient tragedy, the tragic circumstance is determined by the hero's actions. In modern tragedy, however, the tragic circumstance is determined by how the hero understands him or herself. Thus, there is a switch from the external to the internal with regard to what is "tragic." The result of modern tragedy is a change in the hero and not necessarily in his or her circumstances.

111. Kierkegaard (*Either/Or*, 144) suggests that the tragic lies somewhere between absolute subjective guilt and absolute subjective innocence, neither of which interests us tragically. Thus, the concept of guilt is no longer ascetic as it is in ancient tragedy but becomes ethical. This transforms the hero into someone evil and evil becomes the focal point of tragedy. This misses the point of tragic guilt, since proper tragic guilt ought to contain some level of ambiguous innocence.

into thinking that they are, in some senses, an absolute in and of themselves. A calls this mindset ridiculous and suggests that a reflection on the tragic is the only avenue by which one can become truly happy.[112]

An example of how modern tragedy differs from ancient is in A's retelling of the *Antigone*. The modern Antigone strives to discover what is wrong in her family and is forced to keep this painful secret hidden. She continues to mourn over her father's fate and continues to keep her mourning a secret from everyone, including her lover. As long as she can keep her secret, she can live with the pain caused by it. But, if she reveals her secret, she must die because she has betrayed herself. This modern version of *Antigone* clearly expresses the fundamental difference between ancient and modern tragedy, in which modern conceptions of guilt and consciousness differ from their ancient versions.

Another of Kierkegaard's authors—this time named Johannes de Silentio—names father Abraham as the quintessential "Knight of faith," and contrasts him with the ancient tragic hero in *Fear and Trembling*.[113] This work focuses primarily on the Aristotelian concept of discovery or recognition (ἀναγνώρισις), which relieves the religious mystery of fate.[114]

The essential argument that Silentio is making is concerned with what happens to the ancient hero at the moment of recognition. This moment relieves the tension surrounding fate and resolves the contradictions that scandalize the ancient hero.[115] There is, therefore, a telic function to recognition in ancient tragedy, one that orchestrates an end to the story and generates an ethical response. In other words, the ancient hero comes to terms with the power of fate through recognition and chooses an ethical course of action in response to fate. In doing so, the ancient hero responds to the external influences on his or her life by trying to live in accordance with them through ethics. The modern knight of faith also recognizes fate but realizes that he or she cannot

---

112. Kierkegaard, *Either/Or*, 144.

113. I will be using Walter Lowrie's translation of Kierkegaard, *Fear and Trembling*.

114. Greenspan, "Poetics," 66.

115. Greenspan ("Poetics," 66) notes such apparent contradictions in the status of Oedipus as husband and son, father and brother, king and exile.

appease fate through ethics. Instead, the knight of faith accepts the paradox of fate and learns to live with the paradoxes that it presents.

Friedrich Nietzsche (1844–1900 CE)

Nietzsche became an influential voice in the discussion of tragedy after the publication of *The Birth of Tragedy* in 1886.[116] This work is an attempt to philosophically explain how the Greek tragedians—especially Sophocles and Aeschylus—made sense of the world and humanity's existence in it. It argues that the tragic hero struggles to make sense of his or her existence in light of the seemingly unjust and chaotic throes of fate.

Nietzsche dichotomizes the viewing of tragic drama into two categories: the *Apollonian* and the *Dionysian*, named after two Greek deities. These two gods became analogous with two distinct types of art and philosophical thought—Apollo with plastic art and rationalization, Dionysus with music and revelry—both of which Nietzsche thought were expressed in Greek tragedy.

Tragedy is the theatrical expression of the one thing that humanity is inevitably forced to contemplate, and that is death. Nietzsche, like the ancients, understood the importance of thinking about death, which leads to certain philosophical considerations. Life *can* be seen as a series of chaotic, unconnected events that culminate in death, which prompts humanity to create sensible categories that attempt at some ultimate meaning. Such categories in and of themselves leave humanity unfulfilled and thus people become preoccupied with thoughts of the afterlife. Nietzsche blames this type of thought on the Socratic dialectic, which always attempt to neglect life for higher ideals. Such a mindset is constantly deflecting the potential of this life in exchange for a greater reality. One ought, he suggests, instead to be preoccupied with affirming the experiences of this life, both good and bad.

Nietzsche thought that Greek tragedy rejected this Socratic dialectic in favor of an acceptance of fate and suffering. He begins with the *Dionysian*, analogous with music and revelry, as a means by which the Greeks thrived despite death. The *Dionysian* is epitomized in the

---

116. The translation I use here comes from Kaufmann, ed., *Basic Writings of Nietzsche*, 15–144.

chorus, the means by which the audience partakes in the tragedy as an ideal spectator in "absorbed contemplation."[117] This psychological process allows one to be transformed into another character, and, in doing so, one realizes his or her connection with every other audience member. Since each audience member enters simultaneously with the others into another character, individuality is surrendered and "a whole throng experiences the magic of this transformation."[118]

While the *Dionysian* is represented by the chorus, the *Apollonian* is represented by the dialogue. The dialogue in Greek tragedy in turn represents the individual conception of the world. Thus, it stands in contrast to the *Dionysian* collectivizing experience by seeking to define and individualize experience. The true essence and brilliance of Greek tragedy, then, is found in the tension created between individualization and collectivity.

TWENTIETH-CENTURY THEORY OF TRAGEDY

Hans-Georg Gadamer (1900–2002 CE)

Gadamer most explicitly deals with the concept of tragedy in his *Truth and Method*.[119] His theory of tragedy is rooted in his overarching theory of hermeneutics, which, simply stated, was a rather prolific attempt at discerning how we understand (*verstehen*) and what "truth" is.[120]

---

117. Nietzsche, *Tragedy*, 8.62–63.
118. Nietzsche, *Tragedy*, 8.64.
119. I am using the translation of Joel Weinsheimer and Donald G. Marshall.
120. Grondin, "Basic Understanding," 37–39. Gadamer's philosophy of hermeneutics as set forth in *Truth and Method* is based on that of his teacher, Heidegger, but with alterations. Heidegger promoted a more "practical" notion of understanding, which had less to do with cognition and more to do with—as Grondin says it—a "know-how" type of process that reflected a person's capabilities. Therefore, to understand something did not mean that one could grasp a concept, but that one could perform a particular skill. This led to the idea that human existence was always in search of orientation in the world that is realized in action. Gadamer follows Heidegger insofar as he understands truth to be not simply an idea, but a practical concept; a concept that can also be derived from Aristotle's notion of practical understanding (*phronesis*). Unlike Plato who held abstract notions of things like "the good," Aristotle argued that what counts is being able to do "good" in human affairs. Therefore, practical wisdom lies in its actualization and not in abstract theory. Much of what Gadamer has to say about art—and subsequently tragedy—is based in a combination of Heideggerian and Aristotelean "practical" hermeneutics.

The Prevalence of Tragedy

This theory lends itself to much of what Gadamer has to say in *Truth and Method* about the concept of beauty, which is very much a critique of Kantian aesthetics.[121]

Truth is approximated to beauty, and beauty manifests itself in both poetry and painting. How one experiences this beauty, and subsequently truth, is through the concept of *play*. The term *play* refers not to the mind of the writer or audience, but to the "mode of being of the work of art itself."[122] In other words, what an author or audience thinks of the work of art is less important than the world that the art—such as a tragic play—creates. The experience of being drawn into the world of the piece of art is what changes a person. This is why Gadamer can say that "play has its own essence, independent of the consciousness of those who play."[123]

Tragedy is no different. Gadamer identifies an essence of tragedy that has not changed "from Aristotle down to the present."[124] Drawing on Aristotle, Gadamer identifies an aesthetic dimension of tragedy that is common to every form of tragedy, namely the effect tragedy has on its audience.[125] Like Aristotle, Gadamer mentions pity and fear as the emotions common to the tragic, and elucidates them as the kinds of emotions that overwhelm a person and sweep them away.[126] In beholding the powerful and, at times, unforgiving power of fate, the audience is forced to contemplate its own finiteness. In addition, the audience confronts itself and generates a sort of self-knowledge. In other words, the audience is placed into a position in which life is wholly outside of its control, and in doing so is forced to contemplate just how minuscule its life actually is. This place is never foreign but is always reminiscent of—if not identical to—the world of the audience. There is a continuity,

---

121. Dostal, "Introduction," 9.

122. Gadamer (*Truth and Method*, 102) says of play: "We can certainly distinguish between play and the behaviour of the player, which, as such, belongs with the other kinds of subjective behaviour. Thus it can be said that for the player play is not serious: that is why he plays. We can try to define the concept of play from this point of view."

123. Gadamer, *Truth and Method*, 103.

124. Gadamer, *Truth and Method*, 125.

125. Gadamer, *Truth and Method*, 126.

126. Gadamer, *Truth and Method*, 126.

as Gadamer states, that "links the world of art with the existing world and from which even the alienated consciousness of a cultured society never quite detaches itself."[127] This in many ways can be seen as a religious experience, because it forces the audience to contemplate and submit to the forces that control life itself. It is also an exercise in ontology that forces the audience to consider the reasons for its existence.

Northrop Frye (1912–1991 CE)

Frye's *Anatomy of Criticism* provides a modern perspective on Greek tragedy that seeks to further extrapolate Aristotle's categories of *spoudean* and *phaulic*.[128] He begins by describing the *fictional modes* as they are represented by Aristotle, and he names five. The first mode is the fullest sense of *spoudean* in that, if a hero is superior to other characters and to the environment in which they reside, the story is a *myth*—a story about a god. The second mode has a hero who is superior in *degree* to the other characters and to the environment, and whose actions are marvelous, but who is identified as a human being.[129] Such a story is typified as a *romantic* one and corresponds with folk tales. In the third mode, the hero is superior in degree to other characters, but not to his or her environment. The hero here is called a leader, and is of "high mimetic mode," according to Frye, and is typical of most tragedy and epic.[130] The fourth mode regards the hero as equal to the environment and to the rest of us. This type of character is of "low mimetic mode," and we expect the same of the hero that we expect of ourselves in our own experiences. The final mode is called the *ironic* mode, and contains a hero that is inferior in power and intelligence to ourselves.

---

127. Gadamer, *Truth and Method*, 129.

128. Frye, *Anatomy*, 33.

129. Frye (*Anatomy*, 33) characterizes the *romantic* mode by both the qualities of the characters and their actions. For example, the hero must be a prodigy of both courage and endurance. His qualities are unnatural to us, yet perfectly natural to him.

130. Frye, *Anatomy*, 34. This type of hero is primarily what Aristotle had in mind. According to Frye, this hero has powers of expression, authority, and passions far greater than ours but what he does is subject to both social criticism and to the order of nature.

The Prevalence of Tragedy

This mode usually corresponds to the absurd, and grants to the reader the feeling that he or she might find themselves in the same situation.

Turning to tragedy, Frye remarks that tragic stories apply to divine beings who die, such as Hercules, Orpheus, Balder, and Christ.[131] These divine beings must be isolated from their society in some way, and so they must "fall" in some sense. Moreover, the fall of this hero must be involved in some way with a relation to society and with a sense of the supremacy of natural law, thus creating a level of irony. Frye notes that these types of tragedies originate in an environment in which an aristocracy is fast losing its power but still retains a good deal of ideological prestige.[132]

Frye also comments on the emotive response of pity and fear to tragedy and suggests that these two emotions refer to the two general directions in which emotions can move. The types of pity and fear, however, relate to the mode of tragedy being viewed—either away from the object or towards it. This relates to the Aristotelian concept of *hamartia*, in that our emotive responses of pity and fear are not related so much to the hero's actions as they relate to his moral character, but to the consequences of those actions as a moral character. The tragic "flaw" therefore has much less to do with a moral failure than it has to do with the matter of the character being a strong one in an exposed position.[133]

Tragic irony is thus created by the isolation of the hero from his society. Frye identifies two opposite poles of irony combined in tragedy: inevitable and incongruous. Inevitable irony, on the one hand, is the irony of human life, the archetype of which is Adam, who epitomizes human nature under the sentence of death. Incongruous irony, on the other hand, is also the irony of human life, yet all attempts to

---

131. Frye (*Anatomy*, 35–36, 207–8) designates the tragic hero as being somewhere between divine and "all too human." He must be greater than the audience in every respect, but he must occupy a middle position between the audience and something larger, be it God, the gods, fate, fortune, et cetera. The tragic hero becomes the mediator between God and the audience and they are "wrapped in the mystery" of their communion with God, who we can only see through them. God then becomes the source of their strength and their downfall.

132. Frye, *Anatomy*, 37.

133. Frye, *Anatomy*, 38.

transfer guilt to a victim gives that victim something of the dignity of innocence. The archetype of incongruous irony is Christ, who is a perfectly innocent victim excluded from human society.[134]

CONCLUSIONS

The purpose of this chapter has been to draw attention to the wide range of theories surrounding what I am calling a "tragic genre." In doing so, we can begin to see both similarities and differences in the ways that various critics explain their theories of tragic drama. There are, however, two things that should be understood before we move on to an appropriation of the tragic elements in the Gospel of Mark. The first is that emotion is an integral part of tragedy. Beginning with Plato, emotion becomes an obvious concern for most critics of tragedy. Aristotle, however, poses the greatest challenge to defining how emotion and tragedy mix because he fails to explain in any depth how *catharsis* works. The same can be said of Horace, who admits the emotional effect that tragedy can have but, like Aristotle, also fails to offer an explanation as to how. It is not until the eighteenth and nineteenth centuries that we find more in-depth explanations of *catharsis*. This may be in response to Aristotle's apparent lack of explanation, or because the philosophical implications of tragedy that developed during this period require it.

A second point, largely connected to the first, is that tragedy contains a conflict that appears familiar to the audience. What I mean by this is that the quality of a tragic drama is dependent upon how well the audience can perceive the conflict and relate to it. This conflict is what eventually leads to the downfall of the hero in some respect. This theme is most readily taken up by Hegel in the nineteenth century, when he observes that tragedy is characterized by a tension between two goods. The hero is caught between two forces that, that, though both ethically responsible, cannot be reconciled. This type of conflict generates the most tragic scenarios, and, as a result, best captivates the audience.

All tragedies contain these two characteristics, emotion and conflict, and, because we are able to identify them, we can begin to

---

134. Frye, *Anatomy*, 42.

appreciate the ways in which the different tragedians craft their stories. A hero can be caught in an ethical struggle between upholding the laws of the state and obligations to family. In this particular example, Greek religion required adherence to both, and so the struggle becomes tragic since both choices lead to negative results. Tragedy, appearing in a number of different forms, can thus reveal the things that a particular society regards as important.

In terms of the relationship between the tragic genre and the Gospel of Mark, I must make two further points before I begin my analysis in the next chapter. The first is that Aristotle's *Poetics* had little influence in the first century when Mark was written. This is problematic for scholars who want to compare the categories of tragedy found in the *Poetics* with the Gospel of Mark. While the *Poetics* is a valuable document that describes the tragedies of fifth-century Athens, we must be mindful of the fact that by the first century CE, tragedies appeared in a variety of forms. Second, tragedies of the first century were written for a variety of contexts. We learn from an analysis of Seneca's tragedies that a tragic play could be performed in a theatre or in a private home.

3

The Elements of Tragedy

INTRODUCTION

IN THE PREVIOUS CHAPTER, I highlighted some major contributors to the study of tragic structure and theory, establishing that, prior to the first century when Mark was written, Aristotle's *Poetics* had slipped into relative obscurity. This alone has a major impact on how we as biblical scholars compare the Gospels with tragedy, because the ways we think about ancient tragedy may be misinformed. It is possible—as we saw with Seneca—that first-century tragedies began to take on a different form and purpose than those composed in fifth-century Athens.

Something else that was discovered is that, despite how we may interpret Aristotle, the form of tragedy does not influence its meaning and purpose. In fact, even if we narrow our study to fifth-century Attic tragedy, we do not find one common form of tragedy. Instead, tragedies took on a variety of forms that continued to be cultivated and shaped as time went on. We, of course, can tip our hat to Aristotle and to his meticulous descriptions of form in the *Poetics*, but we ought not be constrained by him. What we ought to say instead is that there are core elements evident within tragedy that generate a tragedy's content and form, and I have identified three.

In light of this, the purpose of this chapter is to outline these core elements of tragedy as they appear in the Gospel of Mark. These elements form the plot of every form of tragedy in the ancient world, and they are prevalent because everyone can relate to them. I have already identified death and suffering as two core elements, as well as how the tragic protagonist is often in *Collision* with some other power. In what follows, I will analyze Mark as it addresses both death and suffering, as well as how Mark fashions his story to pit Jesus against the established religious system in order to create *Collision*. What we will see is that Mark forms his story in such a way as to highlight these core tragic elements, and then produces a response to them.

THE CONCEPT OF *COLLISION* IN MARK'S GOSPEL

The concept of tragic conflict, or *Collision*, in Mark's Gospel is an important one. Without lessening the importance of the resurrection—which I hold is of central importance to the Christian faith—the crucifixion and the acts of conflict leading to it are, in my opinion, often overshadowed by a focus on what I call a *kerygmatic interpretation* of the Gospel.[1] Having said this, perhaps the reason why scholars have been unable to come to any kind of agreement on such things as the "messianic secret" or Jesus' famous usage of the title "Son of Man" is because they have overlooked the importance of conflict and how these things operate within the context of tragic conflict in the Gospel (see below). Jesus' proclamation of the arrival of the kingdom of God (1:15) and the miracles associated with his ministry, I suggest, ought to be understood as strategic, polemical statements that reveal Jesus' superiority as the Son of God to the temple, or, literally, God's home on earth.

To me, there appears to be a disjuncture of logic in Jesus' complete failure to convince any of the religious teachers—and in the end even his own disciples—and his cunning ability to perform miracles and persuade large crowds in Mark's Gospel. Therefore, the central

---

1. So much is said in Broadhead (*Prophet, Son, Messiah*, 283–84) when it is stated that the "central task of Jesus is proclamation" (284). Broadhead (284) also provides a number of occasions on which Jesus commands others to go and tell what they have seen and heard. Broadhead has missed the essential purpose of Jesus' proclamations, which are introduced as a paradigm shift from an already existing ideology (1:15), and that ideology is embodied by the temple and its representatives—the religious teachers. Therefore, the entire purpose of Jesus' ministry is to bring about such a paradigm shift, which means that he must constantly be in conflict, or *Collision*, with the temple and its representatives.

thesis of this section—and of this entire study—is that conflict with religious leaders is the necessary narrative tool that Mark uses both to illustrate the ways in which Jesus was in *Collision* with the temple, and to highlight the reasons that brought about his crucifixion. I arrive at this conclusion by asking, "If Jesus had persuaded the religious teachers of his message, would they have crucified him? And if not, how could the all-important resurrection have occurred?" There is a manner by which Mark illustrates Jesus' conflicts with the religious leaders, and, when examined under the lens of tragedy, these conflicts fit extremely well within the concept of *Collision*. Not only this, but also by viewing Mark as a tragedy and accepting the concept of *Collision*, the miracles, themes of secrecy, titles such as the "Son of Man," and exorcisms in Mark's Gospel begin to make more logical sense within the overall flow of the narrative (all of which will be discussed in chapters 4 and 6). And so, this section will both define and articulate the ways in which Mark wrote his Gospel as a tragedy, and how he uses the conflict between Jesus and the religious teachers to bring about the crucifixion event.

Some Examples of *Collision* in Ancient Greek Tragedy

As mentioned in the previous chapter, Hegel's concept of *Collision* represents one of three core elements in tragedy. The content of "tragic action" is therefore provided by the aims of the tragic characters that exist within substantial and justified powers that influence human behaviour. On this point, Hegel expands on what these powers can be:

> family love between husband and wife, parents and children, brothers and sisters; political life also, the patriotism of the citizens, the will of the ruler; and religion existent, not as a piety that renounces action and not as a divine judgment in man's heart about the good or evil of his actions, but on the contrary, as an active grasp and furtherance of actual interests and circumstances.[2]

Tragic characters live and act under the influence of these powers. Hegel defines these tragic characters as following:

---

2. Hegel, *Aesthetics*, 1194.

The Elements of Tragedy

> Throughout they (the tragic character) are what they can and must be in accordance with their essential nature, not an ensemble of qualities separately developed epically in various ways; on the contrary, even if they are living and individual themselves, they are simply the *one* power dominating their own specific character; for, in accordance with their own individuality, they have inseparably identified themselves with some single particular aspect of those solid interests we have enumerated above, and are prepared to answer for that identification. Standing on this height, where the mere accidents of the individual's purely personal life disappear, the tragic heroes of dramatic art have risen to become, as it were, works of sculpture, whether they be living representatives of the substantive spheres of life or individuals great and firm in other ways on the strength of their free self-reliance; and so in this respect the statues and images of the gods, rather abstract in themselves, explain the lofty tragic characters of the Greeks better than all other commentaries and notes.[3]

From this definition we can state two things. The first is that tragedy is concerned with certain powers that have influence on a person. The second is that, though a historical figure may represent many different powers, tragic heroes and their counterparts represent one power and are identified by it. The tragic hero then becomes an artistic representation who embodies a particular thing: faith, justice, love, revenge, et cetera. From this we can state that tragic conflict, or *Collision*, is concerned with two powers, as defined above, and their negative interaction with each other. What makes a plot essentially tragic is its ability to convey the *Collision* between two powers, where each of these powers is justified in its own right:

> The original essence of tragedy consists then in the fact that within such a conflict each of the opposed sides, if taken by itself, has *justification*; while each can establish the true and positive content of its own aim and character only by denying and infringing the equally justified power of the other. The

---

3. Hegel, *Aesthetics*, 1194–95.

consequence is that in its moral life, and because of it, each is nevertheless involved in *guilt*.[4]

The guilt referred to here is the outcome of the hero's opposition to a justified, substantial power.[5] The hero, then, comes into contact with an established order and by his or her existence attempts to subvert it, thus causing *Collision*. In the tragic world, these two powers cannot coexist and one must therefore be destroyed at the expense of the other. Neither power is able to renounce itself nor its intention (lest it become non-tragic) and it finds itself condemned to either total destruction or forced to abandon the accomplishment of its aim.[6]

This brings us to a point from which we can begin considering pity and fear. As was discussed in the previous chapter, pity and fear are, according to Aristotle, the proper emotive responses that an audience

---

4. Hegel, *Aesthetics*, 1196.

5. The tragic hero must be guilty in some sense or else his or her death ceases to be "tragic." Innocent suffering would only be sad and not tragic and it would not be a rational misfortune. Misfortune is only rational, then, when it is brought about by the will of the subject, who is absolutely justified and moral in what he or she does, *like* the powers against which he or she wars. And so, tragedy is concerned with two opposed "rights" that come into collision and the one destroys the other. Both, therefore, suffer loss and yet are mutually justified. Hegel (*History of Philosophy*, 1:446–48) defines them as such: "The one power is the divine right, the natural morality whose laws are identical with the will which dwells therein as in its own essence, freely and nobly; we may call it abstractly objective freedom" (1:446). He goes on to describe the other as, "the right, as really divine, of consciousness or of subjective freedom; this is the fruit of the tree of the knowledge of good and evil, *i.e.* of self-creative reason" (1:446–47). For Hegel, an excellent example of this type of tragic character is Socrates, who exercises self-creative, subjective reason in conflict with the Athenian *polis*, which is understood as an established entity that represents objective freedom. Both are necessary but are constantly in conflict with one another. The *polis* thus understands the Socratic, self-creative reason as a threat to its own stability and must destroy it in order to survive. However, Socrates proves to be the catalyst for paradigmatic change, and the Athenian people later began to understand Socrates as one who had committed no crime. Tragedy, written in this environment, thus becomes symbolic of this struggle between institutionalized patterns of thought and subjective patterns of thought. The tragic hero is thus seen as both great and flawed: flawed in the sense that he or she is unable to adapt to the social norm, and great in the sense that he or she is acting on behalf of a just principle. The hero's guilt is established because he or she refuses to adapt, and as a result the hero desires only that the substance of their actions be recognized, including the consequences.

6. Hegel, *Aesthetics*, 1197.

member ought to experience while viewing tragedy.[7] But pity and fear should be understood as neither a subjective sense of something corresponding to me, nor as being agreeable or disagreeable, attractive or repulsive. In order to grasp the true meaning of pity and fear, we must move beyond a simple, subjective interpretation of these emotions. Instead, we ought to focus on the subject matter by which these emotions are realized. What is a person truly afraid of? Hegel notes two things. The first can be something finite and external to a person. The second is wholly external, and that is the power of the Absolute, or God.[8] Taking both of these into consideration, we can suggest that what a person truly has to fear is the power of the ethical order which is a determinate of his own free reason, as well as the consequences of what might happen if he should turn against it.[9] Pity is likewise understood: we feel pity by watching someone violate an ethical order that we ourselves hold dear. It is for this reason that tragic characters cannot be beggars or rascals; watching a *spoudean* character violate something of intrinsic worth "strikes the heart of a noble person."[10]

How the concept of *Collision* affects the emotions of pity and fear is clearly illustrated in the *Antigone*. Antigone honors the bond of kinship and the gods of the underworld, while Creon honors Zeus alone, the dominating power over public life and social welfare.[11] The *Collision* of these two highly valued powers is observed and the only two results that can suffice are the end of the socio-religious stratum under Creon's rule or Antigone's death. Similar conflicts are found in Euripides' *Iphigenia of Aulis*, Aeschylus' *Agamemnon*, *Choephori*, and *Eumenides* as well as Sophocles' *Electra*. Agamemnon sacrifices his daughter in the interest of the Greeks and the Trojan expedition. In doing so, he severs the bond of love for his daughter and wife. Clytemnestra, his wife and the mother of Iphigenia, prepares the shameful death of her husband upon his return from Troy. Orestes, Agamemnon's son, must honor his

---

7. Aristotle, *Poet.* 1449b.
8. Hegel, *Aesthetics*, 1197–98.
9. Hegel, *Aesthetics*, 1198.
10. Hegel, *Aesthetics*, 1198.
11. Hegel, *Aesthetics*, 1213.

mother but must also defend the right of his father, the king, and thus, murders his mother.

Thus, the tragic complication can end in no other way than this: the two sides of the conflict strive to preserve the justification that each has, yet in doing so end up destroying one another. This establishes a harmony and returns the proper and equal glory to the gods. The true development of the action in tragedy consists solely in the cancellation of conflicts as conflicts, and the reconciliation of the powers that animate the hero and his or her counterpart. Therefore, in the act of the annulling of conflict appears a hidden moment of reconciliation in tragedy, that is, the restoration of tranquility and harmony. Only then, according to Hegel, can our hearts be morally at peace: shattered by the fate of the heroes but reconciled fundamentally.[12]

It should be mentioned that this conclusion should not be viewed as a purely moral outcome where evil is punished and virtue is rewarded. We cannot apply a subjective reflection on what is good and evil; rather, when the *Collision* is complete, the causes that drove both parties in the conflict are satisfied. This is not what we might call blind fate; that is, a purely irrational and unintelligible destiny. The outcome is a purely rational one, and we can say that the supreme power that resides over all things cannot allow one-sided powers to continue to overstep the limits of their authority or the *Collision* that follows in consequence. Essentially, the supreme power—call it God—drives the one-sided powers back within their limits. We know this because irrational compulsion and innocent suffering would inevitably produce in the mind of the observer indignation instead of moral peace and satisfaction.[13] And so, Antigone rises as a hero in conflict with Creon, and both represent the interests of the gods. Antigone is destroyed by Creon, thus annulling her half of the conflict. Then, in order to reestablish harmony, Creon must also be destroyed so that his one-sidedness will not continue to exist. Therefore, Antigone *must* exist in *Collision* with Creon in order to instigate Creon's destruction and thus reestablish a harmony in which all balance is restored. In other words, *one-sidedness is the opposite of balance, and in order for that one-sidedness*

12. Hegel, *Aesthetics*, 1216.
13. Hegel, *Aesthetics*, 1216.

The Elements of Tragedy

to be annulled, another one-sided position must be established in order to cause the downfall of the other which leads to the satisfaction of each god represented. Thus, conflict, or *Collision*, is essential to tragedy's ability to promote a logical, cathartic reconciliation in the audience.

To review, the core element of *Collision* must be in place in order for a tragedy to exist, and it is the *Collision* that makes a tragedy essentially "tragic." *Collision* can occur in a number of ways, but in order for a *Collision* to have its full tragic effect, it must embody a tension between two highly valued powers. As viewers, we are torn between the values of each power; we sympathize with the hero who, despite his or her transgression of the other power, also upholds allegiance to his or her cause. We identify with the power of the hero, yet we fear the repercussions of transgressing the opposite power which inevitably destroys the hero. Thus, the hero appears in a somewhat paradoxical position: in one sense, the hero refuses to acknowledge the validity of the other power, but in another sense the hero embodies the very thing he or she wars against. As a result, the more equally valued each position is, the more tragic a narrative becomes. Thus, the emotive response in tragedy is roused by a sense of being torn between two powers that, in the end, destroy each other. This brings about a sense of *catharsis* in the audience, which is forced to rationalize the impossibility of two opposing, yet equally valued powers existing together. Tragedy also provides a sense of reconciliation in the sense that one-sidedness is abolished, thus leading to a sense of harmony through the appeasement of God.

Some Examples of *Collision* in Mark's Gospel

Turning now to Mark's Gospel, there are a number of ways that *Collision* is illustrated. When reading the Gospel of Mark, it is important to remember that the religious leaders thought of themselves as chosen by God and as a group(s) responsible for upholding God's established temple. Jesus, on the other hand, is revealed to be God's son with whom God is well pleased (1:11). While the conflicts between Jesus and the religious leaders appear most prominent, the real *Collision* of Mark's Gospel exists between Jesus and the temple, of which the religious leaders are representatives. There are two facets of the temple. The first is the temple as God's dwelling place on earth. The second facet is the temple as symbolic of Jewish belief and practice; in other words: the focal point of Jewish *ethos*. It would be uninteresting and non-tragic for Jesus to be continually assaulting the temple physically or verbally. Instead, Mark portrays Jesus engaging with the religious leaders as an illustration of *how* the conflict plays out. Therefore, the religious leaders are secondary to the temple as Jesus' opponent. This is the essence of *Collision* in Mark's Gospel; that is, Jesus as God's son is pitted against the temple as Israel's social, political, ideological, and ethical *ethos*, which is established by God. It might be said that Jesus is pitted against the ill practices of the religious teachers, but this misses the essential point. Whether or not the religious teachers embody "correct" legislation of God's law is of lesser importance than the existence of the temple itself and its function within Jewish society. Jesus would have had the same problem with the temple regardless of whether the religious teachers were doing things "correctly" or not.[14] The essential conflict must then be about the *ethos* that the temple creates, meaning that Jesus, as God's son, stands as a direct challenge to the temple and all it represents. If we place this into the context of tragedy, it becomes readily apparent that Jesus and the temple cannot coexist, and that one must destroy the other. The religious leaders, as representatives of the *ethos* that the temple creates, then become the agents of this destruction.[15]

---

14. This is perhaps most clearly illustrated by the events surrounding Jesus' death in 15:37–38. The curtain that separated the holy of holies from the rest of the temple is torn from top to bottom. Therefore, it must be assumed that Jesus' death signifies the disablement of the temple as the dwelling of God. The secondary nature of the religious teachers is also illustrated by the lack of attention given to them at the moment of Jesus' death. There is no "victory" over them that is signaled. Instead, only the temple is mentioned.

15. This position is argued in Rhoads et al. (*Mark as Story*, 116–136), who suggest that the major conflict between Jesus and the religious teachers is about the interpretation of the law. While such interpretations do come into play, I think that the interpretations and applications of the law, especially with regard to Jesus, emphasize the *ethos* that the temple creates. This becomes apparent when Jesus neglects the implications of the law, especially with regard to purity or Sabbath laws. With this in mind, it becomes difficult to suggest that the only thing driving the conflict between Jesus and the religious leaders is interpretation. Jesus does not offer a different way of interpreting the purity laws, he simply *neglects* them.

The Elements of Tragedy

In what follows, I will illustrate the ways in which *Collision* is presented in Mark's Gospel. I will first discuss Jesus' conflict with the temple followed by his conflict with the religious teachers.

Jesus and the Temple

There are two ways that Mark portrays Jesus' opposition to the temple. The first occurs in ch. 11 when Jesus enters the temple and causes a disturbance. Jesus initially enters the temple in 11:11, and we are told that he simply looks around carefully at everything. It appears that Mark wants to illustrate that Jesus' contempt for the temple was not a random occurrence or impulsive but, instead, that Jesus' actions in the temple were premeditated. It is possible that Jesus, once he saw what was going on in the temple, made a conscious choice to aggressively violate the temple activities. If so, his choice is then to be understood as a premeditated action, one he knew would result in his death (11:18). Jesus' actions in this pericope also demonstrate his contempt for *how* things in the temple were being conducted and his quotations of Isa 56:7 and Jer 7:11 reveal that he understood the activities going on to be somehow incorrect. But why? The area in which Jesus displays his contempt is the court of the gentiles, the area which enabled gentiles to involve themselves in the worship of Yahweh. A simple interpretation of Jesus' actions leads us to conclude that Jesus was somehow angered by the ways in which sales were being made and we could perhaps conclude that some type of unethical business practice was taking place—hence Jesus' reference to the temple as a "den of thieves." But, if we approach reading this pericope in light of the context of Jesus' ultimate conflict, or *Collision*, with the temple, we can interpret it in a different way.

To review, tragedy always involves a *Collision* between two powers, which results in the destruction of one of those powers. In Mark's Gospel, Jesus as the Son of God stands juxtaposed with the temple of God, or, quite literally, the place where God himself dwells and is worshipped. Having God live amongst his people is not wrong and I do not think that Jesus has a problem with this. I also do not think that Jesus has a problem necessarily with how people are worshipping God—this is secondary. The real problem that Jesus has with the temple is its existence as an institution of worship.[16] All of Jesus' efforts until this point—his sermons, miracles, exorcisms, and parables—are towards establishing God's kingdom on earth (further elaborated in chapter 5), making it relevant to all people regardless of social position or race. For it to gain greater relevance and in order to grant humanity true access to God, worship must be deinstitutionalized. Said inversely, the practice of worship in the temple narrows its significance and relevance to all people. Jesus' heralding of the kingdom of God decontextualizes the practice of worship and makes the practice of worship in the temple irrelevant. This is Jesus' strategy in the conflict between himself and the temple: *by decontextualizing the practice of worship, it becomes available to all people in all places, regardless of class, race, or sex.* Therefore, it is not that people were doing something unethical in the temple per se—the issue is much deeper than this. Rather, it is that restricting access to God through temple practices constrains the world from truly experiencing the kingdom of God.

The second way that Mark illustrates Jesus' opposition to the temple occurs in ch. 13, in which Jesus comments on the temple's physical and ideological existence.[17] As Jesus is leaving the temple, his disciples

16. This may be clarified by referring to Hegel's interpretation of "positivist" religion. He defines "positivity" (*Positivität*) as the elements of religion that are its statutes, creeds, dogma, codified moral laws, and theologies. But, in essence, "positivity" means artificially fixing what is inherently fluid. "Positive Law" is posited by a dominant, external authority, and it gives rise to a legalistic frame of mind. "Positive Liturgy" is one that presents rituals and texts as if they were fixed and indisputable facts. Thus, positive aspects of religion take the place of that which they were initially supposed to serve. As a result, people become distant from the God they serve, and people are only in relation with the divine insofar as they operate within the positivist aspects of religion. This, according to Hegel, makes a religion "dead." Jesus seeks to abolish the "positivist" aspects of Judaism by "unfixing" the God who had become "fixed" within the temple through ritual and legalistically-bound adherence to law. Jesus as both fully human and fully God functions to re-associate humanity to God by allowing humanity to identify with God. In doing so, a fluid relationship is reestablished. This is, arguably, the reason why Jesus' identity as the Son of God is so important in Mark's Gospel and why Jesus' opposition to the *ethos* that is created by the temple is essential to the tragic function of Mark's Gospel. For a more detailed analysis of Hegel's thought, see Wake, *Tragedy*, 15–16; Hegel, *Theological Writings*.

17. Discussions concerning Mark's "little apocalypse" are wide-ranging and include a large number of approaches and methods. For a summary of these discussions, see Beasley-Murray, *Jesus and the Future*; Robinson, *Problem of History*, 60–63.

comment on how impressive the stones are that make up the temple (13:1). Jesus replies by heralding the destruction of the temple (13:2), whereupon he expounds the meaning of his words in an eschatological discourse (13:5–36). In this section, Jesus foretells many physical disasters and persecutions, but the most prominent feature of his speech occurs in 13:10, in which he says that the "gospel must *first* be preached to all people." Thus, the relevance of the temple, as the central institution for the worship of God, is destroyed, and its destruction is linked to the spreading of the gospel. Mark is linking the decentralization of worship with a universal spreading of the gospel of God's kingdom. However, much of what Jesus says in this section is rather vague. It is possible that Jesus is warning his disciples against those who would continue to try to institutionalize worship in the way that the temple had done. This can be surmised by Jesus' warning that the disciples will be beaten in synagogues and brought before governors and kings (13:9). If the gospel that Jesus preaches symbolizes a breaking away from the institutionalization and monopolization of worship, it is no surprise that Jesus warns against those who would continue to control worship. Unlike many others who will claim to be the messiah and garner glory for themselves (13:5–6), only Jesus represents a true paradigm shift away from any institutional worship that monopolizes access to God.

Jesus and the Religious Leaders

Jesus is revealed as a teacher, healer, and exorcist of the highest order and this leads to a number of conflicts with members of the crowds, demons, and religious teachers.[18] There is even a point at which Jesus appears in conflict with his own disciples (8:33), which alludes to his relatively unseen conflict with Satan (1:13). While each of these conflicts plays an important part in the narrative of the Gospel, the most prominent way that Mark depicts Jesus' struggle with the temple is by his various interactions with the religious teachers.[19]

---

18. The other forms of conflict (demons, disciples, crowds, etc.) help to form Jesus' strategy for combating the religious teachers. I will speak more about this in chapters 4–6.

19. Five distinct Jewish leadership groups share a desire to have Jesus arrested and killed: Chief priests, scribes, elders, Pharisees, and Herodians. Mark also

Jesus is first contrasted with the religious teachers relatively early on in his ministry in 1:22. We are told that the people who hear Jesus preach are amazed and impressed by the authority by which he taught. The next mention of any conflict between Jesus and the religious teachers of the law occurs in 2:6–10. They accuse Jesus of blasphemy because he forgives a paralyzed man of his sins (2:5). But Jesus retorts by stating that the Son of Man has the ability to forgive sins, thereby challenging the religious tenet that only God can forgive sins.[20] Not long after, Jesus is further challenged by the religious teachers—this time more specifically by the Pharisees—over concerns about purity (2:16), fasting (2:18), and the Sabbath (2:24; 3:2). As usual, Jesus offers a different interpretation of the law, thereby discrediting their arguments and their interpretations of the law. These conflicts also lead to the first intentions to kill Jesus in 3:6.

As mentioned above, the conflict between Jesus and the religious teachers fits within the overall struggle between Jesus as the Son of God and the temple as the center of religious activity and God's dwelling place. The conflicts between Jesus and the religious teachers are therefore an offshoot of his struggle with the temple and the religious leaders, who become agents of Jesus' death, are thus meant to embody the temple. As mentioned, this fits the concept of tragic *Collision*, which states that the tragic hero is overcome and destroyed by the force with which he or she is in conflict.

The conflicts between Jesus and the religious teachers are illustrated in a number of ways. One of the ways is by speech. At various points throughout the narrative, Jesus engages with the religious teachers by way of verbal argument. During these arguments, Jesus displays a superior knowledge of the law, which coincides with his *spoudean* characteristics (below). For example, when confronted about certain

---

separates these five into two smaller conjoined groups: Chief priests + scribes + elders; Pharisees + Herodians. These two groups never encounter one another within the narrative, with the exception of three instances where the Pharisees and teachers of the law are mentioned in conjunction (2:16; 7:1, 5). For a description of the various positions concerning Mark's treatment of Jesus' opponents, see Cook, *Mark's Treatment*.

20. This is the first appearance of Jesus' self-title "Son of Man" (2:10). I will discuss the reasons for Jesus' use of this title in more depth in chapter 6.

purity laws pertaining to ceremonial washing, Jesus offers a rebuttal that challenges the motives of such laws by quoting Isa 29:13 (7:1–7). He continues to manifest the hypocrisy of the religious teachers by further challenging their interpretations on the treatment of mothers and fathers (7:10–11). Jesus then introduces a new concept of purity that dissolves a number of the aforementioned ceremonial laws (7:18–23). From this example we can deduce that Jesus had not only a great knowledge of the law, but also the shrewd insight needed to discern a more critical application of the law. While a more in-depth discussion of Jesus' overall strategy concerning these conflicts will occur in chapters 5–6, for now we can conclude that Jesus' verbal arguments with the religious teachers illustrate a position that is distinct from the temple and thus the religious teachers.

Another way in which the conflict between Jesus and the religious teachers is illustrated is by miracles. This is most clearly portrayed in 3:1–6, in which Jesus is criticized for healing a man on the Sabbath. We are told that Jesus is being watched very closely by the Pharisees to see whether he will break the Sabbath law. When Jesus stands and challenges their position (3:4), they respond with passive-aggressive silence, which prompts Jesus to heal a man with a withered hand (3:5–6). Then the Pharisees immediately leave and make plans to murder Jesus (3:6). It is clear that the Pharisees mean to set Jesus up, so to speak, so that they can in turn persecute his actions. This miracle, and ones like it, are a means to portray the ongoing conflicts between Jesus and the religious teachers, thereby, expressing the overall *Collision* between Jesus and the temple.

THE *SPOUDEAN* ELEMENT OF MARK'S GOSPEL

Some Examples of Spoudean Qualities in Ancient Greek Tragedy

As mentioned above, a *spoudean* protagonist is essential to a tragic drama and this type of protagonist displays some kind of superlative quality. This is essential to the element of *Collision*, as mentioned above, because the tragic hero must have superlative qualities in order to rightly challenge the opposing position. As a result, the tragic protagonist exemplifies a lesson of some kind—there is a political, ethical, or religious purpose for why the author chose to write a particular tragedy. This purpose can be expressed by a line towards the end of the tragedy that expresses its purpose.[21] For example, in the *Antigone*, the chorus concludes the play in this way:

> Toward a happy life, to be thoughtful
> is the first need. One must do the gods
> no impiety. Claims made too great
> bring down great blows on those who have claimed
> too much in their pride
> and at last, in old age, teach wisdom.[22]

This line is applied to Creon, but certainly aims to contrast Creon with Antigone: Antigone has made her tragic choice and died while trying to honor the gods, while Creon has disobeyed the gods and lost his family as a result.[23] It is clear that Sophocles is attempting to emphasize that piety towards the gods is more desirable than not.[24] But Antigone does not simply desire to obey the gods, she seeks to obey their laws under great scrutiny and in the face of certain death, and it is for this reason that we can consider such piety as *spoudean*.

Spoudean qualities are therefore of great cost to the protagonist because they often oppose an established social or religious order. But where and how do these qualities originate in the protagonist? In some cases, the qualities are inborn, while certain others are realized through action or circumstance. In the case of Antigone, it is circumstance: the desire to disobey the state in order to bury her brother is aroused by anger at one brother being honored over the other (Sophocles, *Ant.* 20–39). Antigone understands her job to be a holy one and by not burying the body she dishonors the gods (76–77). Almost immediately the *Collision* is established by Ismene who says that she "does not

---

21. Lattimore, *Patterns*, 16.

22. Sophocles, *Ant.* 1348–53.

23. It is also important to note that Creon seeks to uphold civic laws through his actions against Antigone. Since Polynices has acted against the state which Creon represents, Creon must uphold the law of the gods and punish his impiety by not burying him. What is revealed is a conflict between two individuals for whom, each, the goal is to honor the gods.

24. Lattimore, *Patterns*, 15–17.

have it in her to act against the will of the people of the city" (78–79). This tells us that a social barrier has been created that inhibits certain actions and, if anyone violates this barrier, death will ensue. And so, Antigone's actions reflect her *spoudean* qualities of piety and ethics, but these qualities will cost Antigone her life.

Oedipus provides another example of a tragic hero who displays *spoudean* qualities. The wit with which Oedipus solves the Sphinx's riddle and becomes the king of Thebes is unmatched. As a result, he is counted as being amongst the gods in stature by the citizens of Thebes (Sophocles, *Oed. tyr.* 31–39). He is also considered to be a protector (41), a prophet (43–44), and the best of all living people (46). Each of these epithets are a result of certain circumstances which lead to his becoming king, but also become the basis of his ironic, hubristic downfall. I say hubristic because, in this particular tragedy, it is Oedipus's *spoudean* qualities that oppose the will of Zeus, thus forming the *Collision* in the drama. I say ironic because it is precisely because of these qualities that Oedipus became a savior to his people. And so, Oedipus's actions as a savior, though done in ignorance, are not at first—since he is a savior—to be considered impious to Zeus. However, his actions are eventually considered impious since, through these actions, Oedipus brought a plague upon his city. Thus, is it Oedipus's *spoudean* qualities that are in *Collision* with Zeus, and, like Antigone, it is precisely these qualities that will eventually lead to his death.

Still another example can be found in the character of Prometheus. Supposed to have occurred at a time when humans had just been created by the gods, *Prometheus Bound* epitomizes the philosophical and religious questions concerning the nature of the divine power that lies behind the universe. Can it be said that this power is good? If so, why does evil exist for humankind? Prometheus becomes the "humble servant" who deigns himself to rescue humanity from its plight and suffers at the hands of a jealous Zeus who punishes Prometheus for his benevolence towards humanity. In one sense, the *spoudean* quality of Prometheus is inborn since he is a Titan. In another sense, Prometheus can be seen as an extreme benefactor who aims to serve humanity despite strong repercussions from Zeus. Regardless, the *spoudean* qualities of Prometheus serve as a way for Aeschylus to convey the philosophical and religious questions concerning the origin of good and evil, as well as to maintain a proper sense of *Collision* that characterizes tragedy.

The final example I will present is that of Orestes and Electra. Both Orestes and Electra possess *spoudean* qualities, and these qualities are displayed in a number of ways. For example, Electra first appears in a peasant's lowly hut, dressed in rags and forced to perform menial tasks. She is of lofty birth though unrecognized as such except by the audience. This makes her *spoudean* qualities inborn insofar as her character is concerned. However, she also exhibits an unwavering desire for revenge and justice because her father was murdered by Clytemnestra in an unlawful and sacrilegious way. Orestes, in many ways, mirrors the same kinds of *spoudean* qualities, yet Electra—at least in Euripides' account—supersedes him in in cunning. She, along with the god Apollo, convinces her not so strong-willed brother to commit matricide because her desire for justice is so strong. Yet Euripides' conclusion of the *Electra* warrants several interpretations. There is certainly a *Collision* between Apollo's commands and the laws of the state with regards to matricide, yet there also seems to be a *Collision* between Apollo and the other gods with regards to how heaven perceives his actions. Orestes is eventually pardoned for his crime of matricide, and the question of how humanity lives under divine control is placed at the forefront. Regardless, Orestes and Electra possess several kinds of *spoudean* qualities that lead them down a road of great distress and anxiety, even if they are pardoned from their crime.

The Spoudean Qualities of Jesus in Mark's Gospel

To review, tragedy contains a protagonist that exhibits some kind of superlative quality, and we call these qualities *spoudean*. *Spoudean* qualities are essential to a tragic protagonist, because he or she must be of elevated character. This is primarily because the actions of the tragic hero produce some type of lesson.

One of the questions that arises from a study of character is how much liberty an author can take with regard to developing the narrative and characters.[25] Stories about Jesus had been circulating for at least

---

25. So much is said in Perrin (*Redaction Criticism*, 75) when he states that "The Gospel of Mark is the prototype which the others follow and it is a mixture of

The Elements of Tragedy

twenty years (depending on the date assigned to Mark's composition) by the time Mark wrote his Gospel. Presumably there were many eyewitnesses still alive at the time of Mark's composition who would have remembered the things said and done by Jesus. But the way in which characters are portrayed in tragedy appears somewhat one-dimensional. This is because a tragic hero is an artistic embodiment of a particular thing, be it a virtue or an ethical position. Having said this, there are presumably facets of Jesus' character that Mark left out of the narrative, otherwise we would have a complete story of Jesus' life and ministry. But Mark instead chose to display the facets of Jesus' character that fit best within the narrative he creates. This is perhaps evidenced by the fact that the other Gospel writers choose to display a Jesus who is, at times, quite different from the one we see in Mark's Gospel. We can take from this the notion that, to some extent, the narrative dictates the character.

But how does narrative affect character, and what is the exact nature of their relationship? We are told in the prologue of Mark's Gospel that Jesus is both the Christ and the Son of God.[26] And if we are to believe the final result of the narrative, namely the resurrection, Jesus *must* be the Christ and Son of God.[27] This is emphasized by the

---

historical reminiscence, interpreted tradition, and the free creativity of prophets and the evangelist. It is, in other words, a strange mixture of history, legend, and myth." In Marxsen (*Mark the Evangelist*), special reference is given to the term εὐαγγέλιον ("Gospel") as it related to genre. In Weiss (*Der älteste Evangelium*), such genre-driven analysis is criticized. In Robinson ("*Gattung* of Mark," 101), it is argued that the genre of Mark is an "aretalogy," and that it ought to be thought of as "a narrative of the miraculous deeds of a god or hero" (103). Jesus as a *theios aner* (divine man) was put forward in Smith ("Prolegomena," 174–99) and in Betz ("Jesus as Divine Man," 114–33). See Robbins (*New Boundaries*, 91–136) for a more complete discussion of the progression of thought concerning Mark's potential editorial activities.

26. This is a common feature of tragedy according to Rutherford (*Greek Tragic Style*, 84). He says, " . . . in each (tragedy) the dramatist creates the poetic world with a particular character, and this can best be seen by examining drama from the beginning." Rutherford then notes how Euripides uses a single speech by Dionysus to reveal a number of features of the drama. The prologue of Mark (1:1–13) highlights a number of features that will play a central role throughout the narrative of the Gospel.

27. Lattimore (*Patterns*, 60–61) points out the essential nature of the hero's character as it relates to the narrative. For example, Herakles must be "the greatest of all men" in *The Women of Trachis* in order to make his downfall that much more tragic.

christological features of Mark's Gospel.[28] These epithets are further emphasized in two places. The first place is when John says in 1:7 that he is unworthy even to stoop and tie the sandals Jesus is wearing. This seemingly out of place reference to John's knowledge of Jesus' character fits quite well within the tragic tradition. Even though Oedipus, despite his great intelligence, continually arrives at false conclusions during the play, it is sufficiently established that he is a man of great knowledge who defeated the Sphinx and a man to whom his people turn when they are in trouble. This tells us that he was a man who ruled wisely until the prologue of the narrative. John's comments regarding Jesus' character are meant to establish Jesus as one who is superior to everyone around him and further serve to introduce the circumstance and characters of the narrative. The second place where an epithet that emphasizes Jesus' character is given is the instance of the heavenly voice in 1:11, which is meant to indicate God's authoritative role in the narrative as the *deus ex machina*. Each of these epithets is reinforced and alluded to throughout the narrative in different ways. These epithets also serve as value statements that create a number of expectations for the reader. Much in the same way that Dionysus introduces himself as a god in the opening lines of the *Bacchae*, Jesus is introduced in Mark in such a way as to make the facets of his character prominent in the narrative.

But, as much as Jesus' character appears fixed in light of these epithets, Jesus appears fluid as well, and there are many things about Jesus that we do not know. For example, we are not told much, if anything at all, about Jesus outside of his ministerial activities. What was the nature of Jesus' childhood? How did John come to know about Jesus' character? Why did Jesus come to John's baptism of repentance? It is not that the answers to these questions are not important, but they are unnecessary to the narrative. In fact, it is common in ancient tragedy for the greater historical context of the tragic hero to be left out of the narrative. In one scene, we observe a Jesus who, with superior rhetoric, disarms the religious leaders and persuades the ever-growing crowds

---

Equally, Oedipus must be the most intelligent of all men in order to emphasize the potency of the ignorance that leads to his death.

28. See Marshall ("Jesus as Messiah," 117–43) for a discussion of the christological features in Mark's Gospel.

of his message. Yet, in other scenes, we observe a Jesus who recluses and withdraws into solitary places (1:35, 45). While Jesus *must* appear as a master rhetorician in order to portray the failings and hypocrisy of the religious elite, we are not told why Jesus must withdraw. But, as consistent as Jesus is in his teaching and action, he appears to waver and doubt his call in Gethsemane (14:36). There is a point at which we as observers must consider the privacies of Jesus' personality and escape the logic of the plot, and in doing so, the dramatic element of the story is heightened. Hamlet is Hamlet because of his hesitations and questionings; Antigone is Antigone because she wavers and doubts her conviction that everyone else is wrong. Lattimore suggests that each audience member is free to fill in the outlines of the dramatic people from his or her own experience and imagination.[29]

THE CONCEPTS OF SUFFERING AND DEATH IN MARK'S GOSPEL

As mentioned above, the core elements of suffering and death are prevalent in tragedy. As Aeschylus tells us in the *Agamemnon*,

> τὸν φρονεῖν βροτοὺς ὁδώ-
> σαντα, τὸν πάθει μάθος
> θέντα κυρίως ἔχειν.
> στάζει δ᾽ ἔν θ᾽ ὕπνῳ πρὸ καρδίας
> μνησιπήμων πόνος: καὶ παρ᾽ ἄ-
> κοντας ἦλθε σωφρονεῖν.
> δαιμόνων δέ που χάρις βίαιος
> σέλμα σεμνὸν ἡμένων.

> Zeus, who leads onward mortals to be wise,
> Appoints that *suffering masterfully teach*.
> In sleep, before the heart of each,
> A woe-remembering travail sheds in dew
> Discretion, —ay, and melts the unwilling too
> By what, perchance, may be a graciousness
> Of gods, enforced no less, —
> As they, commanders of the crew,
> Assume the awful seat (176–183).

29. Lattimore, *Patterns*, 63–64.

Of Conflict and Concealment

The ways in which the story pattern is fitted together by the author can vary, but in order for a tragedy to be essentially "tragic," suffering must be illustrated in connection with the *Collision* and the *spoudean* qualities of the hero. This means that each of the core elements mentioned thus far are in close connection to one another and, when combined, have the effect we call "tragic." This combination lends itself to a deeper meaning with regard to the hero's suffering and death, mainly because it is the tragic end to the *Collision* between the two positions represented in tragedy.

Tragic suffering and death can be realized in a variety of ways. As mentioned, *Collision* is defined as the conflict between two highly valued powers. While each of these powers can stand on its own as a justified entity, these powers cannot coexist. Because of this, one side strives to destroy the other (usually the hero is destroyed) in order to reestablish itself as the only valid position. But since such one-sidedness cannot occur according to the rules of tragedy, both positions often suffer due to the conflict, thus restoring a sense of harmony. This section will discuss the ways in which suffering and death are brought about both in Greek tragedy and in Mark's Gospel.

Tragic *Hybris* and *Nemesis*

The suffering and inevitable destruction of both positions in the *Collision* is realized in a number of ways, but it is important to note that tragedy does not allow for one of the powers to exist on its own. This would be considered one-sided, as mentioned, and would reduce tragedy to simply a sad story. To safeguard against such one-sidedness, the ancient tragedians used several concepts by which the hero or his opponent is reduced after the *Collision* is resolved. This is because a *spoudean* character cannot dwell within the normal human realm, he or she exists for the express purpose of the *Collision* that tragedy illustrates. This means that existence after the *Collision* has taken place is not proper to tragedy.

Two such concepts are *nemesis* and *hybris*. Since tragedy is meant to eventually harmonize *Collision*, the position that continues to challenge such harmony simply by its existence *must* be destroyed by some force beyond itself. Since tragic harmony is meant to restore proper honor to the gods, the continued existence of a *spoudean* character is understood as a direct challenge to the gods. This has sometimes been described as tragic *nemesis*—a "direct challenge to divinity, which is a unique taboo of Greek religion and whose understanding is the sole key to Attic tragedy."[30] Thus *nemesis* is often understood as a force that causes some type of destruction but it should be understood as the force which brings about harmony. This is perhaps the most fundamental definition of *nemesis* since there is no one way of illustrating how *nemesis* works. *Nemesis*, by this definition, can affect either the hero or the position with which he or she is in *Collision*—whichever one continues to exist and challenges harmony. This definition helps us understand why Herakles, once he returns from Hades and saves his family, goes mad and murders his family. It also explains why Creon *must* suffer the loss of his son after sentencing Antigone to death. From these two examples alone, we can see that *nemesis* shows no favoritism, being the force by which harmony is restored.

Another term that is used by scholars to describe the way in which the tragedians brought about harmony is *hybris*. This term is often defined as "arrogance" or "pride" but this definition needs more consideration. Because both positions in *Collision* are *spoudean*, they *must* act in accordance with their character. This does away with the idea, one formed because the inner monologue of the hero is not given, that *hybris* is an ignorant assessment of self. Yet, as great as the hero or his opponent may appear, he is always secondary to the gods. And so, *hybris* is meant to describe the actions of a character who challenges the gods and is thus closely associated with the concept of *Collision*. The concept of *hybris* is somewhat convoluted, however, since both sides of the *Collision* are justified precisely because they honor the gods. This means that *hybris* is defined as a direct challenge to the gods by the destruction of the other position in *Collision*. Referring again to the *Antigone*, Creon's actions are justifiable insofar as he is honoring Zeus, but his *hybris* exists in his destruction of Antigone. Likewise, Oedipus is justified because he wants to avenge unjustified murder but is found guilty of *hybris* because he is the murderer. Again, there is no one way to define how the tragedians make use of the concept of *hybris*, but we

---

30. Lattimore, *Patterns*, 25.

can suggest that *hybris* is related to a position's challenge of the gods in the context of *Collision*.

Tragic Glory or *Kleos*

The hidden purpose of tragedy is to bring about a sense of harmony through the reconciliation of *Collision*. Harmony can thus be understood as a restoration of things to their proper places, so to speak, meaning that the gods are appeased and given their proper glory. Glory in ancient poetry is referred to by the word *kleos*, and, as usual, is illustrated in a variety of ways. But, before this concept found its way into tragedy, *kleos* had more to do with the glory of the hero than it did with the appeasement of the gods. Thus, in Homeric poetry, *kleos* is closely associated with death—a death that is considered glorious. Therefore, to "die well" was very much a Homeric virtue, and this can perhaps be best illustrated by a speech of Achilles' found in the *Iliad*:

> My mother Thetis, goddess with silver steps, tells me that I carry the burden of two different fated ways leading to the final moments of my death. If I stay here and fight at the walls of the city of the Trojans, then my safe homecoming will be destroyed for me, but I will have a glory (*kleos*) that is imperishable. Whereas if I go back home, returning to the dear land of my forefathers, then it is my glory (*kleos*), genuine as it is, that will be destroyed for me, but my life force will then last me a long time, and the final moment of death will not be swift in catching up with me (*Il.* 410–16).[31]

As Achilles begins to process the consequences of his decision to either return home safely or to stay and continue to fight the Trojans, he chooses the option that will result in his death. His death will result in a state of being glorious, and the story by which he is remembered will grant him immortality.

---

31. Nagy (*Ancient Greek Hero*, 27–28) also cites and compares Samuel Butler's translation with the rendering provided above. Butler's translation reads "My mother Thetis tells me that there are two ways in which I may meet my end. If I stay here and fight, I will not return alive but my name will live forever: whereas if I go home my name will die, but it will be long ere death shall take me."

The Elements of Tragedy

The death of a hero is often scripted in the sense that he or she foretells their dying in a way that makes their death a prominent feature of the narrative. Death is therefore not something that is feared, but something that is welcomed, since the hero must achieve the ultimate moment of their death. Such a moment is often foretold by the hero and is usually referred to as their *swan song*.[32] This can perhaps be best illustrated by yet another example from the *Iliad*. The newly married Iphidamas forsakes his family and wife to seek immortal glory (*kleos*) for himself in battle:

> Tell me now you Muses dwelling on Olympus, who was the first to come up and face Agamemnon, either among the Trojans or among their famous allies? It was Iphidamas son of Antenor, a man both good and great, who was raised in fertile Thrace the mother of sheep. Kissēs in his own house raised him when he was little. Kissēs was his mother's father, father to Theano, the one with the fair cheeks. When Iphidamas reached the stage of adolescence, which brings luminous glory, Kissēs wanted to keep him at home and to give him his own daughter in marriage, but as soon as Iphidamas had married, he left the bride chamber and went off seeking the *kleos* of the Achaeans along with twelve curved ships that followed him (*Il.* 218–228).

This passage illustrates *kleos* in the sense that Iphidamas, obsessed with the idea of dying in a glorious way so that he can be remembered forever, leaves his new bride and sails to Troy in order to fight and die in glory. And so, heroes—or those who want to be included in a heroic narrative like Iphidamas—seek to die in such a way that their fame can be preserved in narrative. This is because the distinctions between "reality" and "narrative" were tightly intertwined. A hero's narrative *was* his or her history, and it was not simply meant for entertainment. The stories of the heroes, whether preserved in tragedy or some other type of literature, became as real as the events of everyday life. This is reflected in the ways that the heroes were worshipped and how their *kleos* was preserved.[33]

---

32. Nagy, *Ancient Greek Hero*, 32.
33. According to Nagy (*Ancient Greek Hero*, 26), *kleos* can be understood in a

Thus, the *kleos* of a hero later became a central tenet within tragedy and this can best be illustrated by Herakles.[34] Herakles was famous for having completed twelve labors for the goddess Hera, which included a wide range of feats that led to his glorification.[35] This glory resulted in Herakles being accepted into Olympus as one of the gods—crowned with immortality. The concept of death and rebirth is prominent within the legend of Herakles, and it is closely connected to the concept of *kleos*. This is illustrated in two places that feature the story of Herakles. The first place, as narrated by Diodorus (*Bib. hist.* 4.26.1), depicts Herakles descending into Hades whereupon he captures and delivers Cerberus from the place of darkness (death) to the place of light (life). It is not uncommon within Greek tragedy—and in other genres—for a character to enter into Hades only to return again later. Traversing from earth into Hades and back is meant to depict the process of death and resurrection, which was understood as the ultimate form of *kleos*.[36] The story of Herakles' resurrection ends with his being awakened in Olympus, where he is welcomed amongst the gods as one of their own. And so, the immortality that is often expressed in Greek literature with regard to *kleos* is most explicitly illustrated in the life and death of Herakles. Whereas Achilles is immortalized by way of the preservation of his story, Herakles goes beyond the figurative description of immortality and is depicted as literally entering Olympus with the gods.

To review, the concept of *kleos* in epic poetry is very closely associated with the concept of the death of the hero. It is also, as in the case of Herakles, associated with resurrection. The hero seeks to be

---

number of ways. It can be translated simply as "glory," as I mentioned, but *kleos* can also refer to the ways in which a hero is remembered. For example, a tragedy itself can be considered a *kleos* because, when recited, it helps the hero's worshippers remember their deeds.

34. According to Nagy (*Ancient Greek Hero*, 44), the Greek name Herakles can be translated literally as "he who has the glory (*kleos*) of Hera." This is fairly ironic since Heracles is persecuted by the goddess Hera for most, if not all, of his life.

35. The various accounts of Herakles are recorded in the works of Diodorus Siculus and Euripides' *Herakles*.

36. Nagy (*Ancient Greek Hero*, 41–42) explains that Hades became an intermediary place in which a person would travel before moving on to eternal life. And so, it was not uncommon for a hero to venture into Hades and either return to earth or to move on to Olympus.

remembered and to be glorified, and the hero's death is often advertised throughout the narrative either by circumstance or by the hero himself. Two examples of this are Achilles and Herakles, who both clearly illustrate the connection between *kleos* and the death of the hero.

The Event, or *Agōn*, of Tragic Suffering

The achievement of glory in tragedy is put into motion by some event, or *agōn*, that will result in the death of the hero. In tragedy, the *agōn* usually appears midway, and in the form of opposing speeches between both parties involved in *Collision*.[37]

An example of a tragic *agōn* is found in Euripides' *Bacchae*, in which we see Pentheus—the king of Thebes—destroyed by his desire to understand the Bacchic rites that go on in his city. Bacchus, or Dionysus, returns to the city Thebes—where he was born—only to realize that he is neither recognized nor honored. Because the people no longer honor their god, he seeks to reestablish his sacred rite amongst the women of the city. Pentheus seeks to discover the nature of this sacred rite but is killed before he can: the frenzied women, more specifically his mother Agaue, tear his body into pieces before he can recognize Dionysus for who he really is. The *agōn* is, in this tragedy, the point when Pentheus begins to meddle in the affairs of the rite that brings about his suffering and death.

Another thing worth exploring here is the concept of suffering itself, or the *pathos* of the hero. The term *pathos* can mean "experience," "suffering," or "emotion" and refers to the mental state of the hero during the unfolding of the narrative.[38] In the context of tragedy, however, *pathos* means "to experience suffering." According to Nagy:

37. Nagy (*Ancient Greek Hero*, 572) defines *agōn* as either a "coming together," a "competition" (*antagonism*), or an "ordeal" (*agony*). The noun *agōn* is derived from the root *ag-* of the verb *sun-agein*, meaning a "bringing together" of sorts. When people are brought together, it can be thought of as a "competition." Nagy understands the activity of a competition to be the essence of an "ordeal" or an "event." And so, "the concept of 'ordeal' as embedded in the Greek word *agōn* is still evident in the English word borrowed from the Greek, *agony*."

38. Nagy (*Ancient Greek Hero*, 574) explains this is juxtaposed with the term *drân* ("to do") from which we get the word "drama." And so, there is a working opposition between the active function of the *drân* of tragedy and the passive function of the *paskhein* of the hero. According to Nagy, to translate *paskhein* simply as

What is passive *pathos* or *action experienced* by the hero within the world of tragedy is active drama, that is, *sacrifice* and the *performance of ritual*, from the standpoint of the outer world that frames this world of tragedy. Such an outer world is constituted by the audience of the theatre, visualized as a community that becomes engaged in the drama and that thereby participates in the inner world that is the pathos or 'suffering' of the hero.[39]

The *agōn* of the tragedy is the event that causes suffering, which is referred to as the hero's *pathos*. In the case of the *Bacchae*, Pentheus suffers because of the *agōn*, which is his induction into the sacred rite. Little does he realize, however, that the initiation he seeks will result in his death. It can be debated, however, whether the hero of the *Bacchae* is Pentheus or Dionysus, since it is Dionysus who appears in the prologue of the play and introduces the circumstance to the audience. If Dionysus is the hero, then he becomes the one who initiates the downfall of Pentheus since it is by trickery that he involves Pentheus in the rite. This would mean that the *pathos* and *agōn* of the tragedy can be instigated by the hero instead of the hero being the one to suffer it. This does not exactly fit with the idea that a hero's *kleos* is established by his death and suffering but, in this case, it could mean that Dionysus' *kleos* is established by making Pentheus suffer the *agōn* and *kleos*. Thus, it would appear that Dionysus succeeds in establishing his identity amongst the Thebans but does so at the cost of Pentheus. If this interpretation is correct, then it appears as if the concepts of *kleos*, *agōn*, and *pathos* can be intertwined in different ways.

To review, tragedy can often embody a concept of *kleos* with regard to the death of the hero. The hero seeks glorification through death, and his or her death is often advertised throughout the narrative. A hero's downfall is often realized through an event, called the *agōn*, and their suffering is referred to as the hero's *pathos*.

"emotion" is incorrect insofar as "emotion" conveys only one aspect of the general meaning of *pathos*.

39. Nagy, *Ancient Greek Hero*, 575.

The Elements of Tragedy

Some Examples of Suffering and Death in Mark's Gospel

In this section, we will examine the ways in which suffering and death become prominent themes in Mark's Gospel. As with Greek tragedy, the core element of suffering and death is closely associated with other core elements of *Collision* and the *spoudean* qualities of the hero. This being said, suffering and death in Mark's Gospel are realized by the *Collision* that occurs between Jesus and the temple, thereby lending itself to its tragic nature.

Jesus Predicts His Own Suffering and Death

Mark 8:31 signals a new section of the Gospel, and this section contains a number of allusions to Jesus' death and suffering. It begins as such: "Then Jesus began to tell them that the Son of Man must suffer many terrible things and be rejected by the elders, the leading priests, and teachers of religious law. He would be killed, but three days later he would rise from the dead" (8:31). As we have seen, this verse plays a prominent role in the realization of both the *spoudean* qualities of Jesus as well as the *Collision* between Jesus and the temple. For this section, I will focus on the words "the Son of Man must suffer terrible things."

It is clear that Jesus' words in this verse allude to his coming trial and death. At this point, Jesus has established a working ministry in Israel and has gained notoriety amongst Israel's people (7:36–37). So great is this notoriety that Peter assesses Jesus as being the Christ (8:29). There is, however, a disjuncture between Peter's confession and his subsequent rebuke in 8:33. There must have been something about hearing Jesus foretell his death and suffering that confused Peter. Theologically, perhaps, the idea of a dying messiah may not have suited Peter, but what is particularly odd is the way that Peter challenges Jesus' words even when they include a prediction about resurrection. It is possible, of course, that Peter did not believe in a resurrection and discredited Jesus' words in light of this absence of belief. There are any number of reasons why Peter may have challenged Jesus on this occasion; we simply do not know. However, in light of the present discussion, it can be observed that Jesus' prophecy concerning his suffering and death begins to create *Collision* even between Jesus and his disciples. This is important because, not only is there an apparent tension between Jesus and the various teachers of the law, there is a tension now between Jesus and his disciples that raises Jesus to a level beyond where they currently are.[40] At this moment, any thought that the disciples might be equal to, or have a future opportunity to share in Jesus' glory, is dispelled in the mind of the reader (cf. 6:6–13; 10:37). Even though Jesus tells his disciples that a similar fate awaits them (8:34–38), he is now separated from his disciples on a literary level—the hero is displaying his *spoudean* qualities in the face of death. This is evidenced by the fact that Jesus actually does go on to suffer and die, whereas Peter—most prominently over the other disciples—is portrayed as a cowering betrayer who flees from any association with Jesus (14:66–72).[41]

Jesus' prediction in 8:31 also signifies his glorification, which in terms of tragic vocabulary, refers to his *kleos*. As mentioned, a hero's glory is often wrapped up in his or her death. As mentioned above, Achilles and Herakles are the prototypical heroes in this regard. Achilles knew that if he stayed and did battle with the Trojans, his life would be cut short, yet his glory would live forever. We may be able to draw some parallels between Achilles and Jesus here, because, presumably, Jesus did not have to die when he did. He *could* have gone on to performing more healings, more exorcisms and more preaching only to die at a later time. But it seems that Jesus was preparing for the *right time* to die. As for comparing Jesus with Herakles, the most obvious parallel occurs within the context of their resurrections: like Herakles, Jesus dies and then at some point is with God in heaven (14:62).

40. Brant (*Dialogue and Drama*, 51) notices a similar pattern in tragedy and says that recognition often alienates people rather than uniting them. I agree with this point and suggest that such recognitions serve to establish or re-establish the identity and *spoudean* qualities of the hero over the others in the story.

41. Some scholars (such as Beavis, *Mark*, 133–34) have described Peter's rebuke as "not surprising" due to the belief that a suffering messiah was unsavory to a first-century Jew or gentile. While this is probably true, Peter's rebuking of Jesus appears, on the other hand, even more unsettling when read in light of Jesus' prediction of his own resurrection. It is also worth noting that if a suffering and dying messiah was not expected within Judaism during the first century, the concept must have come from another source. Since prediction and foreshadowing of death and resurrection of the hero occur so commonly in tragedy, I think Peter's rebuke has no other place here except for an opportunity for Mark to emphasize Jesus' qualities over the other disciples.

The Elements of Tragedy

However, there is also a parallel between Jesus' returning to be with his disciples, as alluded to in 16:7, and the way that Herakles is depicted as returning from Hades to be with his family.[42]

Jesus' prediction of his own death in 8:31 corresponds in many ways to how Greek tragedy depicts the dying hero. There is a sense in which the hero's death is timely, and his or her death can thus be understood as a method for attaining glory, or *kleos*. This will be further emphasized in the following section which discusses the event of Jesus' suffering and death.

The Event of Jesus' Suffering and Death

Another comparison we can make between Mark's Gospel and Greek tragedy is the *agōn* of Jesus.[43] To review, the *agōn* is typically denoted by a pair of opposing speeches after which the conflict is set into motion. It is closely associated with the hero's *pathos*, or suffering, and can be defined as the event after which a hero's suffering is realized. This is most obviously depicted in the conflicts that arise between Jesus and the religious elite—conflicts that eventually cause Jesus to be tried and killed.

With regards to developing the *agōn*, Mark does several things. As mentioned, Jesus' prediction of his death in 8:31, as well as the other places he refers to it (9:12, 31; 10:33–34; 14:21, 36), all serve to set the tone for the passion narrative. But what is the actual occurrence that sets these things into motion? Jesus' speeches and many miracles no

---

42. Of course, there are many differences between Jesus, Herakles, and Achilles. But, in terms of the timing of their death and subsequent immortality, there is a clear pattern of tragic suffering and death accompanied by some form of granted immortality which leads to glory.

43. In Beck (*Nonviolent Story*, 39), the *agōn* is described as the "determined resistance against the threat of evil that is the narrative's image of social order." The restoration of things to their proper state is essential to tragedy, and Beck argues that Jesus embodies a goodness that both provokes and disturbs. He goes on to say that Jesus "initiates a challenge against certain practices of his day." Such a definition, though not applied to tragedy by Beck, fits our overall concept of *Collision* in Mark's Gospel. While Nagy (see discussion above) wants to limit the *agōn* to the suffering event, Beck applies the *agōn* to the entire narrative of Mark's Gospel. I agree with Beck to an extent, and I do see Jesus as an "active resister," however, I think that Mark's Gospel can best be understood according to the concept of *Collision* as stated in section one above.

doubt irritated the religious authorities to the point of their wanting to murder him (3:6). But there was a definite delay in their actions, evidenced by Jesus' questioning them at his arrest (14:49). If there is one definitive action that put their plans into motion, it is the clearing of the temple (11:15–18). This single action not only disrupted the process of worship, it provoked plans to murder Jesus (11:18). I am singling out this particular action of Jesus over the others because it appears more prominent due to its being premeditated. We are told that Jesus goes into the temple and simply "looks around" (περιβλεψάμενος) in 11:11. This action reveals that Jesus' later actions at the temple were premeditated, thus reflecting a conscious choice thereby setting into motion a necessity of action (see below). After a short segment that includes cursing a fig tree, Jesus appears back in the temple whereupon he begins to cause a disturbance. We are explicitly told that he, over several different occurrences, challenges the religious leaders and their beliefs (11:27; 12:12, 13, 18, 28, 35). It appears as if Jesus chooses just the right time to agitate the religious authorities and does so in front of large crowds to protect himself. Jesus' timing also coincides with the Passover celebrations (14:2), which further emphasizes his conscious choice to instigate certain events *at a certain time* that would eventually result in his death. When examined in the context of the tragic *agōn*, these passages serve to illustrate how Jesus instigates the events that will lead to his death, but also to his glorification, or his *kleos*.

Tragic Choice and Necessity

One further point I would like to make concerning the *agōn* is with regard to Jesus' messianic consciousness as it relates to *choice*. Choice has been called the "archetype of the tragic situation" and it is found where the hero confronts alternatives and must decide between them.[44] Once made, the choice is most often irrevocable and the hero must continue on their chosen path or else they become dramatically incredible. Once Medea, for example, has stated that she will murder her children, she cannot change her mind. Equally, once Agamemnon has decided that he must sacrifice his daughter Iphigeneia, he is guided by necessity

---

44. Lattimore, *Patterns*, 36.

(*anangke*), which leads to a number of events that culminate in his murder. There are instances (see below) in which the tragic choice can be altered, but these are more the exception than the rule.

The concept of necessity is an important one in tragedy because it revolves around the illusion of choice. Interpreters will often confuse this concept and I think this is because there are two forms that necessity and choice can take. The first form is best explained by referencing the Platonic idea that the soul chooses a life that will then be controlled by *anangke*. In this scenario, the soul is responsible for the outcome and God is not. The choice, however, is irrevocable, and is best illustrated by the analogy of an arrow being shot from a bow: "Once you have shot the arrow or bullet," says Lattimore, "not all your goodwill or pity will stop it. That is *anangke*."[45]

A second distinct form renders the act of choosing more illusionary and it can be explained by analyzing the whole of Agamemnon's story. The ultimate choice belongs to Clytaemestra, who, as a result of Iphigeneia's murder, decides that she will stop at nothing to kill Agamemnon. And just before he is murdered, Aeschylus presents a scene in which Agamemnon is persuaded by his own free will to enter a house whereupon he will be killed. Agamemnon's choice is therefore an illusion, and regardless of what he decides to do, he will be killed.

This means that there are two vantage points from which we can view tragic choice: from the perspective of original choice that generates the path along which the narrative must go or from the perspective of illusionary choices that are made but cannot change the path upon which the narrative is going. Either way, once a choice has been made, there are typically no means by which the characters in the narrative can change the course of action.

There are, however, exceptions to this rule, and instances in which the tragic choice is altered. For example, in Euripides' *Iphigeneia in Aulis*, the tragic choice made by Agamemnon to sacrifice Iphegeneia is revoked by Artemis who saves the girl, thus, reversing the *anangke*. Another example occurs in Euripides' *Ion*, in which Ion drags the murderous Creusa to the place of execution where both recognize each other as lost mother and son. And so, recognition can also serve as a

---

45. Lattimore, *Patterns*, 40.

means by which *anangke* can be revoked. But, as mentioned, the typical way in which tragedies unfold is through irrevocable *anangke*; that is, a hero makes a choice, the fatal results from which he or she cannot escape, since to do otherwise would render the narrative meaningless. For example, if Antigone, when she realizes she may have failed, were to alter her course of action and recant, the narrative would be rendered meaningless.

We also find the concept of *anangke* displayed in Mark's Gospel. Mark has chosen to adopt the pattern of the *sacrificial victim*, which is as follows. The welfare of humanity is threatened, and there will be some great disaster unless God is somehow appeased. Usually such appeasement involves the sacrifice of a human victim, and this victim is usually blameless—often a virgin in Greek tragedy. The victim declares him or herself willing to die, and then becomes not so much a substitute for the ordinary animal, but a sacrifice seen as an act of self-devotion.[46]

Jesus declares in 8:31 that he is willing to be this victim and this is further reinforced by a later statement: "For even the Son of Man came not to be served but to serve others and to give his life as a ransom for many" (10:45). Jesus as the Son of Man is ready to become the blameless victim for sacrifice in light of humanity's plight. This is made clear in Jesus' eschatological sermon in Mark 13. Humanity is in a perilous state in which brothers are murdering brothers, fathers are betraying their own children, and children rebelling against their parents in order to have them killed (13:12). Even worse is that the worship of God is replaced by idols (13:14) and the anguish that humanity suffers as a result will be worse than any other time since the creation of the world (13:19). It is clear from this passage that humanity is and will continue to be in a state of peril. The purpose of this passage is thus made clear: the sacrificial victim must give his life for the salvation of humanity, and in order to do so, Jesus will become the very one (the Son of Man) who will save humanity (13:26–27). This places the suffering and death of Jesus into a context: Jesus' death is not simply the murder of a rebellious man who claims to be the messiah, it is, as it can appear in tragic narrative, to be understood as a voluntary choice of honor.

---

46. Lattimore, *Patterns*, 47–48.

The Elements of Tragedy

In addition to Jesus' premeditated actions in the temple, as mentioned above, the concept of Jesus' choice is further emphasized in the garden scene, in which Jesus seems to be unsure of his choice. Jesus cries out to God and asks that God take away the cup of suffering if there is another way (14:36). At this point, Jesus is appealing to the only thing that can stop the tragic choice he made earlier with his assault on the temple: God, the *deus ex machina*. God is presiding over the entire course of the narrative, and we know this because of his vocal appearance during Jesus' baptism (1:11). After his voice is heard, God remains silent and we do not hear directly from him again until 9:7, a passage in which God also verifies Jesus' identity. This makes God the *deus ex machina*, and we are to understand his implied sovereignty during the course of the narrative.

This causes us to ask a number of questions about how conscious Jesus may have been of his own identity. Whether Jesus was aware of his divine sonship prior to 1:11 is uncertain, but it appears as if he knows exactly who he is and what he is doing in 8:31. In fact, he must know. If the concept of *anangke* is at work, Jesus is forced by necessity to play the part of the sacrificial victim. Otherwise, the narrative simply does not make sense. And so, the necessity which prompts his choice to assault the temple, confront the religious leaders, and accept the role of the sacrificial victim guides the narrative.

CONCLUSIONS

This chapter is an attempt to illustrate three ways in which Mark's Gospel embodies the core elements of Greek tragedy. While it has attempted to treat each of these core elements somewhat independently, it is important to note that each of the three core elements listed above work together to create a cohesive "tragic" narrative. Without all of the elements listed, a tragic narrative simply cannot exist.

Perhaps the most prominent element of tragedy is its *Collision*. This is illustrated by two highly valued powers that make incompatible demands. This is what creates the essentially "tragic" nature of tragedy. This occurs in Mark's Gospel when Jesus, as God's son, appears in conflict with the established temple or the *ethos* of Jewish culture. The result of *Collision* almost always leads to the destruction of the hero, which inevitably leads to the destruction of the position with which he or she was in conflict. The result is a restored balance, which disallows the one-sidedness of either position to continue and restores the once misplaced glory to God.

Tragedies often appear during times of historical turmoil and times of great paradigm shift so that the experience of such things is often expressed in the tragedy. The tragedies that appear during these times usually contain a hero who embodies a position of power—as a god or a king—and who has superlative qualities that are called *spoudean* qualities. These *spoudean* heroes effect a change by engaging with an established position in *Collision* that embodies a paradigm shift. As a result, the *spoudean* character often suffers for his or her position in the *Collision* and is eventually destroyed.

Each of these core elements can be found and identified in the character of Jesus in Mark's Gospel. Jesus is God's son and Messiah who appears in direct conflict with the temple and with the religious teachers who represent the temple. Jesus is portrayed as a superior debater, who performs a number of miracles and exorcisms. He also has the ability to effectively teach large crowds and amaze them. Each of these things illustrate Jesus' *spoudean* qualities. Jesus is also brought into *Collision* with the temple, which eventually causes his suffering and death. Thus, the Gospel of Mark embodies each of the core elements of tragedy.

4

Hiddenness and Recognition

INTRODUCTION

It has been argued thus far that the Gospel of Mark was written as a tragedy. In chapter 2 I surveyed a large number of literary theories ranging from Aristotle—who provided the first comprehensive description of Attic tragedy—to modern theorists in the twentieth century. What was found is that Aristotle's description of tragedy, as illustrated in the *Poetics*, was not regarded as the prevalent theory of tragic composition. Instead, all of the tragic literary critics after the second century BCE referred to something else, something not found within the *Poetics*. This reference could be to a now lost document by Aristotle—perhaps entitled *On Poets* or *Poetics II*—or from the work of one of Aristotle's proteges, Theophrastus. This discovery has highlighted a common error in the work of modern scholarship that seeks to judge the tragic content of Mark's Gospel based on Aristotle's *Poetics*: Aristotle's theories of tragedy—as we have them—were not prominent after the second century BCE.

This means that, even if Mark's Gospel was written as a tragedy, it may not exactly follow Aristotle's descriptions of tragedy in the *Poetics*. Indeed, it is more likely that Mark was influenced by a prominent theory of tragedy—the one quoted in virtually every tragic critic before and after the first century—wherein a tragedy is "the encompassing of heroic crisis."[1] While this may appear to be a sparse definition of what tragedy is, this definition actually tells us a lot about tragedy. As argued in chapter 3, tragedy consists of three major elements: a hero of *spoudean* quality; suffering combined with death; and conflict—referred to as *Collision*. When combined, these elements fulfill the Theophrastean definition of tragedy by encompassing "heroic crisis."[2]

Part of what constitutes tragic conflict, or *Collision*, is the tension created by two powers that are highly valued. Applied to Mark's Gospel, this means that the temple, which is opposed to Jesus, is justified in and of itself. The *Collision* occurs when Jesus, who is also independently justified, is brought into conflict with the temple, thereby creating the necessary tension that we call "tragic." In other words, tragic conflict is concerned with the psychological union of opposites, which brings about a sense of catharsis. Just how the conflict plays out will be the topic of this chapter as well as that of chapters 5–6. With regard to the present chapter, I will argue that the tragic conflict, or *Collision*, in Mark's Gospel is illustrated through Jesus' ambiguous use of parables. This, I believe, is tied to what is commonly referred to as the "Messianic Secret." There are several occasions on which Jesus chooses to conceal his identity. These occur mostly within exorcism scenes, when Jesus silences the demons when they refer to him as the "Son of God," but also after certain other scenes in which his identity is recognized.

Therefore, the purpose of the current chapter is to explain the ways in which tragic *Collision* is illustrated by way of the motif of hiddenness and I will proceed to do this in four sections. The first section will discuss the importance of tragic hiddenness as it relates to plot and will provide a number of examples from ancient tragedy. The second section will identify certain motifs of hiddenness in Mark's Gospel and explain the importance of these motifs in terms of plot development. The third section will examine the use of parables but will do so in light of the motif of hiddenness. The fourth section will examine the motif of hiddenness within the exorcisms and explain the necessity of such secrecy in light of tragic *Collision*.

---

1. Keil, *Grammatici Latini*, 1:487.
2. See chapter 3 for a description of Hegel's elements of tragedy.

Hiddenness and Recognition

What will be found is that the previously inexplicable "Messianic Secret" is a feature of the tragic genre and that its appearance serves to motivate the tragic plot. Hiddenness is, therefore, not a historical feature of Mark's Gospel as much as it is a literary one. As a result, we no longer need to explain the motifs of hiddenness through historical methodology, since it makes more sense to consider them in light of tragic plot structure.

TRAGIC HIDDENNESS AND PLOT

The concept of hiddenness in Greek tragedy is a prevalent one and is effectively illustrated in a large number of plays. It becomes an important element of the plot because it creates a dramatic irony that is necessary to tragedy, especially when it is connected to the inevitable suffering of the hero. As with most tragedies, the audience is aware that the suffering and death of the hero is inevitable; in Mark, the audience is aware of who Jesus is and what his fate will be. This diminishes what could be called tragic suspense but what the author has at his disposal are the details that lead to the inevitable, which he might try to avert unsuccessfully.

This is clearly illustrated in Euripides' *Bacchae*. In this tragedy, Dionysus takes the principal role as a god who conceals his identity as a lowly beggar, though not before he identifies himself to the audience. He then progressively manifests his divine presence while remaining hidden through the unfolding of plot. As Vernant has observed, "it is as if, throughout the spectacle, even as he appears on stage beside the other characters in the play, Dionysus was also operating at another level, behind the scene, putting the plot together and directing it toward its *denouement*."[3] From the beginning of the drama, Dionysus appears as a duality: theologically he is presented as a god; on the stage he is presented as a Lydian stranger. This dualism allows Dionysus to be disguised while, at the same time, it allows him to be misidentified as a human stranger which prepares the way for his authentic triumph and revelation as a god. Those who see him as a Lydian stranger see only a foreign missionary, yet the audience sees both the disguise and the god,

---

3. Vernant, "Dionysus," 382.

a revelation that will later be realized. Once Dionysus is revealed for who he really is, he will be a fulfillment of joy for some. Yet for those who do not recognize him, he will be the deliverer of destruction.

From the onset, hiddenness is central to the plot. Even as the drama continues, this enigmatic representation of a god becomes more perplexing: Dionysus reveals himself by concealing himself and makes himself manifest by hiding himself from the eyes of all those who believe only in what they can see.[4] In order for Thebes to accept him, he must change his nature. Thus, he takes the appearance of a human being—distinct from a god—while conducting the actions of a god. This makes him unrecognizable to those who are not prepared to recognize him, and recognizable to those who have learned "to see what must be seen" (924). We must assume that, at any time, Dionysus could reveal himself as a god to those who abuse him. So much is said while Dionysus—still masked—is speaking with Pentheus. At line 500, Dionysus says to Pentheus, "He (Dionysus) is here now and sees what I endure from you." Yet, Dionysus continues to conceal himself in light of persecution *because it is what the plot demands*.

Dionysus cannot reveal himself as a god until he has established his rites but, in order to do so, he must remain concealed despite persecution. Such is the essential nature of tragic *Collision*: the god must remain concealed in order for the conflict to remain believable. If, on the other hand, Dionysus reveals his true nature at the first sign of conflict, Pentheus would be overcome and the story would cease to be tragic because humans cannot withstand conflict with a god. And so, in order for two opposing forces to be rightfully engaged in tragic *Collision*, they must be of equal value during the course of the drama. As Vernant says,

> . . . whether the god rises to heaven, falls to earth, or leaps and flames between the two, whether he is man, flame, or voice, visible or invisible, he is always the polar opposite to Pentheus, despite the symmetrical expressions that are used to describe them both. He brings down to earth the revelation of another dimension to existence and grants our world and our lives direct experience of the elsewhere, the beyond.[5]

---

4. Vernant, "Dionysus," 391.
5. Vernant, "Dionysus," 397.

Hiddenness and Recognition

This "elsewhere" or "beyond" is made manifest in the presence of the concealed god. He is the embodiment of the "other," and his miracles are performed in the familiarity of an everyday setting (449). His ability to shift what seems solid baffles those who watch him with skeptical eye, yet, for those who recognize him, his miracles are prominent amidst everyday existence. This is the nature of tragic *Collision*: the "otherness" of the tragic hero forms the substance of conflict. Dionysus appears as the polar opposite to Pentheus, and acts in a way that is contradictory to Pentheus' understanding. Therefore, Dionysus acts contrarily only to that with which he is juxtaposed—in this case, the beliefs and habits of Pentheus.[6] At the end of the play, Dionysus dissolves Pentheus and, with him, the city's entrenchment within its own boundaries.[7] This victory is then seen as a sign that the "otherness" that Dionysus has promoted is being given its rightful place at the center of the social system.[8]

Visualizing hiddenness as it appears in the *Bacchae* allows us to understand the necessity of such a motif in tragedy. It also allows us to further grasp the concept of tragic *Collision*. Of course, not all tragedies appear the same, nor do they illustrate the concept of hiddenness in the same ways. Yet, the concept of secrecy and hiddenness *do* exist in

---

6. So much is observed by Charles Segal (*Dionysiac Poetics*, 27). He notes that tragedy establishes an opposition between two parallel systems of values: the respective worlds of Pentheus and Dionysus each "incorporate their own forms of reason and madness, good sense and folly, wisdom and delirium" (quotation taken from Vernant, "Dionysus," 403).

7. Christopher Pelling (*Greek Tragedy*, 224–35) has noted how tragedy is often written as reflection of certain civic ideologies. Since tragedies were performed at civic festivals, they often challenge the ways in which a city operates politically (in the case of the *Antigone*), democratically (*Orestes*), or present ideals of domestic harmony or international peacefulness which clash against contemporary reality (*Eumenides, Heraclidae, Supplices*). In one sense, tragedies can be viewed as subversive of civic ideology and can even contradict the context of the festival itself. Yet, in another sense, tragedy can be viewed as ideal. Somewhere in between lies experience and this experience is what tragedy prompts and provokes in the context of those who view it. In any case, tragedy provokes one to consider the ways in which his or her own context can be shaped and reshaped. Perhaps this is the real definition of *pathos*, that is, the emotions that exist as a result of viewing tragedy. See also, Cartledge, "'Deep Plays.'"

8. Vernant, "Dionysus," 402.

Of Conflict and Concealment

many tragedies, and these motifs play a central role in the development of tragic *Collision*.

Let us consider another example of a Greek tragedy whose elements illustrate hiddenness and secrecy as essential to its plot. Aeschylus' *Seven Against Thebes* not only provides a clear example for how hiddenness dictates plot but also shows how this motif functions to promote the element of tragic *Collision*.

As the play opens, we are told that Thebes is at war and its king, Eteocles, is charged with creating a solution to the impending threat. As he is planning his defense, several Theban women rush into his quarters and, in their excitement, begin to visualize the enemy spilling over the walls even though the battle has not yet begun. Eteocles deals with the women by telling them to return home—a common recommendation whenever a tragic hero comes upon an excited chorus.[9] Yet they fail to heed his advice and take the role of the chorus throughout the rest of the drama.

As for the threat that resides outside of the city, its role is juxtaposed with that of Thebes. Within Thebes, we see valiant fighters who rely on courage; outside of Thebes, the opposing threat is illustrated as a beast full of idle threats. Within Thebes, caring women convey the outcomes of war; outside of Thebes, shields and chariots represent the symbols of war. Within Thebes, there is food, warmth, and life; outside of Thebes, there is blood, fire, and death. These juxtapositions serve to heighten the gravity of the threat that looms without. But Aeschylus continues to compare them. Thebes is understood as a "city which pours forth the speech of Greece" (71) and the opposing army is "an army of another tongue" (170).[10] And there is a reason for this: the enemies of Thebes *must* be barbarian in speech because it is what the plot dictates; to have it any other way would discontinue the tragic nature of the drama. To be a Greek meant to be tied to the cities which your fathers cultivated and lived within. To lose the city meant to lose what

---

9. Rosenmeyer, *Masks of Tragedy*, 12.

10. According to Rosenmeyer (*Masks of Tragedy*, 13), it is possible that Aeschylus, in contrasting the Argives with the Thebans, is conjuring up memories of the Persians who had recently invaded Athens. Doing so allows the audience to become further entrenched in the tragic nature of the drama, thereby heightening the emotional response to what will happen.

it was to be Greek. The opponents, on the other hand, cannot share in this legacy and are seen as vagabonds who wander without a place to call home. The enemies of Thebes also must violate the religious rites of the city. We are told that the seven enemy champions have engaged in unholy practice with regards to animal sacrifice: " . . . who cut a bull's throat into a black-rimmed shield, and dipped their hands into the gore of the bull, and swore their oaths to Ares, Enyo, and blood thirsty Terror . . . " (43). This description brings to mind images of enemy barbarians drinking the blood of their sacrificial victims which was meant to validate their purpose.[11] What is more, the enemy champions do not swear by the gods of Thebes: they have no city, no gods to honour and no heritage to be rooted in—the ingredients of a perfect enemy.

Each of these juxtapositions is meant to heighten the battle that is to follow, but it also allows for the motif of hiddenness to be brought to light. Amid the acute differences that Aeschylus has carefully illustrated, there is an ironic twist: Eteocles must challenge the greatest of the barbarian warriors, a warrior who, as it turns out, is none other than his brother, Polynices.

Polynices is different from the other barbarian warriors. He is a moral agent who prays to Justice and who carries her image on his shield. The image shows a woman leading a man in full armor (644), and it is thought that this is meant to symbolize how Justice leads her champion back to his native city to enjoy the freedom of his home.[12] The symbol intensifies the battle between Eteocles and Polynices because it is no longer Theban against wretched barbarian, it is now brother against brother. This places stress on the character of the brothers who, as legend states, still operate under the curse of their father Oedipus. At once, Eteocles is removed from his kingly duties and is forced to contemplate the once hidden and now revealed danger: the curse and its promise of death.

As such, the brothers engage in battle and are both killed. Their death marks the end of the curse that once hovered over the city. As it turns out, it was not the impending barbarian threat that threatened slavery, it was the hidden reality of the curse. Aeschylus uses the image

11. Rosenmeyer, *Masks of Tragedy*, 14.
12. Rosenmeyer, *Masks of Tragedy*, 37.

of war as an occasion during which he can reveal the true pollution, or *miasma*,[13] and it is only through the sacrifice of their king that such pollution can be alleviated.[14]

Seven Against Thebes allows us to understand a different way by which tragic *Collision* is illustrated, as well as the ways in which the motifs of hiddenness and secrecy are utilized to create the plot. Without hiddenness, we cannot perceive the proper tension that is created by brother battling brother. But, more importantly, without hiddenness, we cannot fully appreciate the revelation of the true danger to Thebes: it is not the impending barbarians that are the most dangerous; it is the revealed curse that truly enslaves the city.

Hiddenness and Recognition

Along with the motif of hiddenness, tragedy contains a number of occasions during which the motif of secrecy is lifted and recognition occurs. Aristotle calls this type of recognition ἀναγνώρισις, and he defines it as: "a change from ignorance to knowledge leading to friendship or enmity, and involving matters which bear on prosperity or adversity."[15] Though Aristotle plays no significant role in Mark's composition, as was argued in chapter 2, his definitions are worth consulting because of his careful analysis of fifth-century Attic tragedy.

Aristotle delineates six types of recognition scenes: (1) recognition through tokens; (2) recognition that is contrived by the poet; (3) recognition through memory; (4) recognition by reasoning; (5) recognition based on wrongful inference; and (6) recognition that emerges from the events themselves.[16] From this list, we can see that there are

13. See Nagy (*Ancient Greek Hero*, 525–41) for a discussion of tragic *miasma*.

14. Lattimore (*Patterns*, 47–49) calls this type of story a "sacrifice play" and he argues that the self-immolation of the hero lurks "beneath Eteocles' choice in *The Seven* … " (47). There are, of course, many different expressions of this type of play. Examples include the *Iphigenia in Aulis*, *The Heracleidae*, *The Phoenician Women*, the *Hecuba*, and the *Andromedas*. At times, however, the self-immolation is not public but private as in the case of Ajax, Antigone, and Alcestis. What ties each of these characters and their plays together is the pre-set pattern in which "death is necessary, and in which the hero sees this, consents, and makes the act his own" (49). See also, Nagy (*Ancient Greek Hero*, 537–38).

15. Aristotle, *Poet.* 1452a 29–32.

16. Aristotle, *Poet.* 1454b–c. Hubbard's translation (found in Russell and

many different ways by which recognition can occur and very seldom do two tragedies manifest the same type of recognition scene.

The recognition scene is an important aspect of tragedy because, as Aristotle suggests, it serves to thrust the plot towards an ending, even if somewhat surreptitiously at times. It is best accompanied by some type of reversal of plot, which means that the recognition itself forces the characters within the drama to act differently in light of the new information they have discovered.[17] An example of this occurs in Sophocles' *Oedipus Rex*, in which Oedipus is forced into self-mutilation because of what he has discovered. Another example can be found in the *Seven*, mentioned above, in which Eteocles recognizes the power of the curse as well as his own death upon seeing his brother. Yet another example is found in the *Odyssey*, in which Euryclea recognizes Odysseus by way of the scar on his leg. In each of these examples, recognition thrusts the plot towards a particular end, making ἀναγνώρισις an essential aspect of plot.

But recognition is not simply an aspect of plot; it is, in essence, the necessary element of plot. In order for a plot to be "tragic," it must impose on its audience some type of emotive response. Aristotle calls this response either "pity" or "fear,"[18] and refers to it as a type of *catharsis*, or emotional release—a topic to which he never returns in the *Poetics* (see chapter 2).

Despite the lack of an Aristotelean definition of *catharsis*, we can still appreciate the nature of these emotions, and I say this for two reasons. The first is that *catharsis* must be associated with a realization of

---

Winterbottom, eds., *Classical Literary Criticism*, 51–90) emphasizes five types and places recognition through false inference in a subcategory of recognition through reasoning. For clarity, I have separated them into six distinct categories. For a similar format, see Russell and Winterbottom, eds., *Classical Literary Criticism*, 70–72.

17. Aristotle, *Poet.* 1452a 22–23.

18. Aristotle (*Poet.* 1385b 12–16) defines pity as: " . . . a pain from some apparently evil, either destructive or painful, happening undeservedly which someone himself might expect to suffer or any of those that belong to him [to suffer], and this when it appears near." Aristotle (*Poet.* 1382a 21–25) defines fear as: " . . . a pain or disturbance from imagination of imminent evil, either destructive or painful. For not all evils are feared, for example whether one is to become unjust or stupid, but whichever make possible great pains or destructions, and these if they are not far off but appear nearby so as to be imminent."

a certain type of emotion, or *pathos*, and that emotion, whatever it may be, is one that is associated with tragedy—as opposed to the types of emotion associated with comedy, for example. One could then argue that the success of a tragedy depends on whether the audience is able to perceive these types of emotion over other types, like those associated with comedy, and whether a tragic type of emotion is aroused by watching other dramas also understood as being tragic. This definition suggests that tragedy is distinguished from other genres by the emotion that it produces and not necessarily by the poetic formula, per se. This means that two tragedies can differ from one another in terms of form and still be considered tragic because of the common emotions produced by both. This is why Lattimore stresses the fact that tragedies can have different forms of plot and still be called "tragedies."[19]

Yet, these tragic types of emotion can even be appreciated out of context, and a twenty-first-century audience is still able to appreciate a tragedy as being tragic almost 2,500 years after it was written. This is precisely why Hegel's definition of *Collision* is helpful here, because one is able to appreciate a conflict between two opposed and highly valued powers. Thus, in many ways, the perception and nature of tragedy resides intrinsically within the human experience: because we can fathom the emotional tension between two highly valued powers, we are able to appreciate the same types of emotion that an Athenian might have experienced so long ago.

This leads to my second point about *catharsis*, and that is its ability to generate emotional tension—that Aristotle called "pity" and "fear"—which is then ameliorated by tragic *Collision*. Tragedy, though it may appear otherwise in certain stories, contains within it a sense of restoration. I touched upon this concept in chapter 2 and suggested that the amelioration of tragic conflict restores the nature of things to its pre-conflict state. Odysseus may have suffered much on his long journey home but his destroying the suitors brings about a sense of restoration of that which was lost. Similarly, Eteocles, much like Jesus, must accept his own demise in order to restore Thebes to its pre-Oedipean state.

So much can be seen in Mark's Gospel. There are a number of recognition scenes in which Jesus is correctly identified as either the

19. Lattimore, *Patterns*, 1.

Hiddenness and Recognition

Son of God or Messiah. Yet, Jesus continues to conceal himself, often commanding silence from that those who have recognized him. This has often been referred to as the "Messianic Secret" (dealt with in more detail below) but this is a misnomer. Instead, Jesus must remain concealed precisely because he is the Son of God. This seemingly paradoxical aspect of Jesus' ministry is often misinterpreted because it makes little historical sense. However, viewed from a tragic aspect, hiddenness and secrecy are commonplace. This is because Jesus cannot reveal himself too soon, lest the plot become unbelievable.

With regard to recognition, Mark chooses to place a number of recognition scenes within the plot, each of which I will deal with in detail below. However, these recognition scenes are unequivocally linked to Jesus' identity as the Son of God and Messiah. It will be argued that there are three kinds of recognition scenes in Mark, which are all characterized by conflict. These can be understood as conflicts on a micro-level in comparison to conflict on a macro-level, which is characterized by Jesus and the temple. Each of these levels develops *pathos* in the audience because we are aware of who Jesus is from the beginning of the Gospel. Just as Dionysus appears to the audience and reveals his identity and purpose in the prologue of the *Bacchae*, so Jesus appears and reveals his identity and purpose in Mark's opening chapter. This is characteristic of tragedy in which the protagonists and their cause are to be made known to the audience. The purpose for this is *pathos*: knowing certain information allows the audience to perceive the tension created by the conflict within the plot. Revealing the identity of the protagonist and their cause also allows for the audience members to form their conceptions of the two "goods" being represented—Jesus as the Son of God and the temple as the center of all religious activity, culture, and the believed residence of God himself.

In order for Jesus to dissolve the temple and make it obsolete through the tearing of the temple curtain, his identity must remain concealed in order for him to be mistakenly killed. Since he is a god, he is unable to remain dead, and his resurrection is the act by which the temple is rendered obsolete and the "kingdom of God" is established. Therefore, all parables and exorcisms, concealments, and recognitions revolve around the center which is Jesus' abolishment of the temple, and each of these things serves to make alive by dying, to make accessible by restricting, and to pronounce and yet conceal.

HIDDENNESS, THE "MESSIANIC SECRET," AND THE PLOT OF MARK'S GOSPEL

This section will apply the concepts of tragic secrecy to a discussion of Mark's Gospel. What will be shown is that secrecy is essential for the plot of Mark's Gospel because Jesus cannot exceed the expectations of his character or else the story ceases to be tragic. This section will begin, however, by discussing scholarly conceptions of Wilhelm Wrede's "Messianic Secret."

The "Messianic Secret"

In 1901, Wrede published *Das Messiasgeheimnis in den Evangelien*, or "The Messianic Secret."[20] In it, he sought to establish that a motif of hiddenness could be found in Mark's Gospel and that it was theologically and not historically motivated.[21] The basic question that Wrede

---

20. The first edition appeared in 1901 as *Das Messiasgeheimnis in den Evangelien* and was reprinted in 1963.

21. When Wrede began his career, the Gospel of Mark was considered to be a purely historical account of Jesus' life and ministry. This is probably due to the advancements of Strauss and Baur on the historical critical approach to reading Scripture. This approach was also used by Eichhorn, who had outlined a historical critical approach to the New Testament and who influenced Wrede considerably during his career. The force that lay behind Wrede's *Messiasgeheimnis* was this historical critical method and Wrede used it to arrive at a "pure" history. This is evidenced by Wrede's statement, "The first task can consist only in examining the account in the context of its own spirit asking what the narrator intended to say to the readers of his own time" (*Messiasgeheimnis*, 2). This statement is meant to create a distinction between "history" and "what the narrator had to say." Such distinction is evident in Wrede's *Messiasgeheimnis* when he concludes that the "idea of the Messianic Secret is a theological presentation" (66). This means that, as those closest to Jesus became more aware of his Messianic identity, the less he wanted to openly talk about it. This explains why Jesus commands his disciples not to speak of the events at the transfiguration (Mark 9:9) until after his resurrection. To safeguard against any accusation that the church falsely applied certain Messianic traits to Jesus, Mark created the "Messianic Secret" to dissolve the apparent tension between a post-Easter church who understood the messiahship of Jesus and a historical Jesus who never talked about his messianic identity. This theory contradicted the contemporary notion of "history," and Wrede's theory was mostly rejected for the first ten years after he wrote

was interested in answering was whether Jesus regarded himself as the Messiah or not.[22] At the forefront of the discussion is the question of historicity: did the historical Jesus purposefully add an element of hiddenness to his teaching, or is the element of hiddenness a creation by the Gospel writers? Each of the scholars that I will mention from this point on struggle to answer this question. For Wrede, who first noticed the motif of hiddenness in Mark's Gospel, it was a matter of theology. For Wrede's earliest critics, it was instead a matter of history. After more than a century, Wrede's theory still looms within Gospel studies, and a huge amount of scholarly literature has been devoted to either refuting,[23] supporting, or re-shaping his theory.[24] Even today, the question of why a motif of hiddenness exists in Mark's Gospel is still without an agreed upon answer.

Wrede divides his book into three parts. The first part is concerned with the criticism of the "psychological lives" of Jesus, which suggest that Jesus gradually became aware of his messianic identity. This awareness would then have begun at his baptism, been further realized during the Caesarea-Philippi pericope, and come to full awareness during the transfiguration. Wrede demonstrates that there is no such development within the Gospel and argues that there is a clear manifestation of messiahship throughout the entire Gospel coupled with a definite tendency to withhold it. Wrede then argues that Mark chose to conceal the messiahship of Jesus in order to reflect the theological tendency of the early church.[25] As mentioned, the transfiguration becomes the central point of Wrede's theory because, after it happens, Jesus warns his disciples not to talk about it until the resurrection occurs. It makes sense why Mark would want to represent Jesus as the Messiah, but the

---

it. For an excellent summary of the varying scholarly views from 1901–1975, see Blevins, "Messianic Secret."

22. Wrede, *Messiasgeheimnis*, 1; Räisänen, *'Messianic Secret'*, 38.

23. Among those who first disagreed with Wrede are: Barth, *Die Hauptprobleme*; Schmiedel, *Die Hauptprobleme*; Scourer, *Das messianische*; Soden, *Die wichtigsten*.

24. Weiss (*Die Geschichtlichkeit*) agreed with Wrede that Mark's presentation was largely ahistorical but thought that the substance of Mark was a valid representation for a life of Jesus. Schweitzer (*Historical Jesus*) accepted the theory but refused to attribute it to Mark.

25. Blevins, "Seventy-Two Years," 192–200.

reason why Mark decided to include a motif of secrecy appeared as a mystery to Wrede, which he titled "the Messianic Secret."

The second part of Wrede's book is concerned with how the later Gospels represented the secrecy motif. He demonstrates that Matthew corrects the inability of the disciples and instead idealizes them. Luke portrays the disciples in a way similar to that in Mark, but explains their inability to recognize Jesus in light of certain Jewish messianic expectation.[26] John follows closest to Mark by demonstrating that belief in the resurrection was the prominent factor in the formation of the early church's conception of the Messiah.

The third part of Wrede's book is concerned with the historical and dogmatic conclusions to be drawn from the Messianic Secret. Wrede imagines two groups within the early church: one who wanted to show claims of messiahship in the accounts of Jesus, and the other who noticed a lapse of such messianic claims during Jesus' life. Mark tried to compromise between the two groups by creating a secrecy motif.

Turning now to the evidence, a motif of secrecy is evident in several places throughout Mark's Gospel: Jesus commands the demons to keep silent when they recognize him (1:25, 34; 3:12); those who are healed by Jesus are commanded to keep silent (1:44; 5:43; 7:36; 8:26); the disciples were commanded to keep silent concerning Jesus' identity (8:30; 9:9). As mentioned, the crux of Wrede's argument is based on 9:9, when Jesus commands Peter, James, and John not to speak of what they have seen until the Son of Man has risen from the dead. So, while the inner circle of Jesus' cohort becomes aware of his true identity, everyone else will become aware *after* the resurrection. This makes the question of Jesus' identity a theological one based on the resurrection and helps to explain why Jesus never referred to himself as Messiah throughout his ministry. Therefore, the "Messianic Secret" is an attempt by Mark to account for an absence of messianic claims made by Jesus himself.[27]

And so, Wrede came to three principle conclusions.[28] The first is that there is a distinct motif of hiddenness in Mark, which he called

---

26. Blevins, "Messianic Secret," 194.
27. Dunn, "Messianic Secret," 93.
28. Dunn, "Messianic Secret," 93.

Hiddenness and Recognition

"the Messianic Secret." The second is that certain elements of that motif, namely the exorcisms, are non-historical and should lead us to the conclusion that the motif of hiddenness is a construction of Christian or Markan theology. The third is that such theological interpretations of the hiddenness motif are the attempt of early Christianity to "read back" messiahship into the life of Jesus.

Although echoes of Wrede's work can still be heard in New Testament studies today, there are a number of problems with his ideas. The first is how he addresses the issue of whether Mark invented the "Messianic Secret," asking why the historical Jesus would purposefully withhold his true identity. The fact of the matter is that we do not know and cannot know the answer to this question. One can make any number of assumptions about what could have happened but, until we discover a document with which to compare Mark's use of hiddenness, we cannot know for sure whether the historical Jesus employed it or not. The same critique can be applied to those who argue that the Gospels portray an accurate description of Jesus' life—again, we do not know for sure. And so, we should look with some skepticism at Wrede's theory that the historical Jesus made no claims of messiahship because we are unable to know for certain.

The second problem with Wrede's theory concerns the title "Messianic Secret." This title is a misnomer primarily because Jesus' commands for silence are not always in conjunction with messianic claims. It can be argued, however, that things like miracles or parables can be understood in messianic terms but it would be a fallacy to suggest that because we understand Jesus' messianism in light of those things everyone else did too. In short, we ought to be careful not to ascribe "messianic" qualities to things which may not have been unanimously understood as "messianic." To call the motif of hiddenness a "Messianic Secret" is therefore incorrect. Instead, we should simply accept Wrede's observation that, at times, Jesus wanted to remain hidden. But to answer the question "why," by asserting messianism as its answer, is incorrect. This is perhaps why there is no unanimous agreement amongst scholars as to why a motif of hiddenness exists in Mark's Gospel. For this reason, it is better to understand why Jesus uses secrecy in light of tragic conflict, or *Collision*. More will be said on this below.

In what follows, I will survey a number of scholarly opinions concerning the "Messianic Secret." As mentioned, there is little consensus with regard to why a secrecy motif exists in Mark's Gospel and the dichotomy of history versus theology still looms large.

Scholarly Opinions Concerning the "Messianic Secret"

In the second edition of his commentary in 1966, Taylor addresses the issue of the "Messianic Secret." While he mentions that Wrede's theory has been rejected by most modern scholars, the influence of Wrede's theory still exists. He departs from Wrede by suggesting that the "Messianic Secret" is historical rather than merely a work of art.[29]

Taylor offers several pieces of evidence to validate his assertion. The first is that Jesus' crucifixion would have been largely unintelligible unless he was condemned as a messianic pretender.[30] The sign that is hung above Jesus' head during his crucifixion signifies namely that Jesus would not have been sarcastically labelled as the "king of the Jews" unless there was some messianic tension during his ministry.

Additionally, the narratives of Peter's confession, the entry into Jerusalem, and the trial before the Sanhedrin all illustrate the presence of a messianic tension during the ministry of Jesus. Taylor suggests that Jesus' messianic identity has more to do with his actions than his status. This means that his works of healing, his exorcisms, his victory over Satanic powers, his suffering, dying, resurrection, and future return are all to be understood in messianic terms.[31] The completeness of his messianic identity, however, lies in the occurrence of the resurrection. Taylor, then, understands the commands for silence and hiddenness to be evidence of Jesus' mindset that, even though he was already the Messiah, he could not fully identify with being the Messiah until his resurrection had occurred.

Taylor's criticisms of Wrede are also not without their problems. The first problem is that Taylor does not effectively explain why Jesus demands silence. If, as Taylor suggests, Jesus' messianic identity is effectively understood throughout his ministry—so much that it creates

---

29. Taylor, *St. Mark*, 124.
30. Taylor, *St. Mark*, 123.
31. Taylor, *St. Mark*, 123.

Hiddenness and Recognition

a tension—then it makes no sense why Jesus would command secrecy concerning it.

This leads us to the second problem, and that is Taylor's appeal to Jesus' subjective mindset. In order for Taylor to justify his position, he needs to prove that Jesus was thinking exactly what Taylor suggests he was. Since the text does not explicitly state what Jesus was thinking, this is impossible.

A third problem with Taylor's explanation of the "Messianic Secret" is that the occurrences of commands for silence do not make sense historically. One example of this is the pericope of Jairus's daughter. It does not make historical sense for Jesus to command secrecy concerning the resurrection of a girl that everyone knew was already dead. This lack of historical sense extends also to the exorcisms: if a demon screams the identity of Jesus aloud, it makes little sense why Jesus would command secrecy since those around him would also hear the demon's words. It makes more sense to consider these occurrences in light of their being literary devices that are meant to allow Jesus to avoid self-designation—more will be said on this below.

Each of these problems reveal Taylor's tendency to regard Scripture in light of his preconceived theological categories. This leads him to interpret the messianic identity of Jesus historically in light of a number of problems, as discussed above. While it is not my intention to suggest that Jesus' messianic identity was not a historical phenomenon, I am suggesting here that Mark's Gospel portrays that identity in a literary way.

In 1967, Hay takes up the topic of the "Messianic Secret" in light of the "Jesus of history and the Christ of faith" controversy and challenges two assumptions: that the messianic secret is the creation of Mark, and that Mark was primarily concerned with what is now known as the problem of the Jesus of history and the Christ of faith.[32] Because Wrede held that the pre-Markan tradition was non-messianic, Mark had to compensate for it by creating the hiddenness motif. Hay sides with Conzelmann who thought that the pre-Markan tradition was indeed messianic, and that Mark created the secrecy motif to ameliorate its

---

32. Hay, "Messianic Secret," 18.

effect.³³ However, Hay concludes that the "Messianic Secret" neither impairs nor enhances the messianic nature of the tradition.³⁴ This means that, as far as the hiddenness motif is concerned, Mark has no intention of bridging the gap between a historical Jesus and a Christ of faith.

Hay concludes by suggesting that any hiddenness motif that exists in Mark's Gospel came to him from a tradition that already featured this motif. He also argues that the motif neither impairs nor enhances the picture of Jesus as Messiah because not all of the pericopes that contain the motif are concerned with Jesus' identity as the Messiah. This means that, while Conzelmann was correct in asserting that the motif was pre-Markan, he was incorrect insofar as the purpose of the Gospel is concerned. Hays argues that "a Gospel did not appear in order to provide a link between opposing views of Jesus; we have no evidence that the evangelist knew of such a problem."³⁵

The "Messianic Secret" came into being, therefore, as a means of explaining who Jesus was. This does not tell us how the hiddenness motif functions within the Gospel, however, and it is a position from which later scholars such as Dunn and Aune separate. If Jesus' identity as Messiah became obvious by way of the miracles he conducted, then there would be no need for a hiddenness motif—the motif becomes redundant. What is more, if Jesus' identity as the Messiah was made clear after the resurrection, why would the earliest believers need to perpetuate a hiddenness motif? It seems unlikely, contrary to Hay's thesis, that a pre-Markan tradition would maintain redundancies that had no effect on the overall story of Jesus.³⁶ It is more probable that

33. Conzelmann, "Gegenwart und Zukunft"; Hay, "Messianic Secret," 18.

34. Hay, "Messianic Secret," 19.

35. Hay, "Messianic Secret," 27.

36. This is contra Steele ("Theology of Hiddenness," 185), who argues that a "theology of hiddenness" can be derived from Mark's Gospel. The perspective of the early church, which was one of a group experiencing persecution, is reflected in Mark's Gospel: the cognitive dissonance between the church's faith and its experience is given answer. He concludes by arguing that the theme of secrecy "both affirms them (the earliest believers) in the midst of apparent failure and reframes their self-image as the people to whom God has given the secret of the kingdom." While this is possible, it is not provable since Steele is appealing to the subjective mind-frame of the earliest believer, which is not accessible.

Hiddenness and Recognition

Mark created the motif to serve a particular function within the narrative and not as a means of conveying a theological truth about Jesus' identity as the Messiah. I will discuss this in more detail below.[37]

In 1970, Dunn addressed the "Messianic Secret" in a negative way. He criticized each of the three strands of argumentation that I outlined above with regards to Wrede's theory by pointing out that the resurrection does not exclusively allow one to correctly interpret the life and ministry of Jesus. Instead, Dunn finds it more compelling to think that the motif is a historical reminiscence of the failure on the part of the disciples to correctly recognize Jesus, and he suggests three reasons for this. The first is his observation that the disciples continually failed to comprehend who Jesus was. Dunn argues that "the natural and unexceptional slowness of unlettered men whose rigid and closed system of thought made it difficult for them to adjust to new teaching."[38] This, of course, is an argument from silence, since we cannot be sure exactly why the disciples did not grasp Jesus' teaching—especially with regard to the parables—beyond what the text tells us. The second reason why Dunn discredits Wrede's theory is the number of explicit references to Jesus' messianism throughout his ministry. These include Jesus' use of the title "Son of Man," various references and fulfillments of Old Testament messianic expectation and the description of Jesus as the "Son

---

37. I am not arguing, as Fowler does, that the "Messianic Secret" is not a characteristic of the text itself but rather that it resides in the reader's experience of the text. Fowler (*Let the Reader Understand*, 156) says, "The Messianic Secret is best understood as a variety of closely related experiences that occur when the reader of Mark's Gospel encounters the indirect rhetorical strategies of the narrator's discourse." This is an inference drawn from his explanation of irony in Mark's Gospel: the reader's reception of irony cannot be a facet of the text and is instead a reaction by the reader to the narrative. This is to say that the secrecy motif found in Mark's Gospel is nothing other than a creation in the mind of the reader and is a rhetorical tool used by the author to create a level of irony in the reader's mind. He justifies this by pointing to the plethora of opinions regarding the "Messianic Secret" and suggests that no solution has won critical acclaim. I disagree with him on this point and suggest that the "Messianic Secret" has less to do with a creation in the reader's mind and more to do with its function within the narrative. While irony may reside in the reader's mind, the secrecy motif does not. Instead, secrecy functions as a way for Jesus to avoid self-designation which, as we will see below, is critical for the plot: Jesus cannot supersede the confines of his character before the resurrection or the plot ceases to make sense.

38. Dunn, "Messianic Secret," 96.

OF CONFLICT AND CONCEALMENT

of David"—a title for which Jesus did not command silence. The third reason is that Jesus' commands to silence ultimately failed. This means that the messianic nature of Jesus could not be understood primarily in light of the resurrection, since the news of what Jesus was doing spread far and wide (1:25-28, 43-45; 7:36).[39]

Dunn concludes by stating that "to speak of a Messianic *secret* is misleading and unjustified."[40] He instead argues that Jesus' messiahship was not rendered a secret at all and was a "cautious disavowal of false (messianic) views."[41] It appears that Dunn is attempting to preserve the historical authenticity of Mark's Gospel by discrediting certain claims made by Wrede,[42] more specifically Wrede's argument that the exorcisms are stories created *ex nihilo* for the purpose of developing a messianic theology.[43] While I understand the desire to preserve "historicity," I do not think that Dunn adequately does so here. To speak of a "Messianic secret" as Wrede does—and subsequently Dunn—is to render the data as purely historical phenomena from which certain theological implications can be drawn. Doing so prevents either scholar from explaining the presence of commands to silence without making arguments from silence (e.g. the disciples being unable to make sense of Jesus in light of their closed system of thought or there being no explicit messianic claims during Jesus' ministry). To think of the commands to silence as anything other than literary features renders the text absurd: it presents Jesus as commanding something that is impossible (e.g., the command

---

39. Dunn, "Messianic Secret," 100.
40. Dunn, "Messianic Secret," 115.
41. Dunn, "Messianic Secret," 115.
42. Dunn follows in the footsteps of one of Wrede's earliest critics, Albert Schweitzer. Schweitzer (*Historical Jesus*, 337) disagreed with Wrede on his conclusions but agreed with him with regard to the inconsistencies between the public life of Jesus and his messianic claim. He suggested that Mark's Gospel must either be either a historical or a literary document since each position is incongruous with the other. If one subscribes to a literary interpretation of the Gospel, as Wrede did, Schweitzer thought that any messianic claim made by Jesus in the Gospel had to be interpolated and therefore of no historical value. See also Aune, "Messianic Secret," 4–5.
43. This was rejected by Sanday (*Life of Christ*, 70–71), who criticized Wrede for jumping to conclusions too quickly. He pointed out that Wrede saw any appearance of contradiction or incoherence in the narrative as evidence of the material being ahistorical.

to keep the resurrection of Jairus's daughter a secret). The question, which I will answer below, then becomes: how are we able to read the commands for silence without generating arguments from silence? Unfortunately, Dunn falls into the same trap as Wrede in this regard.

Also writing in 1970, Aune agrees with Wrede that there is a lack of explicit reference by Jesus to his messianic nature but disagrees in that this lack of reference does not indicate historical inaccuracy in Mark's Gospel. Jesus did not claim to be the Messiah because he could not, not until his resurrection and exaltation had taken place.[44] This makes Aune's "solution" to the "Messianic Secret" primarily eschatological.

But this raises the question of whether Jesus knew about his messianic status before the resurrection occurred. To answer this question, Aune observes three things that point towards Jesus' messianic self-awareness. The first is Jesus' attitude towards the Old Testament. Though Jesus often placed his teachings above those of the Torah, Jesus viewed the Old Testament as the authoritative word of God. Jesus read the Old Testament and defined his person and mission in light of it.[45]

The second thing that Aune observes is Jesus' attitude towards determinism and predestination. Jesus' life and thought were "controlled by the will of God as it was revealed to him through the Old Testament."[46] Aune appeals to 2 Sam 7:12–14 and Zech 13 and suggests that these two passages must have had significance for Jesus. It appears that Jesus combined the meaning of being "raised up" as a king with the concept of resurrection and therefore believed that God would crown him as king upon his resurrection (Rom 1:4).

The third observation that Aune makes in relation to Jesus' self-awareness of his messianic status is how Jesus understood the concept of Messiah. Much like those at Qumran, Jesus understood Isa 52:7 as describing the Messiah as one who would bring "glad tidings" (Mark 1:15).[47] In addition, Ezek 34:16 represents a messiah who would actively seek the lost ones of Israel. Therefore, Aune understands Jesus'

---

44. Aune, "Messianic Secret," 31.
45. Aune, "Messianic Secret," 22.
46. Aune, "Messianic Secret," 22.
47. See 11QMelch.

miracles and exorcisms in light of these passages and suggests that Jesus understood his messianic status.[48]

Like Dunn, Aune disagrees with Wrede's "Messianic Secret" insofar as Jesus clearly did make public messianic claims about himself. The problem that faces both Dunn and Aune, however, is that Jesus never explicitly states that he himself is the expected messiah. Instead, Jesus often avoided such self-designations and often preferred to use the title "Son of Man" with regards to certain messianic expectations. As will be discussed in chapter 5, Jesus creates a level of confusion when he uses this term because it is uncertain why Jesus prefers the term over the use of a personal pronoun. Even if messianic expectations are explicitly illustrated in the miracle stories, the problem of whether the miracle pericopes are historical or literary in nature is prominent.

Räisänen's book *The 'Messianic Secret' in Mark's Gospel*, composed in 1990, offers a negative appraisal of Wrede's theory. Räisänen provides an analysis of Wrede's major arguments as well as a summary of the various critiques Wrede received in the years after his theories were published. Räisänen then discusses what he calls the "Parable Theory," focusing on the Parable of the Sower as his main text. He then goes on to analyze various other commands for silence and hiddenness, including the commands Jesus gives after performing healing miracles and exorcisms and gives to the disciples after the transfiguration .

Räisänen concludes by suggesting that the commands for secrecy given to the demons and to the disciples constitute the "Messianic Secret" proper.[49] These secrets concern Jesus' nature and identity: in both examples, Jesus is identified as either Messiah or Son of God. Räisänen also notes that Jesus' commands in both examples are not disobeyed as they often are after healing miracles. This means that secret healings should not be considered part of the "Messianic Secret" because they have less to do with Jesus' identity and more to do with his abilities.[50]

In addition to the healing miracles, Räisänen argues that the "Parable Theory" ought to be distinguished from the "Messianic Secret." He suggests that 4:11–12 is most likely related to the negative attitude

48. Aune, "Messianic Secret," 27–30.
49. Räisänen, *'Messianic Secret'*, 242.
50. Räisänen, *'Messianic Secret'*, 243.

Hiddenness and Recognition

of certain Jewish people with regard to the preaching of the gospel. He also suggests that the Parable of the Sower ought to be understood as "one attempt among many to overcome the painful experiences in spreading the word . . ."[51]

HIDDENNESS AND PARABLES

The parables in Mark's Gospel should be included in a discussion concerning hiddenness because of Jesus' seemingly cryptic quotation of Isa 6:9–10 (Mark 4:11–12). Because Mark's Jesus chooses to teach in such a cryptic way, scholars have put forth a large number of hypotheses to explain why he does so. Part of the discussion is hinged on Mark's use of the "Messianic Secret," which leads scholars to interpret the parables in light of Jesus' supposed historical use of hiddenness. However, reading the so-called "Messianic Secret" as a historical phenomenon has led scholars to make a number of incorrect assumptions with regard to why Jesus did this. I have suggested, instead, that the appearance of hiddenness is a literary phenomenon that belongs within the scope of the tragic genre. Understanding how the parables function in accord with the motif lends itself to an understanding of their overall meaning within the plot of Mark. In other words, one cannot attempt to ascertain a meaning for the parables in Mark's Gospel independently from the plot. This section will therefore argue that the motif of hiddenness, which defines tragic plot, is illustrated in Mark's parables.

The Parable of the Sower as Epitome of Hiddenness (4:1–20)

The Parable of the Sower is the first instance when Jesus employs hiddenness with regard to his teachings.[52] Jesus quotes Isa 6:9–10, which signals the motif, and then explains the parable to his disciples (4:13–20). There are several immediate questions that I want to address: (1) Why does Jesus choose to teach about the kingdom of God in parables, and is there an identifiable motif of hiddenness within these parables? (2) If a hiddenness motif can be established, can we apply this motif to

---

51. Räisänen, *'Messianic Secret'*, 243.

52. On this point, Beasley-Murray (*Kingdom of God*, 128) notes that " . . . contemporary discussions of the parable reflect great confusion as to its meaning." Yet, because Jesus provides an explanation, this parable is quite prominent.

OF CONFLICT AND CONCEALMENT

all of the parables or only to a select few? (3) Again, as alluded to in the introduction to this section, what does Mark accomplish by including a hiddenness motif in the parables?

The answer to the first and second questions were addressed by Jeremias in his 1947 book *The Parables of Jesus*.[53] In it, he argues that the *logion* in vv. 11–12 cannot be referring to the parables themselves, and are instead referring to Jesus' preaching in general.[54] Jeremias then concludes that, to those who are on the outside, the words of Jesus remain obscure because "they do not recognize his mission nor repent."[55] This is based on his Jeremias' interpretation of Isa 6:9–10 in which a two-fold issue is presented: the offer of mercy and the threat of judgment inseparable from it.[56]

I am in agreement with Jeremias insofar as the motif can be applied to most, if not all, of Jesus' ministry in Mark's Gospel (see subsequent chapters for examples). However, I depart from Jeremias on the basis that the motif is not primarily meant to be a commentary on the disbelief of those who reject Jesus—this is a byproduct. Instead, I think that the primary purpose of the parables, and in particular the parable of the sower, is to contribute to an overall greater theme of subversion:

---

53. For Jeremias (*Parables*), the parables must then represent some type of *Sitz im Leben* to which Jesus addresses his teaching. His work here builds on that of C. H. Dodd (*Parables*), who was amongst the first to argue that the parables represent an authentic part of the historical Jesus' ministry and must be interpreted as being a part of that setting. Jeremias' goal was to look behind the text in order to discover this life setting, thus recovering the original meaning of the parables. This was a reaction to Jülicher (*Die Gleichnisreden Jesu*) who saw the chronological distance between Jesus and the composition of the Gospels as evidence for potential adaptations of Jesus' parables. Jülicher had legitimate concerns, but his theories must remain conjecture because—as is the case for Jeremias' theories—we have no pre-Markan material to which Mark's Gospel can be compared. See also Stein, *An Introduction*, 58; Gowler, *What are They Saying*, 3, 22; Davies and Allison, *Matthew*, 1:209.

54. Jeremias (*Parables*, 17–18) argues that vv. 11–12 were not spoken by Jesus in the context of the parable. Mark misunderstood Jesus' use of the term παραβολή and inserted vv. 11–12 into the middle of the parable and its explanation to the disciples. He bases his conclusion on several translations of Isa. 6:9–10 that lead him to translate v. 10 as: "unless they turn and God will forgive them" (17). This is difficult to accept beyond mere speculation, however, since we have no pre-Markan material to which to compare the Gospel, it is ultimately an argument from silence.

55. Jeremias, *Parables*, 18.

56. Jeremias, *Parables*, 18.

Hiddenness and Recognition

the parables exist as linguistic expressions of the kingdom of God that are meant to subvert the existence of the temple, thus, fulfilling their role in tragic *Collision*. This answers the third question posed above and suggests that Mark's purpose for utilizing the motif is to present Jesus, who constantly subverts the temple's existence and function within society, as a viable opponent to the temple.

But how exactly does Jesus do this in the Parable of the Sower? On this point, I find it frustrating that many of the early twentieth-century interpreters, Jülicher included, attempt to draw connections between the *Sitz im Leben* of Jesus and the parables he taught. The problem that each faced and eventually succumbed to, however, was that any interpretation of a moral or theological "lesson" *must* be read into the text.[57] The very existence of allegorical or metaphorical approaches to the parables are evidence of this because, for almost two thousand years, readers of the parables had no other choice but to deduce subjective meaning from the parables[58] since Mark does not provide exact clues that lead to a particular meaning.[59] Attempts to situate a *Sitz im Leben* for the parables probably occurred because Jesus tells his listeners that those on the "outside" will be unable to comprehend his message and are therefore not a part of the kingdom of God. So, one of two things has happened: the overwhelming number of conflicting interpretations appear as evidence that most people are on the "outside"; or the purpose of the hiddenness of the message has another purpose other

---

57. Hooker ("Mark's Parables," 88–89) notes that the parables seem "unduly puzzling," and, as a result, would necessarily involve some form of allegorization in order to interpret them.

58. Marcus ("Blanks and Gaps," 247–62) addresses the lack of meaning in the parables and suggests that these represent what he calls a "gap." Following Sternberg (*Poetics*, 191–92), a gap is defined as a deliberate ambiguity in the narrative and such gaps are common within biblical parables. An author may leave a gap intentionally open to various interpretations but these interpretations fall, more or less, within the narrative framework and ideological coherence that would be clear to the original audience. When applied to the Sower parable, several gaps are identifiable: the nature of the "word," the identity of the "sower," and the "method of sowing" (Marcus, "Blanks and Gaps," 253). Marcus does a good job of identifying clear gaps in scholarship yet fails to convincingly argue for an interpretation that is not itself completely subjective. See also Stern, *Parables in Midrash*, 75.

59. For a discussion of the various approaches to reading parables, see Blomberg, *Interpreting*, 33–81; Thiselton, *Hermeneutics*, 35–59; Parris, "Metaphors."

than deciding who is "in" or "out." It could be argued, therefore, that attempting to conjure a "historical Jesus" from the parables in Mark's Gospel becomes nothing other than an attempt to satisfy an interpreter's theological aim.[60]

The distinctions found in the Sower parable appear paradoxical to Hooker, who notes that the disciples—those to whom the secret of the kingdom of God had been given—clearly did not understand anything that had been said.[61] They fail to understand the power of Jesus (4:40-41; 6:37, 49–52; 8:4, 14–21); they are mystified by his teaching (7:18) and with the concept of suffering (8:32-34; 9:32-34; 10:32, 35-41); and they fail him at critical moments (14:32-42, 47, 50, 66-72). Yet, those "outside" respond positively to Jesus (5:34; 7:29; 9:24; 10:13-16; 14:3-9; 15:39).[62] Hooker is right to note this distinction, yet in no instance does anyone ascribe the titles Son of God or messiah to Jesus.[63] As a result of the paradox, scholars have been unable to unanimously agree on why Jesus would choose to obscure his words rather than make them clear.

Perhaps we are asking the wrong questions with regard to this problem; perhaps the tension exists because we are reading the sower parable as history instead of observing how it functions within Mark's narrative. Historically speaking, Jesus' purposeful obscuration of his teachings makes little sense. In addition, Jesus commanding silence with regard to his miracles and exorcisms—as we will see—makes little historical sense, either. Yet if we read the Gospel literally—realizing that the commands for silence serve the plot, then these paradoxical problems disappear. Much like the story of Dionysus recounted above, whose identity and message must continue to be obscured for the plot

---

60. On this point, Herzog (*Parables*, 14) adapts a quotation by Schweitzer (*Historical Jesus*, 4): "It was not only each [intellectual movement] that found its reflection in [the parables]; each individual [interpreter] created them in accordance with his [or her] own [ideological passion]." The quotation, as translated by Montgomery, reads as follows: "But it was not only each epoch that found its reflection in Jesus; each individual created Him in accordance with his own character. There is no historical task which so reveals a man's true self as the writing of a Life of Jesus."

61. Weeden, *Mark*, 23–32.

62. The groupings of verses mentioned here come from Hooker, "Mark's Parables," 91.

63. A possible exception being Blind Bartimaeus in 10:48 who calls Jesus the "son of David."

to make sense, Jesus' identity must likewise continue to be obscured until the resurrection.

What I am proposing here is that the sower parable becomes another example of how Jesus is continually subverting the temple's *ethos* and he does so by generating distinctions. As mentioned above, using the example of the *Bacchae*, the tragic protagonist must be distinct from his or her opponents in appearance. Yet Jesus' identity is not discovered by interpreting the meaning of what he says. This approach has yielded a number of problems because scholarship has not agreed on a single meaning for the sower parable. Instead, Jesus' identity and purpose are discerned by the distinctions that he makes. In other words, distinctions create identity. The religious leaders have already attempted to identify Jesus through association with Beelzebul (3:20–30), but Jesus renounces such associations. In the next section (vv. 31–35), Jesus continues to identify himself by creating more distinctions. Here, Jesus refuses to be identified by familial relations, and instead claims that anyone who does God's will is kin. Mark is identifying Jesus by illustrating that which Jesus is not: he is not in league with demons nor is he motivated by familial associations.

The Sower parable, as the first in-depth exposition of the kingdom of God, appears in series with these two pericopes and is also concerned with creating identity through distinction. In order to establish the distinctions, Jesus separates those people who understand his message from those who do not. Since the meaning of the parable is vague—as illustrated above—I understand the vagueness with which Jesus describes the kingdom of God as a method by which he obscures its meaning, thereby making it available to everyone. This is unlike the temple which places numerous restrictions on God's availability to humanity. Therefore, the parable of the Sower is a means by which Jesus creates identity. However, he does not do so by creating rules or regulations, as in the case of the temple, but by universalizing access to the kingdom of God, a method that is therefore understood as an act of subverting of the temple.

With regard to the plot and why this method fits within it, we can make two observations. The first observation concerns the tearing of the temple curtain in 15:38. At the moment of Jesus' death, the temple

Of Conflict and Concealment

curtain is torn in two, illustrating in a physical way that God is decontextualized from the temple. Not only does this decontextualization abolish the temple and its purpose, it also suggests that now everyone, regardless of their life situation or who they are, has access to God. The parable of the sower, as well as the other parables, functions in a way similar to this because Jesus is also decontextualizing access to God by obscuring his meaning. The second observation is that Jesus would not have been crucified if everyone had recognized him as the Son of God and Messiah at any point during his ministry, so hiddenness plays a necessary part in moving the plot toward the crucifixion. This may also explain a secondary function for why Jesus chooses to obscure his meaning through parables, and that is because he wants his identity and purpose to remain hidden until God has been decontextualized from the temple.

Therefore, the parables have less to do with deciding who is "in" the Christian faith and who is "out"—a dichotomy that would leave most of us "out." Instead, the parables—especially that of the sower—serve to do two things: (1) obscure Jesus' identity and purpose; (2) subvert the temple by offering universal admittance into the kingdom of God. We are now in a position to ask what Jesus means by the "seed" or the "word" (4:3, 14)—something that scholars are quite hesitant to do.[64] The "word" must then represent a recognition of, or participation in, the kingdom. This makes sense in light of Jesus' explanation of those who receive the "word": they produce a harvest of thirty, sixty, or even a hundred times as much as has been planted (v. 20). If the temple

---

64. Linnemann (*Parables of Jesus*, 119) simply defines the "word" as the gospel of Jesus. Crossan (*In Parables*, 39–44) seems less interested in a discussion about the meaning of the word and instead focuses on discovering anomalies in the text. Kistemaker (*Parables*, 38) ambiguously defines the word as the "word of God." Jones (*Parables*, 68–83) avoids defining the word, but seems to suggest that it might be Scripture. Pentecost (*Parables*, 53) describes the word as the actual words of Jesus, though he does not give much attention to its definition. Wenham (*Parables*, 44–45) defines the word as a "revolution" but does not explain in detail exactly what is meant by revolution. Hooker ("Mark's Parables," 89) defines the word as the report about Jesus himself. Juel (*Master*, 59–63) avoids defining the word except that it somehow refers to the kingdom of God. Marcus ("Blanks and Gaps," 251–52) notes that the identity of the seed is not given and is an intentional "gap" in the narrative that allows for multiple interpretations. Blomberg (*Interpreting*, 288–95) avoids an explicit definition, but follows Kistemaker, who calls the word the "word of God."

Hiddenness and Recognition

constricts access to God, the kingdom allows complete access to God. The analogy of harvesting greater amounts refers to how much more effectual the kingdom is than the temple. Contrarily, those who are unable to receive the word for the reasons listed, are those who cannot, or are unable to, decontextualize God from his current context in the temple.

This also makes sense in light of the parable that Jesus tells immediately after the sower (4:21–23). Here Jesus is using light as a metaphor for the "word" instead of "seed" and he suggests that "everything that is hidden will be brought into the open, and every secret will be brought to light" (v. 22). If we attempt to interpret this by associating knowledge with being "in" and ignorance with being "out," it does not make sense. There is no reason for Jesus to purposefully obscure his words and exclude people in the sower only to suggest that everyone will later be included—one would negate the other. Instead, Jesus is suggesting that the "word," which is again the decontextualization of God from the temple, will reveal more about God than the temple and its laws could reveal.[65]

The sower parable illustrates an important aspect of our discussion of Mark as tragedy. In it, Jesus explicitly announces a motif of hiddenness which is prevalent within most, if not all, tragedies. This is because some aspect of truth must be hidden in order for the plot to proceed. If it is revealed too early, then the plot ceases to make sense. Such is true of Jesus' identity. It can be argued that the parables serve to illustrate Jesus' identity as the deliverer of the kingdom of God. However, if Jesus is revealed too quickly as the Son of God or Messiah, then the plot collapses and it has no effect. Instead, Jesus must continue to obscure his identity. In addition to this, the parables serve to decontextualize God from the temple, which forms the basis of tragic *Collision*. Therefore, the sower parable ought to be interpreted in light of the plot and not by way of some type of universal truth.

---

65. The same can be said for the parables that occur in 2:18–22. Here Jesus utilizes a number of metaphors to make his point: just like old clothing cannot be patched with new cloth and new wine cannot be placed into old wineskins, so the people of God cannot have access to God via the temple and its ways. Instead, Jesus is suggesting that the temple, which has always "housed God," will become obsolete through decontextualization.

HIDDENNESS AND RECOGNITION

This section will discuss three kinds of recognition that occur in Mark's Gospel. The first kind are those moments of recognition that come by way of demonic exorcism.[66] The second kind comes by way of Peter's recognition of Jesus as Messiah. The third kind comes by way of the Centurion's recognition of Jesus. As mentioned above, recognition scenes hinge on the audience's true perception of Jesus' identity as the Son of God and Messiah, which are revealed in Mark's introductory chapter. This creates a level of *pathos* by which the audience can perceive the tension created by the conflicts. It will, therefore, be argued that recognition in Mark's Gospel is a necessary component of plot and serves to illustrate Jesus' true purpose in Mark's Gospel: to dissolve the temple and its contextualization of God.

Demonic Recognitions

Bilezekian notes the importance of the demonic exorcisms and suggests that these are part of Mark's plot known as the "Complication."[67] Bilezikian also notes how the demons regularly recognize Jesus' true identity while the crowds are capable of only "dumb amazement."[68] This continual cycle of exorcism, recognition, and amazement, however, never leads to the crowd confirming the true identity of Jesus. This is not only quite odd, but it also leads one to question why Mark would choose to make such situations prominent within the plot if they do not convince anyone of Jesus' identity. Bilezikian argues that the exorcisms serve to illustrate Jesus' mastery over the forces of Satan, but this can only be an assumption since Mark's Gospel never explicitly states

---

66. Wire (*Performance*, 92) notes that exorcisms are more prominent in Mark's Gospel than either Matthew's or Luke's and exorcism is largely absent in John's Gospel. What is more, Matthew and Luke seem to follow Mark with regard to exorcisms where they abbreviate the stories or even omit them altogether. This could mean that Mark's use of the exorcism narratives differs from that of Matthew and Luke, further pointing to the fact that they could be used as a function of tragic plot.

67. Bilezikian (*Liberated Gospel*, 59) follows Burkill (*Mysterious Revelation*, 6), who notes that the first half of the Gospel (1:1—8:26) is marked by Jesus' secret identity, whereas the second half (8:31—16:8) is characterized by Jesus' messianic function as the suffering Messiah.

68. Bilezikian, *Liberated Gospel*, 60.

Hiddenness and Recognition

this reasoning.[69] Bilezikian does, however, take notice of an important detail: though the crowds never recognize Jesus' true identity, his exorcisms often provoke a negative response from the religious teachers (especially 3:20–30). This tells us that there is a direct relationship between some of Jesus' exorcisms and the religious leaders who represent the temple.[70] Therefore, it is an assumption that the exorcisms serve primarily as an assault on the demonic world—something that is not defined nor discussed at length in Mark's Gospel. Instead, based on the text, it seems more plausible to suggest that the reason why Mark sometimes portrays the religious leaders as taking such offence to Jesus' exorcisms is to continue to establish a negative relationship between them and Jesus. This fits with the theory that Jesus' main adversary in the Gospel is the temple. Demons, on the other hand, play a very minor part in Jesus' ministry and, even though Satan is mentioned briefly in the opening chapters, he does not play a major role throughout the Gospel. It would be incorrect to assume, then, that the primary purpose of the exorcisms is to establish Jesus' dominance over the demonic world—this would be a byproduct of what Jesus is doing.

But what does the text say about exorcisms? The first exorcism is found in 1:21–28 and occurs in the synagogue in Capernaum. Immediately, a man who was possessed by an evil spirit began shouting at Jesus while he was teaching (1:21). The demon(s) identifies Jesus as "Jesus of Nazareth" and "Holy One of God" (1:24) and asks whether Jesus has come to destroy it. Jesus interrupts the demon and silences it, commanding it to come out of the man. The language employed by the demon here is a vocabulary of violence (ἀπολέσαι, "to destroy"), suggesting that the demon understands the interaction as combative. Yet we are not told whether Jesus "destroys" the demon, only that the

---

69. Bilezikian, *Liberated Gospel*, 60.

70. I should also like to add here that Jesus does not ever convince any of the religious leaders of who he is. The only exception might be Joseph of Arimathea—a prominent member of the Council—who asks for Jesus' body after the crucifixion (15:43). Not much is mentioned about Joseph, however, and we are not told if he is convinced of who Jesus is. Rather, we are told that he was "waiting for the kingdom of God." The answer to the question of why Jesus fails to convince of his identity is not that he *cannot*: the religious leaders exist for the purpose of representing the temple, with which Jesus is in direct conflict. Therefore, the characters in the story must remain consistent.

demon is commanded to "come out" of the man (ἔξελθε). This led to much amazement and Jesus then began to heal many others and drive out demons (1:34). Yet Mark adds the phrase "he (Jesus) did not allow any of them to speak because they knew who he was."[71] Historically, this makes little sense because, presumably, others would have heard the demons identifying Jesus. A less detailed account of these phenomena occurs in 3:11–12 and Jesus responds in a similar way: he commands the demons not to reveal who he is. This has led a number of scholars to assume the presence of a "Messianic Secret," a theory that was discussed above. Since the "Messianic Secret" is largely based on interpreting the Gospel historically, I do not think that it applies here. Instead, the hiddenness that Jesus employs with regards to exorcisms is very similar to tragic hiddenness which was explained by way of the *Bacchae* above. In addition, this scene functions as a proper recognition scene in that it alludes to Jesus' true identity—even if ironically by an unexpected source.[72]

This is illustrated even more clearly in the dramatic story of Jesus' encounter with Legion (5:1–20). Mark's version of the story differs significantly from that of Matthew (8:28–34) but is rather similar to that found in Luke (8:26–39). Mark, however, tells us that Jesus encounters a man possessed by many demons who correctly identity him as "Jesus, son of the Most High God" (5:7). The demons beg Jesus not to torture them (5:7) and Jesus drives them into a large herd of pigs grazing nearby (5:13). With regard to tragic recognition, this scene functions in an ironic way similar to that in 1:21–28. This irony may be what Bilezikian refers to as the complication of tragedy and is illustrated by the ways in which Jesus is rejected despite his spreading fame as a healer and exorcist. For example, even after Jesus rids the man of Legion, the spectators pleaded with Jesus to go away. Even Jesus' closest friends and family, as

---

71. In 1858, Alexander (*According to Mark*, 26) noted that Jesus did not let the demons speak " . . . either because he did not need their testimony and would have been dishonoured by it, or because a premature annunciation of his Messianic claims would have defeated the whole purpose of his mission." Whether or not Jesus would have been dishonored by these demonic expressions is impossible to know, yet Alexander notes the importance of silencing the demons for the completion of Jesus' mission.

72. Bilezikian, *Liberated Gospel*, 60.

Hiddenness and Recognition

well as those he grew up with in Nazareth (6:1–6),[73] do not recognize Jesus—yet the demons do.[74]

Each of these things adds to the irony and complexity of Jesus' ministry but it also makes one wonder why Jesus never convinces, or even wants to convince, anyone of who he is. This means that the purpose of Jesus' ministry, according to Mark, was not to convince of his identity.[75] Instead, the plot continually builds towards his journey to Jerusalem, his final interactions with the religious leaders, and his eventual crucifixion and resurrection.

Peter's Recognition

Peter's recognition of Jesus as Messiah alludes directly to the incipit in 1:1, which is the only other time in the Gospel that the title is used in a positive light.[76] Somewhat ironically, however, Peter's successful recognition is partially wrong since Jesus sharply corrects his false expectations of what being the Messiah means.[77] This correction may be equated with the positioning of the two-fold healing of the blind man (8:22–26), which scholars often equate with the "blindness" of the

---

73. Bilezikian, *Liberated Gospel*, 60.

74. A third example of exorcism occurs in 9:14–29. In this example, Jesus does not have the same type of interaction with the demon that he does in 1:21–28 and 5:1–20. Instead, the emphasis seems to be placed on the boy's father, who asks Jesus to help him overcome his lack of faith (v. 24). It is possible that this exorcism is then a commentary on the lack of faith that many struggle with since the possessed boy is unable to hear or speak (v. 25). The fact that Jesus waits until a large crowd has gathered before he conducts the exorcism takes away from the validity of the "Messianic Secret" but one must also keep in mind that Jesus is becoming increasingly aggressive and provocative as the time to travel to Jerusalem approaches. Thus, this exorcism does not seem to fit the usual recognition pattern that the previous ones do and is being used by Mark here to accomplish another goal.

75. English (*Message*, 60) suggests the same, but arrives at a different conclusion. He points out that " . . . Jesus did not intend to *prove* who he was by his acts of authority and power."

76. Evans, *Mark 8:27—16:20*, 9. The other two times are negative pronouncements found in 14:61 and 15:32.

77. Hooker (*St. Mark*, 203) describes this point of the story as divisive between those who recognize Jesus' true identity and those who do not. See also Bilezikian, *Liberated Gospel*, 77.

disciples to fully grasp what the messiah is meant to do.[78] Yet, once Peter correctly identifies Jesus as the Messiah, Jesus tells his disciples not to tell anyone about him (v. 30). Again, Jesus' command for hiddenness does not make historical sense, and we must assume that its inclusion is meant to portray an element of plot instead.[79]

Concerning plot, Peter's recognition scene can be considered the central turning point of the Gospel for two reasons.[80] The first reason is that Peter correctly identifies Jesus as the Messiah, and the second reason is that, after Peter's recognition (8:27–30), Jesus immediately begins to predict his death and resurrection using the pseudonym "Son of Man" (8:31). This gnomic usage of the Son of Man title is important because it lends credibility to the theory that Jesus' primary goal is not to convince his disciples of who he is as much as it is to dissolve the temple. Despite Peter's attempts at recognizing him, it also reveals that Jesus wants to continue the motif of hiddenness, which, as mentioned, must continue until his crucifixion and resurrection.

The Centurion's Recognition

The final recognition scene that I want to examine is that of the centurion in 15:39. It is the only instance in the Gospel where a human agent uses the title "Son of God."[81] Not only does this recognition scene

---

78. Hurtado, *Mark*, 133.

79. Hare (*Mark*, 99) calls this command for silence "historically comprehensible" because, if word got around about Jesus' identity, it would mean that he would die before his ministry was complete. This opinion is incongruent with the idea that Jesus had to die in order to complete his mission. What is more, if Jesus did not want his disciples to spread the word about his identity, it makes just as much historical sense to argue that Jesus should not have asked a question concerning his identity to his disciples. It is much more plausible to suggest that this scene serves as a proper recognition scene and that Jesus' continual commands for secrecy fit properly within tragic plot.

80. Boring (*Mark*, 231) calls 8:22—10:52 a transitional section that binds part 1 and 2 of the Gospel together, though he warns that this particular transition should not "divide" as much as "bridge" or "hinge" two sections that overlap and connect. Moloney (*Gospel of Mark*, 171–72) identifies a shift in Jesus' teaching from parables to conditional formulae concern surrounding passion predictions. Collins (*Mark*, 397) notes the transitional nature of 8:27—10:45 that focuses on the "blindness" of the disciples.

81. Hurtado, *Mark*, 269.

Hiddenness and Recognition

allude to the incipit, it may have also had a particular meaning to a Roman audience—since the Roman emperor was thought of as the son of God,[82] portraying a centurion admitting Jesus as the Son of God would have had prominence.[83]

With regards to tragic recognition, this scene fits well with what might be called "recognition accompanied by reversal." The centurion's recognition signifies a reversal of events: as Jesus hangs on the cross and is dying, several people pass by and mock him. Some even mock his words concerning the temple: "You said you were going to destroy the temple and rebuild it in three days" (v. 29). This mention of the temple is prominent because, as has been mentioned, Jesus' main opponent in the Markan tragedy is the temple. It appears as if Jesus has lost the conflict, and that the *Collision* will continue to be one-sided.[84] But it is at this point that the reversal takes place. Jesus dies (v. 37) and the curtain in the temple is torn from top to bottom (v. 38).[85] It is now revealed that Jesus' death does not signify defeat,

---

82. Evans ("Mark's Incipit," 67–81) argues that a number of elements in Mark resemble those found in the Roman Imperial cult. Porter ("Paul Confronts," 170–75) states references to the Emperor as a divine son of God can be found in a number of places: *IGR* 1.901, 4.309, 315; *ILS* 1:107, 113; P.Ryl. 601; P.Oslo. 26. According to Kim ("Anarthrous," 221–41), Augustus as *divi filius* also appears in literature. See also, Virgil, *Aen.* 6.791–793; Philo, *Flacc.* 74; Philo, *Legat.* 148, 149.

83. The *Priene Calendar Inscription* is a collection of inscriptions found in Asia minor that were erected in celebration of Augustus' birthday in 9 BCE. As Porter ("Paul Confronts," 167) points out, calling the whole collection the "Priene Inscription" is a misnomer, since parts of the collection were found in a number of areas such as Apamea Kibotos, Dorylaion, Maionia and Eumeneia. Porter goes on to affirm that "there are a number of features of the calendar inscription that Mark's Gospel holds in common to indicate that the Gospel was written in direct confrontation of the imperial cult." If this is so, Mark's description of Jesus as the "Son of God" would have resonated with an audience familiar with similar descriptions of the Caesars. It is not surprising then that Mark would have a centurion identifying Jesus as the "Son of God" thereby increasing the dramatic irony of the crucifixion scene.

84. Tragic *Collision* suggests that a tragic hero rises up for the purpose of challenging a one-sided position. Jesus appears as a challenge to the temple and is destroyed by it. The temple must then itself be destroyed or invalidated, otherwise the gospel story becomes simply a sad story about a misunderstood Jesus. However, Mark's resurrection narrative combined with the occurrence of the tearing of the curtain are meant to invalidate the temple, thereby validating Jesus' position as the advocate of the kingdom of God.

85. Moloney (*Gospel of Mark*, 329) notes a connection between the tearing of the

but victory, and the temple is made obsolete because it no longer contextualizes God. Once the reversal is observed, a recognition takes place[86] and Jesus is correctly recognized by a human agent as the "Son of God" (v. 39).[87]

CONCLUSIONS

This chapter has attempted to do three things. The first was to elucidate the concepts of tragic hiddenness, concealment, and recognition in several tragedies. Most prominent are the *Bacchae* in which Dionysus purposefully conceals his identity as the Son of God in order to bring about proper worship of himself in Thebes. He then reveals his identity through a number of miracles and actions. Another example is the *Seven Against Thebes*, in which hiddenness and recognition are used to further the plot and create a sense of *pathos*.

The second thing was to summarize various theories concerning the apparent motif of hiddenness found in Mark's Gospel. It provided a summary of Wrede's "Messianic Secret" and provided a number of scholarly opinions concerning it. It was shown that a historical approach to interpreting the Gospels is, and has been, wrought with false assumptions as well as misleading observations concerning the plot of Mark's Gospel. Instead, I suggested that Mark, and especially his motif of secrecy, be interpreted in light of tragic hiddenness and recognition.

This third thing was to explain how parables, exorcisms, and various recognition scenes validate my theory that Mark was written as a tragedy. Each of these things are meant to conceal Jesus' identity as the Son of God until his crucifixion and resurrection. This is not a historical phenomenon, but rather a tragic one according to which Jesus must remain concealed in message and deed in order for the plot to remain

---

curtains and the rending of the heavens in 1:38. Jesus is called the "Son of God" in both instances, as is access to God.

86. Some, including MacDonald (*Homeric Epics*, 142), have suggested that the centurion is being sarcastic and is joining with the mockers. This does not explain the curious use of "Son of God" here, and it does not explain why the centurion says it after Jesus has already died.

87. See Beavis (*Mark*, 232) for various interpretations of the centurion's recognition.

tragic. If Jesus is revealed too quickly, the plot no longer has force, and its sense of meaning is lost.

5

Miracles and Tragedy

INTRODUCTION

IN CHAPTER 3, I argued that tragedy consists of three core elements: *Collision*, a *spoudean* protagonist, and suffering coupled with death. These elements work together to create a narrative that is essentially "tragic," a narrative that cannot exist without all three being present. By developing a "universal" definition of the tragic, we are able to avoid the problem of great diversity amongst our existing tragedies. We are also now even closer to concluding that Mark's Gospel is essentially tragic, and that Mark has carefully crafted his Gospel to fit a tragic genre. The purpose of the present chapter is to further illustrate the ways in which Jesus is in *Collision* with the temple in Mark's Gospel through his acts of miraculous healing.[1] Therefore, much like the motifs of secrecy that were presented in the previous chapter, the healing miracles function to illustrate Jesus' goals as parts of the plot. I will also argue that the healing miracles in Mark's Gospel function as a continuation of Jesus' efforts to subvert the *ethos* that the temple creates.

When one conducts a survey of scholarly literature that analyzes the healing miracles in Mark's Gospel, one will discover a tendency to *exclusively* justify the healing miracles by way of historical

---

1. A number of Jesus' actions outside of healing can be considered "miracles." Such examples include exorcisms, which I discussed in chapter 4. For now, I will use the term "miracle" to refer to the acts of healing in Mark's Gospel.

Miracles and Tragedy

methodology. I think this is an honest attempt to uphold the historicity of Jesus' miracles and make a case against the skeptical view that the miracles are not historical occurrences. I am not one that adopts this skeptical view, but I do think the miracles have a literary purpose in Mark's Gospel. In other words, Mark attempts to convince his readers not by convincing them that Jesus existed within history and that he conducted miracles, but instead by conveying the truth about Jesus through a carefully crafted plot.[2]

Having said this, there are a number of challenges to Historical Jesus research with regard to Mark's miracles. The first is that Jesus' miracles are not discussed in-depth anywhere outside of the Gospels. While there are numerous accounts of healing miracles scattered throughout the New Testament, Jesus' miracles are not mentioned outside of the Gospels.[3] I think this lends support to the idea that the miracles function more as vehicles of plot.

The second challenge is linked to Christology. It could be argued that the miracles in Mark's Gospel serve to verify the messianic identity of Jesus and should therefore be treated primarily as records of historical phenomena. This is problematic because no other New Testament writer appeals to the miracles of Jesus in order to construct their Christology. Rather, they appeal to the resurrection. Each of these challenges supports the idea that the miracles in Mark's Gospel are used as literary devices that serve the plot. But how does this happen? Mark's Gospel presents Jesus as the Son of God and the Messiah (1:1), who is at once responsible for ushering in the kingdom of God on earth. Through a series of healing miracles, Jesus establishes a certain power that both exhibits and validates the kingdom of God. However, even though many are impressed by the miracles that Jesus conducts (2:12), not everyone is. Jesus' miracles are at once challenged by the religious leaders,

---

2. Brant (*John*, 12–13) suggests something similar with respect to John's Gospel: "Whatever genre category we impose on our reading of the Gospel of John, it is helpful to recognize that ancient writers did not think of invention of events or details or speeches as a distortion of the truth but rather as conveying truth."

3. The only exception is Acts 2:22, "Fellow Israelites, listen to this: Jesus of Nazareth was a man accredited by God to you by miracles, wonders and signs, which God did among you through him, as you yourselves know." Though this verse mentions miracles, it does not go into any detail about them.

who begin looking for ways to kill him (3:6). This may be due to the fact that Jesus heals on the Sabbath, an action that violates Scripture and is deserving of death (Exod 31:14). Yet Mark is deliberate about juxtaposing Jesus to the religious leaders, continually drawing distinctions between them with regard to the authority by which they teach (1:22). We may be able to then explain the frustration that the religious leaders express towards Jesus as mere jealousy but in doing so we succumb to validating something in the text that is not present. Instead, we must accept that Mark is deliberately setting up the conflict that will define Jesus' ministry, a conflict that I have chosen to interpret in terms of tragic *Collision*.

Interpreting the healing miracles in terms of *Collision* makes sense when we consider the function of the miracles within the narrative of Mark. In chs. 2 and 3 they breed contempt. In chs. 5–9 they force Jesus to act outside of several purity laws as regulated by the temple. In ch. 11 they symbolize the death of Jewish institutionalized religion. More will be said of each miracle grouping below, but for now we ought to understand the miracles in Mark as being defined by the way they juxtapose Jesus with the temple and religious leaders. In this way, the nature of both the kingdom of God and Jesus as its advocate can be defined. We can also suggest that, since the kingdom and Jesus are defined in terms of their juxtaposition to the temple, Jesus' efforts with regard to the miracles are always an effort to subvert the temple.

This chapter will proceed in the following way. It will first discuss relevant scholarship with regard to the healing miracles in Mark's Gospel and also offer critiques of this scholarship. Following this discussion, it will then group the healing miracles into workable categories according to function, at which point I will offer several comments concerning the relationship between miracle and *Collision*. In the same way, this chapter will then discuss the function of the exorcisms as they relate to *Collision*. It will then conclude with a number of remarks concerning the discussion.

HEALING MIRACLES IN MARK'S GOSPEL

This section will discuss both the relevant scholarship concerning the Markan healing miracles, as well as how these miracles function within

Miracles and Tragedy

the Gospel according to tragic *Collision*. As mentioned above, studies concerning healing miracles—or miracles in general—are often done in conjunction with Historical Jesus studies. This has led some scholars to derive certain christological features from the healing miracles. This is ultimately confusing, since studying Jesus by mixing historical and theological criteria often produces a muddled picture of what is happening in Mark.

Scholarship Concerning Markan Healing Miracles

Van der Loos' treatment of miracles is extensive and crosses into several disciplines, such as philology, medicine, and philosophy.[4] According to Van der Loos, miracles are largely religious phenomena that appear in many, if not all, of our world religions. With this in mind, Jesus' miracles did not take place "in a world in which his deeds were regarded as new and unprecedented."[5] This makes the study of miracles somewhat contextual but it also adds the difficulty of assessing the "miraculous" in a pre-scientific world. To the ancient, everything was charged with mysterious forces that could be regarded as "miraculous." But to the modern scientific mind, the "miraculous" can be regarded somewhat differently. This modern mindset can be tempted to reject the miraculous *a priori* because of its historical connection with religion. However, to reject a miracle in favour of science is to suggest that modern science understands the phenomena within the universe perfectly and without question.

There is, however, a certain skepticism concerning miracles that seems justified. It was Cicero who said, "nothing can happen without a cause; nothing happens that cannot happen ... what was incapable of happening never happened, and what was capable of happening is not a miracle."[6] This quote epitomizes a familiar skepticism that tells us that as much as miracles were accepted as part of everyday life in the ancient world, there were perhaps just as many skeptics then as now.

The more prominent question with regard to Jesus' healing miracles—at least for this study—is what purpose they had. Van der

---

4. Van der Loos, *Miracles*.
5. Van der Loos, *Miracles*, 6.
6. Cicero, *Div.* 2.28.

Loos creates three aspects into which we can place Jesus' miracles: the messianic aspect, the prophetic aspect, and the priestly aspect. Each of these aspects places Jesus' miracles into a Jewish tradition that links Jesus with several important figures within Judaism. Furthermore, Van der Loos treats the miracles as proofs of identity for Jesus.[7] This seems to fit within Jewish tradition since many of the prophets proved their credentials through miracles.[8] I am hesitant to take this view however, since, as Van der Loos himself points out, the ancient world was full of miracle workers.[9] Therefore, we cannot ascribe messianic status to Jesus based on miracles alone unless we also entertain the idea that several others occupied the same office as Jesus.[10]

In addition to being proofs of identity, Van der Loos suggests that the miracles serve to display mercy and arouse faith. Both of these functions seem fairly obvious since we have verbal confirmation on several occasions that Jesus' healing miracle served to either show mercy or arouse faith (1:40–41; 5:36; 10:47–48). The question then becomes what it is, exactly, that one is putting their faith into. Van der Loos suggests that the miracles function as a way of expressing the nature of the kingdom of God,[11] but, again, this begs this question as to

---

7. Van der Loos, *Miracles*, 241. This position was also held by Origen (*Cels.* 2.52), Thomas Aquinas (*Summa Theologica* 3.43.3), and John Calvin (*Commentaries* 32.2: Matt 12:16).

8. Van der Loos, *Miracles*, 241. This is also attested by John Locke, who regarded the miracles as credentials which God gave his messengers. For information on Locke's position, see Tennant, *Presuppositions*, 80.

9. For a general bibliography concerning miracle workers within Jewish literature, see Fieberg, *Jüdische*; Guttmann, "Significance," 363–406; Safrai, "Pietists," 15–33; Van der Loos, *Miracles*, 139–50; Neusner, *Life of Yoḥanan*; Vermes, *Jesus the Jew*, 58–82; Vermes, "Ḥanina ben Dosa," 178–214; Nadich, *Jewish Legends*, 194–200, 255–59; Brown, "Synoptic Miracle Stories," 55–76.

10. On this, see Cairns, *Faith that Rebels*, 70; Hunter, *Works and the Words*, 55.

11. Kallas (*Synoptic Miracles*, 77–102) argues that the healing miracles serve as "physical anticipations" for the coming kingdom of God. Therefore, the words of Jesus concentrated on the announcement of the kingdom of God, while the miracles showed what the kingdom would look like. While I agree that the words and miracles serve the same purpose, I disagree that they reveal exactly what the kingdom of God is, or looks like. If this is so, then we must also agree that any miracle that accomplished the same purpose also reveals what the kingdom looks like. While it may be true that God was working through *every* miracle in Mark, Mark devotes absolutely no space to talking about any other miracles other than those produced by

Miracles and Tragedy

what exactly this kingdom is.[12] It is true that we can make any number of value judgments with regard to the kingdom of God based on how the miracles are described in Mark—either theological or historical. But the problem with doing so is that it paints an incomplete picture and we are left wondering what the real differences are between Jesus and other healers. That is, unless we attempt to save our position with some type of theological statement that suggests Jesus as being superior to the other healers. It is much more plausible to suggest that Jesus' miracles, as well as the kingdom of God, be defined in another way.

If there were several other healers who had an ability similar to that of Jesus, then we cannot necessarily define the kingdom of God based on the occurrence or the outcome of the miracles alone.[13] We also must keep in mind that a person could be healed by observing certain commands within the Torah (1:44). This makes it much more difficult to define Jesus' miracles, as well as the kingdom of God, by the miracles themselves. I suggest here, as I did in previous chapters,

---

Jesus. It is less problematic to suggest, as I am here, that we define Jesus' miracles by the elements present within the narrative. Since Jesus is juxtaposed with the temple and its advocates, it makes sense that Jesus' miracles are in response to the current *ethos* created by the temple establishment.

12. Van der Loos (*Miracles*, 251–52) notes that it is possible to observe the "behaviour" of the revelation of God in miracles as well as the "result" of this function of the kingdom of God, though the "how" of the function as such is, and remains, an absolute secret. He goes on to suggest that the miracles serve to identify two powers: the Jesus' power as Messiah as well as his militant power against the things that cause sickness and possession. He concludes by suggesting that Jesus has come to smash the forces of disease, sin, and death, and to dethrone Satan.

13. More prominent legends concerning miracle workers appears in Philostratus of Athens's *The Life of Apollonius of Tyana* written in the third century CE, and Hierocles' *Lover of Truth*, also written in the third century. It is said that Apollonius, who lived during the first century, performed a large number of miracles and was even resurrected. As a result, several parallels have been made between the healing miracles of Apollonius and Jesus, with such scholars such as Bultmann (*Synoptic Tradition*, 218–44) and Dibelius (*Tradition to Gospel*, 70–103) going as far to suggest that the miracles found within the Gospels are Hellenistic in origin. Evans (*Jesus and His Contemporaries*, 245–50), on the other hand, suggests that the value of the parallels between Jesus and Apollonius have been exaggerated and that many of the sayings and actions of Apollonius are ostentatious. He instead promotes the idea that better parallels can be found between Jesus and the rabbinic traditions, the Old Testament, and some of the pseudepigrapha. See also Conybeare, *Philostratus*; Harris, "Apollonius of Tyana," 189–99; Bowie, "Apollonius of Tyana," 1652–99.

that Jesus' actions gain meaning when juxtaposed with the temple. This means that the miracles of Jesus are best understood when examined as actions done in contrast to those of the temple and its representatives. Doing so helps us avoid the problem of over-complication: in order to make Jesus particularly unique, we need to establish a number of theological categories in order to interpret the miracles. Doing so, as we have seen in the case of Van der Loos, conflates the reading of the text, and confuses history and theology with narrative.

Twelftree's study concerning miracles has been classified within the "Third Quest for the Historical Jesus" and appeared in 1999. In it, Twelftree aims to examine the miracles from a historical perspective, and it is an attempt to fill the gap in a perceived lack of scholarly interest in Gospel miracles.[14] With regard to the miracles in Mark, Twelftree gives them prominence because they make up approximately one-third of the Gospel material.[15] Though the amount of attention Mark gives to miracles is rather extensive, Twelftree finds their exact purpose to be "far from clear."[16] Though several explanations exist, Twelftree is confident in suggesting that the miracles are predominantly pastoral and that they serve to encourage readers in their evangelism and life together.[17] I agree that the miracle stories could have functioned this way, but there is little, if any, mention of Jesus' miracles within the rest of the New Testament. This does not mean that the Early Church disregarded Jesus' miracles, but there is a significant lack of evidence—at least within the New Testament—that the Early Church thought of the miracles the way Twelftree suggests they did.

The problem that Twelftree faces is that he is constrained by his approach to historicity. This is not to suggest that the miracles that Jesus performs in the Gospel of Mark are not actual events that occurred in history—quite the opposite. But the problem we face is that, because we do not have any pre-Gospel material that discusses them,

---

14. Twelftree, *Miracle Worker*, 13, 17.

15. Twelftree (*Miracle Worker*, 17) designates the miracle discourses as accounting for one-half of the first ten chapters of Mark, making this proportion greater than any other Gospel.

16. Twelftree, *Miracle Worker*, 17.

17. Twelftree, *Miracle Worker*, 58.

Miracles and Tragedy

any conclusions based on "historical" criteria are ultimately ones based on arguments from silence. This is as true for the most cynical interpretations of Jesus' miracles, which suggest they did not actually happen, as it is for those interpretations that suggest they did. Instead, we must approach the miracles of Jesus as they function within the narrative of the text. This may mean that we must accept a relative amount of historical obscurity regarding the miracles, but it helps us to avoid arguing from silence.

We also need to be careful not to suggest, as Twelftree does, the way in which the earliest Christians received and used the miracle stories. Again, since we have little attestation within the rest of the New Testament with regard to the miracles, it is impossible to know exactly how the earliest Christians interpreted Jesus' miracle stories. One might argue that the miracles played a role in developing Christology during the early years of the church[18] but I am hesitant to make any assessment of how the earliest Christians incorporated the miracles into Christology because we simply do not have any evidence outside of the Gospel accounts.[19]

The question then becomes what purpose the miracles stories serve in Mark. Since I am not interested in arguing for the historical

---

18. This is a position held in several places. See Dawson, *Healing, Weakness and Power*; Edwards, "Markan Sandwiches," 193–216; Van der Loos, *Miracles*; Burkill, *Mysterious Revelation*, 41.

19. As much can be said of interpreting the miracles *a priori* through a doctrinal lens, Achtemeier ("Miracles," 471–91) argues that we must be careful not to use doctrinal material to interpret the historicity of the healing event. This is because miracle stories often have theological interpretations added to them at later stages in the tradition—he names several traditions from Epidaurus and Apollonius of Tyana. He argues this even within the Gospels and suggests that the differences found in the Markan accounts from those found in either Matthew or Luke indicate later theological categories added for the sake of interpreting the story. This is not to suggest that the miracle stories are ahistorical, but the historicity of Jesus' miracles cannot be affirmed or denied based on later Christian interpretation any more than those of Apollonius of Tyana. I am taking this a step further and suggesting that the historicity of the miracle event within Mark is secondary to how the miracle story functions within the plot. As has been argued thus far, Jesus is in *Collision* with the temple, and so the miracle stories must function within this narrative scheme. To judge a miracle based on a later Christology, therefore, is problematic and wrought with shortcomings with regard to how the narrative progresses. See Achtemeier ("Miracles," 471–91) for the full argument.

circumstances surrounding early Christology here, I am inclined to suggest that the miracles in Mark function primarily as a part of the plot. This means that we must accept the miracle stories as they appear in the Gospel, and not how we want them to function outside of the Gospel—more will be said on this below.

Twelftree concludes his discussion of the miracles in Mark by linking the miracles to the question of who Jesus is.[20] This is problematic. Since Twelftree is ascribing a strict methodology of historicity to the Gospel, the miracles really serve to reveal who Jesus is because no one ever really recognizes Jesus in Mark. He is then forced to appeal to the later thinking of the earliest Christians about the miracles, which, as discussed above, is an argument from silence. If we apply Twelftree's historical methods too rigidly to Mark, we must conclude that no one ever came to understand Jesus based on the miracles. He can argue, however, that certain demons identify Jesus during the exorcism dialogues and that this identification says something about who Jesus is. But the non-exorcism miracles do not lead to the correct identification of Jesus.[21]

---

20. Twelftree, *Miracle Worker*, 93.

21. Twelftree (*Miracle Worker*, 93) does note that there is a diminution in the miraculous when Jesus' miracles were not met by faith. But what is the nature of faith in Mark's Gospel? The connection between faith and healing is apparent when Jesus attempts to conduct a number of miracles in Nazareth (6:1–6) and is unable to do so due to an apparent lack of faith on the part of those he attempts to heal. Though faith is at times not mentioned in conjunction with a healing miracle (1:34; 3:1–5), faith is most often linked to Jesus' healing acts. This leads to the conclusion that the prerequisite for healing is having some type of faith in Jesus, though it is not exactly clear what the nature of this faith is. For example, we cannot say that the nature of faith is a belief in the true person of Jesus, as Twelftree suggests, because no one truly recognizes Jesus at any point in the Gospel nor does anyone appeal to Jesus as the Son of God or as the Messiah with regard to healing. We also cannot say that healing always occurs as a result of Jesus' ability or willingness since, in the example of 6:1–6, neither of those things produces healing results. Yet, in the example of the leprous man in 1:40–41, Jesus' willingness actually does play a central part in healing. It appears that there is no constant condition that we can call "faith" in Mark's Gospel as it relates to healing miracles, therefore, making it difficult to create a theological category called "faith." Instead, it is more plausible to suggest that the healing miracles function independently of one another and that each has a purpose within the narrative. More will be said about their purpose below when I deal with each of the healing miracle stories.

Miracles and Tragedy

There are two possibilities, then, as to why little is made of Jesus' miracles in the New Testament outside of the Gospels. The first, and perhaps most cynical interpretation, is that the miracles did not actually happen historically as the Gospels record them; the miracles would then function rhetorically within the Gospels as a means to convince later readers of Jesus' authority. The second is that Jesus' miracles did occur historically as the Gospels present them, but the earliest Christians had little interest in discussing the miracles outside of the Gospels. This may be due to the fact that the earliest Christians were more interested in establishing the person of Jesus instead, but still does not explain why the Gospels devote so much space to describing the miracles.

Broadhead's analysis of the Markan miracle stories is propelled by the apparent divide between reading the Gospels as history or as literature.[22] Broadhead faces this juncture and suggests that strategies for interpretation must be shaped to highlight the narrative identity as well as the christological focus of the Gospels. He builds upon the prior work of Bultmann, Dibelius, Wrede, and Marxsen and attempts to re-evaluate the role of the miracle traditions in the New Testament.[23]

Broadhead separates the miracle stories into several sections (1:1–3:7a; 3:7—6:6; 6:6b—8:27a; 8:27—10:52; 11:1—13:37; 14:1—16:8) that each have an observable structure and specific characterization for Jesus. For example, 1:1—3:7a contains six miracle stories that are concerned with the characterization of Jesus as a powerful proclaimer who dies at the hands of his opponents.[24] Mark 3:7—6:6, on the other hand, portrays Jesus as a mighty teacher.[25] Each section also contains a number of literary motifs and roles that interact through action. So, Jesus is often portrayed as a coming (action) miracle worker (role) who heals (motif).

Broadhead concludes by suggesting that the miracle stories in Mark's Gospel function "to produce a distinct narrative portrait of

---

22. Broadhead, *Miracles and Christology*, 23.

23. Broadhead, *Miracles and Christology*, 24. Wrede, *Messiasgeheimnis*; Dibelius, *Tradition to Gospel*; Dibelius, *Gospel Criticism*; Bultmann, *Theology of the New Testament*; Marxsen, *Beginnings of Christology*.

24. Broadhead, *Miracles and Christology*, 87.

25. See Broadhead (*Miracles and Christology*, 208–10) for the full description of each of the sections and their characterizations of Jesus.

Jesus."²⁶ But this begs the question as to what particular aspect of the miracle stories paints Jesus as unique? Broadhead himself notes, and subsequently rejects, the idea that the miracle stories often place reference to Jesus' miracles in the same league as other θεῖος ἀνήρ stories.²⁷ It is also true that several other people—before, during, and after the first century—were regarded as miracle workers. This produces a lot of doubt regarding Broadhead's theory that the nature of Jesus as Messiah can be derived from the miracles alone. Instead, we need something by which we can compare and contrast Jesus as miracle worker within Mark in order to fully understand how a Christology is being portrayed. This is where Broadhead's study begins to fall apart. Since Mark does not make any comparison between Jesus and other healers—except an allusion in 1:44 to the healing that went on in conjunction with the temple—we can know very little about how unique Jesus' miracles are or what sets Jesus apart from any other healer. Therefore, we are unable to gain any real meaning for what a miracle is nor what it means that Jesus is doing the miracles. To aid this, one might be tempted to analyze certain parallels or differences between Jesus and other miracle workers in order to justify his uniqueness and power. However, again, Mark makes no reference to any other miracle worker—the disciples notwithstanding (6:13). Since Broadhead wants to analyze the narratology of Mark's Gospel, and that means reading Mark as the "primary object of investigation,"²⁸ he is constrained by the fact that his method provides no real evidence for what it means that Jesus is a "mighty proclaimer," for example.²⁹

It makes more sense, I suggest, to identify Jesus in light of his conflict with the temple. By doing so, we can clearly state what a miracle means and the impact it has on the plot. Stated another way, Jesus can be better understood as a "mighty proclaimer," or as the Son of God

---

26. Broadhead, *Miracles and Christology*, 208.

27. Kingsbury, "Mark's Christology," 243–57; Polhill, "Perspectives," 389–99; Betz, "Jesus as Divine Man," 114–33; Reitzenstein, *Hellenistic Mystery-Religions*; Gallagher, *Divine Man*; Holladay, *Theios Aner*.

28. Broadhead, *Miracles and Christology*, 24.

29. Broadhead, *Miracles and Christology*, 208.

Miracles and Tragedy

when we are able to compare him to an observable opponent instead of inferring what certain miracles could be illustrating.

This relates to what I said at the beginning of this chapter, which was that miracles in Mark's Gospel function as aspects of plot. Yet, we have seen a number of studies that attempt to argue that the miracles in Mark's Gospel are exclusively historical. As mentioned, this may be an attempt to preserve the authenticity of the claim that Jesus was a historical figure and that he performed miracles. My goal here to not to dissuade from the opinion that Jesus was a historical figure or that he performed miracles. My goal is to suggest that the miracles are elements of plot in Mark's Gospel, and that this has little bearing on the historicity of Jesus or the miracles he performed. What I have suggested instead is that historical methodology provides no real way forward for understanding Jesus' miracles in Mark.

In what follows, I will examine the healing miracles in Mark's Gospel and suggest a way that each relates to tragic plot. This means that each of the miracles attempts to offset Jesus from the temple and, according to the paradigm of *Collision*, each provides a means by which Jesus can effectively juxtapose the *ethos* of the temple.

JESUS' HEALING MIRACLES

If Jesus appears in order to represent the kingdom of God, and his position is in *Collision* with the temple, then we should expect to find some tension between Jesus' healing miracles and the temple establishment.[30]

30. While arguing for a unique genre for Mark, Kee (*Community*, 17–29) makes an attempt at demonstrating why Mark's Gospel has little in common with certain Hellenistic genres (aretalogy, tragedy, "origin myth," Hellenistic romance, comedy and martyrologies). While devoting less than a page to his critique of each genre, he concludes in favor of Mark being entirely unique, thus lacking in an adequate number of parallels with the Hellenistic genres listed just above. His treatment of miracles is then restricted to Old Testament examples—throughout which no consideration of genre for these Old Testament passages is ever made—leading the reader to surmise that Kee is actually arguing for a historical genre for Mark. His analysis also lacks any criteria by which he can assess even Old Testament parallels. He concludes by saying, "The features that Mark does share with Hellenistic rhetorical forms serve only to make the general and obvious point that Mark was influenced by the predominant Hellenistic culture of his time, but they tell us nothing about Mark's specific and distinctive aims" (29–30). This conclusion is quite misleading since he gives no treatment of the many miracle stories that do occur within Hellenistic literature.

OF CONFLICT AND CONCEALMENT

As mentioned in chapter 3, the temple is represented by the various offshoots of religious leaders that Jesus encounters throughout his ministry. These religious leaders frequently challenge Jesus with regard to his healing miracles, thus heightening the element of *Collision*. Each of the healing miracles thus has two purposes: (1) to establish Jesus' *spoudean* quality as the Son of God, and (2) to establish Jesus' position as contrary to the temple, thereby subverting its purpose and existence.[31] As mentioned in chapter 3, Jesus *must* be of *spoudean* quality in order to establish himself as a proper opponent to the temple.[32] And so, each of the healing miracles also provide a means by which Jesus is set apart

---

Furthermore, Kee never does tell the reader what the intention of the miracle stories is in Mark's Gospel. This, again, leads the reader to conclude that Kee is not arguing for a unique genre, but for a history instead.

31. According to the research conducted by Eve (*Jewish Context*, 243–71; see also for a complete discussion of miracles in the Second Temple period), there was relatively little interest in healing miracles during the Second Temple period (the exception being Sir 38:1–15 and certain sections of Philo). Instead, there appears to be considerably more interest in spectacular miracles of national deliverance that is often metaphorically communicated (see 2 Bar. 73:2). This makes the healing miracles of Jesus particularly unique amongst the Jewish literature in the Second Temple period. No other figures contemporary to Jesus are portrayed in the same way that the Gospels present Jesus (though miracles are often attributed to biblical characters such as Isaiah, Moses, Elijah, and Elisha) and miracles of healing are not prominent except in the Gospels, the closest comparison being Artapanus's Moses. There is some evidence, however, that healing as a divine prerogative can be thought of as a polemic against idols. In the Epistle of Jeremiah, it is observed that "they (idols) cannot restore sight to a blind man; they cannot rescue a man who is in distress" (6:37). This tells us that a Jewish interpretation of miracles does include healing—as a polemic against an opposing position. I argue here that this is what Mark is doing. The miracles in Mark's Gospel are thus meant to validate Jesus, thereby, subverting the authority of the temple.

32. In Krook (*Elements of Tragedy*, 36–37), it is argued that the tragic hero "represents the furthest of human possibility" (37). So, while the hero is representative of all humanity, he or she is paradoxically exceedingly unlike humanity. If Jesus were to appear in heavenly form, the narrative would not be believable because there would be no earthly establishment that could withstand a conflict with him. Neither would the concept of *Collision* work here—God must remain as the *deus ex machina* in order to make the conflict real. Instead, Jesus must appear as a human, but also as the Son of God in order for the *Collision* to take place. This makes the narrative believable, and it designates Jesus as the proper *spoudean* counterpart to the temple. It is also possible that the *spoudean* elements of Mark's Jesus have often led scholars to confuse the genre of Mark's Gospel; this may certainly be said of aretalogy, but also of certain biographies as well.

from the rest of the characters in the narrative, thereby heightening the tragic effect of the narrative.

It is important at this point to note again that the healing miracles of Jesus do not receive much attention in the New Testament outside of the Gospels. This is rather confusing considering how prominent the miracles are in the Gospels and I think it poses some problems for Historical Jesus research as mentioned above. This leads me to believe that the healing miracles—specifically the ones found in Mark's Gospel—are *not* meant to be understood primarily as historical reports but instead have a narrative function. As mentioned, this does not negate their occurrence within history, but reveals the possibility that the miracles in Mark's Gospel serve a distinct purpose. While some have suggested that this purpose is christological, I have found this explanation to be problematic since no other New Testament author uses the healing miracles to make a case for Christology. This, of course, does not negate a christological function, but a strong case for Christology cannot be made on the occurrence of healing miracles alone since many miracle workers other than Jesus are purported to have conducted healing miracles.[33] Therefore, if one is to rely on the histo-

33. There are also a number of Jewish healers that are said to have performed healing miracles both before and after the time of Jesus. Evans (*Jesus and His Contemporaries*, 213–44) notes five: Ḥoni ha-Me'aggel (first century BCE), Abba Ḥilqiah the grandson of Ḥoni (late first century BCE), Ḥanin ha-Neḥba the grandson of Ḥoni (early first century CE), Ḥanina ben Dosa (first century CE), and Eleazar the Exorcist (first century CE). In addition to these Jewish holy men, several Jewish rabbis are said to have performed miracles. Among them are Rabbi Simeon, Eliezer (late first century CE), Aqiba (late first century), Judah the Prince (early third century CE), Joshua ben Levi (early third century CE), and Rabbi Yose the Galilean (mid second century CE). With regard to each of these, Evans concludes that "what becomes clear is that Jesus' ministry of healing and exorcising blends in well against his Jewish environment" (243). While what Evans is suggesting *may* be true, it is not entirely conclusive based on the evidence that he provides. There are very few allusions to be found between the stories of Jesus and those of other Jewish healers and no criteria is provided by which we can even assess any similarities. Therefore, the best thing Evans can suggest for his case is that miracles are also included in Jewish literature. However, he cannot be ethnically biased when assessing the authenticity of miracles; for example, he cannot suggest that because miracles occurred within a Jewish context, they are more authentic and therefore are more likely to lend themselves to the authenticity of Jesus' miracles. In fact, suggesting that Jesus' miracles fit best within his Jewish environment could very well take away from the authenticity of Jesus' miracles and point toward clever redaction on the part of the Gospel

ricity of the miracles to explain Christology, they must also generate theological arguments to negate why God did not work through other miracle workers—this seems to me to be an extremely tedious venture.

This is why I suggest that the healing miracles fit better within the context of tragic *Collision*. This not only helps us to sidestep potential issues surrounding historical criteria for establishing the authenticity of healing miracles in Mark's Gospel, but it also avoids the problems of Christology—or negative Christology, in the example of Apollonius. We are then allowed to interpret Christology *as Mark portrays it* by its negative relationship to the temple and the religious authorities. This makes sense, as we will see, because Jesus conducts healing miracles in contradiction to various socioreligious rules and regulations. It also fits the general theme of tragic nonrecognition that is obvious in the Gospel: though the crowds are amazed at Jesus' miracles, even seeking him out on many occasions, the crowds never proclaim him as the Son of God or Messiah. This tells us that Mark is not using the healing miracle stories to show how the crowds are convinced of Jesus' identity. Instead, Jesus' person is revealed through consistent *Collision* and juxtaposition to the temple.

While I dealt with the themes of recognition and nonrecognition and how they are essential to tragedy in chapter 4, let it suffice to say for now that nonrecognition is essential to Mark's narrative.[34] Jesus is

---

authors. Instead, it seems more plausible to define the nature of Jesus' miracles by the elements found in Mark's Gospel: Jesus' continuous conflict with the temple and its representatives.

34. The closest parallel between a tragic figure and Jesus in this regard is Dionysus. In Euripides' *Bacchae*, Dionysus appears as a human being having been changed in shape from "God to man" (4) in order to eventually make himself known to his people in Thebes. As the son of Zeus (the son of God), Dionysus aims to reestablish proper worship of himself through the institution of various rites. He is eventually arrested, without resistance, by a guard who recognizes that he has produced a number of miracles. Pentheus, however, does not recognize Dionysus as the son of God and questions him (496–506), and when Dionysus proclaims that he is akin to God, Pentheus orders that he be arrested. Dionysus is later freed from his chains and is proclaimed as God's child who will conquer all (596–603). At a later point, a number of miracles occur surrounding Dionysus' freedom (672–774). All of this is not to suggest that Mark somehow copied the *Bacchae* while writing his Gospel, but it does tell us that, within other tragedies, miracles are conducted by a misunderstood, unrecognized son of God.

Miracles and Tragedy

juxtaposed with the temple and its representatives, and both of those positions cannot be anything but juxtaposed. This means that the religious leaders *must* continue to be unpersuaded by Jesus' healing miracles in order to heighten the tragic nature of the narrative. As a result, the healing miracles—always to be understood antagonistically to the existence of the temple—serve as a way of exemplifying Jesus' position against the temple.

In what follows, I will discuss several of Jesus' healing miracles and how they correspond to the overarching element of *Collision* in Mark's Gospel.[35] As a result, each of the healing stories can be fitted into two categories: one that serves to reinforce Jesus' *spoudean* character, or one that directly challenges the religious leaders and the temple.

The Healing of a Man with Leprosy (1:40-45)

Though this is not the first recorded healing miracle within the Gospel,[36] the healing of a man with leprosy represents the first dialogue during a healing miracle in Mark's Gospel. It also represents an introduction, of sorts, because it is the first of three healing miracle stories (1:40-45; 2:1-12; 3:1-5) that is related to an interpretation of the law. Though Jesus himself does not violate the law in this pericope, the healed man

---

35. The best way to understand Jesus' healing miracles in Mark's Gospel is in the context of *Collision* and I think there are two good reasons for this. The first reason for is that Jesus never actually works in the same ways that contemporary healers did. For example, Jesus never seeks to identify the agent responsible for the sick person's condition, instead he focuses on the sickness itself. The second reason is that Jesus never urges people to avoid potential health hazards that may have causes their sicknesses—such as, as Eve (*Jewish Context*, 352) jests, cold floors or cold breezes. Instead, he urges them to ensure that their friendships and social networks with each other and with God are in order. This tells us that the healings in Mark were meant to promote a harmonious social and religious environment contrary to the one that existed at that time. Therefore, Jesus did not heal simply for the sake of healing, but his healing miracles are meant to be seen in the context of restoring some type of order that had become disrupted. It follows logically that, since the temple was the center of religious and social operations in Judaism, Jesus was trying to subvert this order by providing another avenue of social and religious conduct.

36. We are told that Jesus heals Peter's mother (1:30-31) as well as several others around the area of Capernaum (1:34), yet we are not told about any dialogue Jesus may have had with them.

does. Thus, this story may act as a segue for introducing the religious leaders, which in turn introduces their ensuing conflict with Jesus.

The exact geographical location for this healing miracle is uncertain.[37] We are told that Jesus begins traveling throughout Galilee (1:39) and then returns to Capernaum days later (2:1). Therefore, unlike the story of Blind Bartimaeus (see below) in which geographical location is related to the interpretation of the pericope, there is little geographical information from which we can discern a context and potential meaning for this pericope.

There are, however, a number of internal features from which we can discern a probable explanation for why Mark chose to include this story. As the story goes, Jesus is moved with compassion and Jesus heals the man's leprosy.[38] He also enjoins the man to be secretive about his healing and to follow the law of Moses by presenting himself to the priest. According to Lev 14:2–32, a person who had been healed of leprosy must present himself or herself to the priest and offer a number of sacrifices to be made pure so that he or she could reenter the community.[39] It must be noted that the prescribed actions in Lev 14 are not healing actions, but are meant only for the process of purification. How a person is actually healed is not stated—the text is ambiguous. This is why Jesus tells the man that his actions will be a public testimony that he has been cleansed (1:44).

But the man does not follow Jesus' admonition, immediately leaving and telling others about what had happened. In addition to defying Jesus' orders, the man forgoes the actual command from Moses: a person who is cleansed must remain apart from the community for seven days (Lev 14:8). This separation is probably to be understood as preventative measure so that, if the disease reappears, the marginalized person would be less likely to infect others.[40] But, disregarding

---

37. Hiebert, *Portrait of the Servant*, 59; Gundry, *Apology for the Cross*, 95.

38. According to the UBS4 apparatus, some manuscripts read ὀργισθείς, while a majority read σπλαχνισθείς (ℵ, A, B, C, L, W, Δ, Θ, 0130, 0233, f^1, f^{13}, 28, 33, 157, 180, 205, 565, 579, 597, 700, 892, 1006, 1010, 1071, 1241, 1243, 1292, 1342, 1424, 1505, 2427, *Byz* [E, F, G, Σ]).

39. Lane, *Mark*, 87.

40. Slusser ("Healing Narratives," 597–99) also notes that any person considered unclean would not be allowed to enter the synagogue premises, "much less to

Miracles and Tragedy

this policy, the man goes immediately into the public sphere in order to proclaim the miracle.

There are two things to observe from this sequence of events. The first, as I have mentioned, is that the man is so overcome by the event that he disregards both the law of Moses and the command of Jesus. The second, related to the first, is that Jesus' healing miracle was apparently so effective that the man saw no need to heed the law of Moses. In addition, the crowds, who are persuaded by the man and who find Jesus in Capernaum several days later (2:1), are seemingly unaffected by the man's disobedience to the law. This could explain—though not absolutely—the introduction and appearance of the religious leaders during the next pericope (2:6); because the man had been healed and refused to follow the prescribed method of cleansing, the religious leaders were present in order to investigate the things that were happening.

This theory may not fully explain the presence of the religious leaders in the next pericope (2:6) but the proximity of the introduction of the religious leaders to the three healing miracles in 1:42, 2:1, and 3:5 is nonetheless noteworthy. While the ensuing conflicts in 2:11 and 3:5 are directly related to Jesus' violation of the law, the healing miracle in 1:42 is the opposite: Jesus heals the man and sternly warns him to observe the law with regard to his purity. The man's violation of the law may therefore provide a segue for introducing the religious leaders—who are representatives of the law—into the narrative. If this is true, then the healing miracle in 1:42 has less to do with the conflict between Jesus and the temple via the religious leaders and may simply be a means of "setting the stage," so to speak, for conflict.[41]

While this is the preferred interpretation, some have suggested that the healing miracle in 1:42 be read symbolically instead.[42] According to this argument, the leprous man is a symbol for the religious leaders and their weakened relationship with God. Jesus is thus meant to heal the religious leaders. I am not convinced by this argument,

---

participate in corporate worship" (598).

41. Lane (*Mark*, 89) suggests something similar: "It serves to terminate the preaching tour of the Galilean villages and provides the point of transition to the five accounts of controversy which follow (2:1—3:6)." Hurtado (*Mark*, 31) notes that this incident serves to create later difficulties for Jesus.

42. Slusser, "Healing Narratives," 598.

however, because a healing of the religious leaders never actually occurs in the Gospel; there is never a time when Jesus convinces the religious leaders of his message. Instead, Jesus continues antagonistically with the religious leaders until his crucifixion, at which point the curtain in the temple is torn—a more appropriate application of symbolism that represents God's absence from the temple. To reiterate, there is never a point at which Jesus' opponents are "healed," so to speak, and this thus tells us that a symbolic reading of the healing miracles, one that implicates Israel and the religious leaders, does not reflect the narrative that Mark has established. Instead, a more pragmatic reading of the healing miracles, one that places Jesus in an antagonistic position to the temple and its representatives and reflects *Collision*, is preferred.

The Healing of the Paralyzed Man (2:1–12)

The healing of the paralyzed man[43] represents the first of two conflict stories with regard to Jesus' healing miracles.[44] It appears, however, that the controversy has less to do with the actual act of healing than

---

43. A "quadrigal" reading of this passage is put forth in Blackburn Sr. ("Jesus' Healing," 43–48). Here Blackburn argues for four types of readings: literal, allegorical, tropological, and anagogical. Aside from the literal, which is self-explanatory, the allegorical, tropological, and anagogical meanings are held in high esteem by Blackburn who advocates for multiple meanings for a text, as the "triune God continues to reveal himself and his purposes to the world" (47). This, however, is an example of a study that fails to recognize the importance of plot with regard to how a story appears. Therefore, because context can be abandoned in favour of an allegorical meaning, for example, nothing is stopping an interpreter from interpreting the text in any way that suits him or her.

44. Dewey ("Literary Structure," 394–401) has noted that the controversy stories that occur in 2:1—3:6 have been often understood as a series of stories compiled by Mark or by some earlier editor, especially in Albertz, *Streitgespräche*, 5–16; Dibelius, *Tradition to Gospel*, 219; Taylor, *St. Mark*, 91–92. Dewey argues that 2:1—3:6 is a literary unit that follows a chiastic structure: A, B, C, B`, A`. This structure then adds meaning to Mark's stories, making Mark a writer of "considerable literary skill" (401). Dewey's point is well taken, and I agree with her to the extent that Mark's narrative is cohesive and points towards the crucifixion at several points. However, pointing out the structures of Mark's narrative, as intriguing as it is, does not point towards an overall purpose of Mark's Gospel. Instead, the controversies, especially those surrounding the healing story in Mark 2, are better understood as occurrences in the greater context of tragic *Collision*. It is clear that Jesus is challenging both the religious leaders' interpretations of Scripture and the reason behind their interpretations, which is the temple establishment. See also, Lightfoot, *Message of Mark*, 31–47.

it does with Jesus' words regarding the healing: "my son, your sins are forgiven" (v. 5).[45] This healing miracle therefore becomes the means through which a dialogue about the improper source of forgiveness can take place. This dialogue is yet another example of how Jesus is in *Collision* with the temple and how it is played out through his debate with the religious leaders. The reason why the religious leaders take exception to Jesus' words is because it was their belief that only God can forgive sins (v. 7).[46]

According to certain Jewish traditions, this is correct. In Exod 34:5–7, we are told that God himself descended in a cloud and spoke to Moses saying that he *alone* forgives iniquity, rebellion, and sin (v. 7). In Ps 103:3, we are told that God forgives all sins and heals all diseases. Again, in Ps 131:4, we are told that God offers forgiveness in favor of respect. God speaks more explicitly in Isa 43:25 where he says that "I alone" forgive transgressions, a point that he later repeats when he tells Israel that he has swept their sins away like a cloud (Isa 44:22).

It is important to note that the response given by the religious leaders who were present was a *correct* one regardless of whether or not they recognized Jesus as the Son of God.[47] This is essential if we are to

---

45. There is a close connection between sin and sickness in Jewish tradition. For his lying and greed, Elisha's servant is afflicted with leprosy (2 Kgs 5). Other passages equate sickness, or a threat of sickness, with sin (Num 12; 16:41–50; Deut 28:15, 22, 27–28, 35, 59–61; 2 Sam 12:15). There are also a number of allusions to sickness being the cause for sin in the New Testament (1 Cor 11:29–30; Acts 5:1–11; 12:21–23). God is seen as the ultimate healer (Gen 20:17; Exod 15:26; 2 Kgs 20:5; Ps 6:2; 30:2; 103:3; Isa 19:22, 30:26). Turning to the help of physicians instead of to God signaled a lack of trust in God (2 Chr 16:12). Sickness and healing are thus ascribed to God, as explicitly stated in Deut 32:39: "I am the one who kills and gives life; I am the one who wounds and heals." Angels are also at times responsible for sickness (2 Sam 24:16; 1 Chr 21:1), as well as Satan (Job 1:6–12; 2:1–6; 2 Cor 12:7–8). See Lohse, *Mark's Witness*, 58.

46. See Hunter, *Saint Mark*, 38.

47. There is some debate with regard to this issue. As Daniel Johansson ("Jesus and God," 43) states in his recent doctoral dissertation: "In their view, Jesus commits the worst sin possible against God—blasphemy—by infringing on the divine prerogative to forgive sins" (43). He separates himself from Otfried Hofius ("Jesu Zuspruch," 38–56), who argues that, on several occasions within Second Temple literature, human agents are able to forgive sins. Hofius points to five Hebrew and Aramaic texts which could suggest human agency with regard to forgiveness. Johansson dismisses these examples on the basis of the ambiguity, with regard to verbal mood,

regard Mark as a tragedy: a tragic narrative dictates that each position in *Collision* be a justified one. This means that the tragic nature of Mark rests in the tension that exists between two essentially good things. Following God's law and respecting his words is a *good thing*—precisely the thing that the religious leaders were seeking to do. However, from the perspective of the reader who knows that Jesus is the Son of God, we perceive tension between these two highly valued things.

This means that the theme of nonrecognition (see chapter 4) becomes essential to the Gospel's narrative flow and purpose. In order for the narrative to make sense and to be tragic, the religious leaders—as representatives of the temple—*must* take offence to Jesus. If we reverse the scenario to one in which the religious leaders are convinced of Jesus' message, then we have lost the plot—tragic or otherwise. Instead, the tragedy of Mark's narrative is that Jesus, as well as the religious leaders, must act in accordance to their positions in the *Collision*, which culminates in the destruction of both positions.

Thus, the healing stories that we will continue to examine will exemplify this very thing, namely, that Jesus continues to be unrecognized by the religious leaders despite his healing miracles. In addition to this, the healing miracles exemplify a position that is contrary to the temple—as evidenced in 1:44—and Jesus' performance of miracles are to be understood as a polemic against the temple's position in the *Collision*.

The Healing of a Man with a Deformed Hand (3:1–6)

Similar to previous healing miracles, Jesus' healing of a man with a deformed hand attracts negative attention from the religious leaders making it the second of two healing miracles that are characterized by conflict. The reason for conflict is that Jesus is conducting a healing miracle on the Sabbath, which is a violation of the law (3:2). Like the healing of the paralyzed man, Jesus is breaching an interpretation of the law that prohibits certain actions. This miracle also shares a common theme with the previous pericope concerning harvesting grain

---

that leaves translation open to interpretation (43). I tend to agree with Johansson here, and suggest that what is explicitly stated in the text supersedes what may be read into the text from other contemporary sources.

Miracles and Tragedy

on the Sabbath (2:23–27), which is also concerned with violating the law, and should thus be read in context of all the conflicts that occur in 2:1—3:6, each of which are characterized by some form of lawlessness on the part of Jesus.[48]

Jesus enters a synagogue on the Sabbath and encounters a man with a deformed hand. We are then told that Jesus is being watched closely by the religious leaders so that they could accuse him of violating the law (3:2). Taking note of his accusers, Jesus invites the man to stand in front of everyone while he questions them concerning the Sabbath. They remain silent, however, presumably because they want to continue to watch and see what Jesus will do.[49]

Just how Jesus violates the Sabbath here is unclear. Hendriksen argues that the violation occurs when Jesus heals a man whose life was not in danger.[50] Taylor thinks that the religious leaders had some rabbinic practice in mind which stated that a person could only receive medical attention if their life was in danger.[51] This is not plausible, however, since the Talmudic references he gives postdate the composition of Mark's Gospel. Vermes argues that healing by word alone would not constitute a Sabbath violation. Further, in that Jesus simply asks the man to extend his hand, Jesus here heals neither by word nor by action.[52] Hurtado notes that many activities were forbidden on

---

48. Guelich, *Mark*, 133; Moloney, *Gospel of Mark*, 60.

49. In the 1986 edition of his commentary on Mark, Mann (*Mark*, 242) argues that the silence of the religious leaders here is a result of their being confounded. Moloney (*Gospel of Mark*, 70–71) follows Guelich (*Mark*, 133–39) and suggests that Jesus places the religious leaders into an impossible situation. However, an examination of the other Synoptics' renditions may shed more light on what is happening here. Matthew's rendition of the pericope does not include silence at all, and instead portrays the religious leaders as asking Jesus the questions (Matt 12:9–14). Luke's rendition is more closely related to Mark's though he does not specifically mention silence (Luke 6:6–11). Based on these parallel accounts, I contend that the silence in Mark's rendition is not a result of their being confounded, otherwise, if it was prominent, we would find mention of it in either Matthew or Luke. Their silence is rather a continuation of their motive to trap Jesus in his action since this pericope is concerned with working on the Sabbath, not with talking.

50. Hendriksen, *According to Mark*, 114.

51. The tradition that Taylor (*St. Mark*, 221) had in mind can be found in *m. Šabb.* 18 and *m. Yoma* 8:6.

52. Vermes, *Jesus the Jew*; Beavis, *Mark*, 64.

the Sabbath, especially at Qumran, and interprets Jesus' questions as challenging whether the Sabbath was actually important enough to stop performing his ministry.[53]

Despite the various scholarly opinions regarding how Jesus violated the Sabbath law, the exact reason remains unclear. However, if we consider what transpires in light of Exod 31:12–17, the motion to kill (ἀπολέσωσιν) Jesus in 3:6 makes more sense. God tells Moses that anyone who desecrates the Sabbath will be put to death, and anyone who works on that day will be cut off from the community (Exod 31:14; 35:2; Num 15:32–36). Therefore, whatever the reason of the religious leaders, it was justified in the Pentateuch.

The plot to murder Jesus (3:6) is important to our concept of tragic *Collision*. If we recall the definition of *Collision* from chapter 3, it requires that two highly valued positions be pitted against one another. A *spoudean* hero rises up against some type of formidable opponent only to be destroyed. But in doing so, the opponent is also rendered obsolete in order to maintain a level of harmony. I have previously argued that Jesus rises up as the *spoudean* hero of the Markan tragedy in order to challenge the temple establishment. The religious leaders are therefore its representatives and are often found to be in direct confrontation with Jesus. However, Jesus' real opponent is the temple since it is the temple that is specifically portrayed at Jesus' crucifixion as becoming obsolete.

The plot to kill Jesus because of his violations of the law fits well within this concept of *Collision*. Not only must the temple's representatives destroy Jesus, Jesus must make efforts to render the temple obsolete. By violating Sabbath laws and reducing the level of dependence upon the temple as the center of religious worship and well-being, Jesus challenges the temple as God's dwelling place on earth, suggesting that everyone can approach God without restriction at all times.

The Healing of the Bleeding Woman (5:24–34)

While on his way to heal Jairus's daughter, Jesus presses through a large crowd that has gathered around him (5:24). At one point, a woman

---

53. Hurtado, *Mark*, 51.

approaches Jesus who has suffered from some type of bleeding for twelve years[54] and who has been unable to be healed by any doctor (vv. 25–26). As she approaches Jesus from behind, she reaches out to touch him with the belief that she will be healed. She touches his robe (v. 28) and is immediately healed of her bleeding (v. 29).[55]

According to the purity laws found in Lev 15, a woman who was subject to bleeding for an irregular amount of time was considered to be impure.[56] In addition, everything that the woman touched also became impure, along with anyone else who happened to touch the same things she had (15:26–27). After the bleeding stops, the woman remains impure for seven days, after which she must offer two turtledoves or two young pigeons to the priest at the entrance of the tabernacle (15:29), who then offers one as a sin offering and the other as a burnt offering (15:30). The priest would then purify the woman before God for the ceremonial impurity caused by her bleeding (15:30).

Based on Mark's description of both the woman and her situation, her bleeding would have caused her great physical distress and excluded her from certain Jewish ceremonies. In addition to these things, her social situation would have become worse due to the stigma of sin that surrounded prolonged sickness. As a result, she would have been socially and religiously alienated.[57] Knowing these things provides a clearer picture of how grave the situation was for this woman, as well as the great purity risk she constituted in large crowds.

Jesus' miraculous healing of this woman further illustrates the ways in which Jesus seeks to render the temple obsolete. In this example, we have a woman who is marginalized due to her ceremonial uncleanliness, who Jesus reestablishes physically, socially, and religiously. In doing so, Jesus illustrates that God is accessible to everyone without the need for ceremony and laws concerning uncleanliness.[58] Again,

---

54. Guelich (*Mark*, 296) also notes the unspecified nature of the bleeding.

55. Moloney (*Gospel of Mark*, 109), Gaiser ("In Touch," 5–15), and Beavis (*Mark*, 95) all discuss the concept of touching Jesus in order to be healed.

56. See Selvidge, "Purity Regulations," 619–23.

57. Lane, *Mark*, 191–92; Hurtado, *Mark*, 88.

58. Hurtado (*Mark*, 88) hints at this when he asks "And though Jewish ritual requirements forbade her to touch any holy thing, she is delivered precisely by touching Jesus, the Son of God! Could this be intended by Mark as a dramatization

this should be interpreted in light of Jesus' continual conflict with the temple, which is characterized by the concept of tragic *Collision*.

The Resurrection of a Dead Child (5:21–43)

The resurrection of Jairus's daughter shares two characteristics with the previous miracle stories in Mark's Gospel. The first characteristic is that Jesus ignores a number of issues related to purity as he does when he heals the hemorrhaging woman (5:24–34). The second characteristic is that Jesus commands secrecy much in the same way that he does after healing the leprous man (1:40–45). However, Jesus begins to do something rather different after he resurrects the young girl—Jesus begins to withdraw from the crowds after he conducts a healing miracle. Withdrawal occurs at other points within the Markan narrative, but this is the first time it occurs in conjunction with a healing miracle. Withdrawal also becomes a theme in the following two miracle stories (7:33, 8:23), leading us to question why it has become a prominent feature in these stories. In addition to the theme of withdrawal, Jesus' demand for silence can also be found in the following two stories (7:36; 8:26) leading us again to question its prominence. Thus we could group these three healing stories together based on similar themes of withdrawal and secrecy: the resurrection of Jairus's daughter (5:21–43), the healing of the deaf man (7:31–37), and the healing of the blind man (8:22–26). However, I will deal with each independently.

The raising of the dead child is the first miracle in this group of three. After proclaiming that the child is not dead but asleep (5:39), Jesus withdraws from the crowd, taking with him only the child's parents, in addition to Peter, James, and John.[59] Jesus speaks to the child in Aramaic and the child is resurrected, after which she stands up and

---

of the emphasis that Jesus' ministry involved a transcending of the ritual definitions of clean and holy?"

59. Beavis (*Mark*, 97) notes that it is possible that the child was simply in a coma and not dead, hence Jesus' words "the child is not dead, but asleep" (5:39). Thus, this miracle would be a resuscitation and not a resurrection. However, both Matthew and Luke interpret the story as a resurrection account (Matt 9:18; Luke 8:49–50). In addition, Beavis notes that there are a number of parallels between this miracle and Elijah's raising of the widow's son (1 Kgs 17:17–24) and Elisha's restoration of the Shunammite woman's son (2 Kgs 4:18–37).

moves around the room (5:42).⁶⁰ Jesus then commands that they keep what just happened a secret and orders that the child be fed (5:43).

There are three things to note about this particular healing miracle story. The first is the state of uncleanliness that would have occurred as a result of touching a dead child. According to Num 19:11–13, anyone who touches a dead body is considered ceremonially unclean and must be removed from society for seven days. For those who touch a dead body and do not follow the proper procedures for purification, that person will be cut off from the community completely. Once again, Jesus defies the laws of ceremony that characterize the function of the temple, thus rendering them obsolete.

The second thing to note is that Jesus' withdrawal occurs twice (5:37, 40). The first occurs when Jesus separates from the crowd, taking only Peter, James, and John (v. 37). The second occurs after Jesus and his three disciples had entered the home of the synagogue leader (v. 40). Presumably the synagogue leader could be considered one of the religious leaders that Jesus is in constant contention with. This might explain why those present at his house had such a negative reaction to Jesus' comment concerning the girl's state (vv. 39–40). It is more likely that their reaction is due to Jesus' seemingly outrageous comment that the child was not dead but sleeping. Regardless, it is at this point that Jesus "drives out" (ἐκβαλών) everyone from the room except for the child's parents and his three disciples.⁶¹ We cannot be entirely sure why Jesus asks everyone to leave, but it is possible that this exclusion is

---

60. The interpretation given here by Hooker (*St. Mark*, 151) is, again, not helpful: "The miracle of resurrection can only be understood by those who believe in the one who has himself been raised from the dead." Since the concept of resurrection was commonplace both in the Jewish and Greco-Roman worlds, it is implausible to suggest that this miracle can only be understood by a future believer. This is an argument from silence and does not help to explain why secrecy is being employed here. For an excellent summary of resurrection in both Greco-Roman and Jewish literature, see Porter, "Jesus and Resurrection."

61. It is possible to see Mark's use of this lexeme as an allusion to the various exorcisms that Jesus conducts (1:39). However, I do not think the appearance of this particular verb alludes to any exorcism any more than it does to the Spirit's driving Jesus into the wilderness (1:12). This particular verb may denote an expression of forcefulness, but no metaphorical meaning should be derived from its appearance in this healing miracle story.

related to his commands for silence (5:43). If this is true, then we can assume that Jesus is avoiding self-designation.

The third thing to note is that Jesus commands the event be kept secret (5:43). The command for secrecy here, however, appears to be an impossibility: how could one keep the resurrection of a dead child a secret when everyone knew she was already dead? But what, then, is the purpose of such a command? Historically speaking, it is possible that Jesus wanted to avoid further negative attention from the religious leaders and therefore commanded that no one share the details of what had happened. This is, however, an argument from silence. It may be more helpful to interpret Jesus' command for secrecy not simply in terms of its historical occurrence, but instead in terms of how it functions within the narrative. It appears that the demand for secrecy here works in much the same way that the Son of Man title operates: the theme of secrecy represents a means by which Jesus can avoid attention and self-designation (see chapter 4).[62]

The Healing of a Deaf Man (7:31–37)

The healing of the deaf man, unique to Mark, could be considered the second healing miracle in this series of three healing miracles that include both withdrawal and secrecy. Until this point in the narrative, Jesus has healed a variety of diseases, but this particular instance is the

---

62. The motif of secrecy is most often found in relation to the exorcisms, though it does appear in conjunction with four further miracles. These are: the healing of the leper (1:44), the raising of a dead child (5:43), the healing of a deaf man (7:36), and the healing of the blind man (8:26). Hooker (*St. Mark*, 184–85) has noted that the miracles linked with secrecy may symbolize Christian faith—sight, hearing, resurrection—which become realities after the resurrection of Jesus. Hooker also suggests that, though they cannot be spoken of with understanding at the time of their occurrence, they point forward to events and spiritual changes which still lie in the future. This interpretation points more towards a narrative function for the miracles, though it still does not fully explain why Jesus demands secrecy for something that obviously cannot remain secret—the resurrection of the dead child, for example. Hooker explains this by suggesting that "it is only those who believe in the risen Lord who can understand the full significance of what was taking place in Jesus' ministry" (185). I think this is an unconvincing argument, since, because it is one from silence, she cannot prove this argument to be true. Much like Jesus' use of the Son of Man title, the secrecy here functions as a means to avoid self-designation, which would violate the element of *Collision* (see chapter 3).

Miracles and Tragedy

first time Jesus encounters deafness. Hurtado notes that Mark uses a specific word to denote the man's "speech impediment" (μογιλάλον) which is also found in the Greek translation of Isa 35:5–6. This passage talks about deaf people miraculously being able to hear again, which Hurtado notes as the source to which Mark is alluding.[63] Hooker notes that this healing occurs after Jesus has urged the crowds to listen carefully to his teachings (7:14–16) and following an occasion on which Jesus appears frustrated by the disciples for their lack of understanding (7:17–18).[64] Jesus is located in a gentile region, which could continue the theme of his disregard for ritual purity since it is placed after a debate concerning purity in 7:1–20.[65] In addition, like the resurrection of the dead girl, this healing miracle story also includes a command of secrecy as well as a withdrawal from the crowd.

We are told that the crowds begged Jesus to heal the man and, once he agreed, Jesus led the man away from the crowds to perform the miracle (7:33). Guelich notes that this could be related to the "messianic secret."[66] Withdrawal in this passage is thus linked to a command for secrecy (7:36), both of which are related—as they were in the previous miracle (see above)—to an avoidance of self-designation. Thus, Jesus' disregard for purity laws in combination with secrecy and withdrawal prove that, yet again, Jesus is working to render the temple obsolete.

The Healing of a Blind Man (8:22–26)

Arriving in Bethsaida, Jesus is approached by a group of people who want him to heal their blind friend. At once, Jesus leads the man out of the village, where he proceeds to heal him. Again, we note here that Jesus withdraws from those around him before he conducts the miracle.[67] He also commands that the man not return to the village on his way home from the healing. This means that this particular healing miracle

---

63. Hurtado, *Mark*, 117.
64. Hooker, *St. Mark*, 184.
65. Hurtado, *Mark*, 117.
66. Guelich, *Mark*, 394.
67. Cole (*St. Mark*, 132) takes this to mean that the man, so bewildered by the crowds, was unable to somehow focus on Jesus and thus needed to be taken to a place of quiet. This is an argument from silence and is unable to be proven.

is the third of three miracles in series that contain withdrawal and a command for secrecy.

This healing miracle also takes place in two parts. Jesus spat on the man's eyes and laid his hands on him, a method that only partly restores the man's eyesight. Jesus places his hands on the man's eyes a second time and he is able to see completely. This is not suggesting that Jesus is somehow unable to heal him completely the first time but may instead point to three different possible interpretations.

The first interpretation links this healing miracle with the two feeding miracles that occur in close proximity to it (5:30–44; 8:14–21). The partial healing of the blind man would then represent the disciples' *lack of* understanding after the feeding of the five thousand and the fully healed man represents the disciples' understanding after the feeding of the four thousand. I am skeptical of this interpretation, however, since we are not told that the disciples do fully understand after the second feeding miracle. Indeed, the continued ignorance of the disciples becomes especially prominent in the next pericope concerning Peter's recognition (8:27–33). And so, it is difficult to say with certainty that the dual attempt to heal the man is figurative for the disciples' faith or understanding.

The second interpretation is closely linked to the first, and that is, the partial healing of the blind man represents Peter who is unable to fully grasp the concept of the suffering messiah (8:27–33). Not much needs to be said here, however, because the reason why this interpretation is non-convincing is because there is no natural point in the narrative at which Peter *does* understand fully. Instead, Peter betrays Jesus and disappears from the narrative completely. It is even non-convincing to argue that Peter's correct designation of Jesus as messiah in 8:29 is analogous to the blind man's full sight—Peter clearly does not fully understand.[68] To argue that Peter obviously did understand due to

---

68. This position is held by Moloney (*Gospel of Mark*, 164), Hurtado (*Mark*, 134), and Beavis (*Mark*, 132). Guelich (*Mark*, 436), who writes before both Moloney and Beavis, notes that the disciples are never fully "healed" of their misunderstanding within the narrative. Gundry (*Apology for the Cross*, 418) does not mention any of the interpretations listed above. Taylor (*St. Mark*, 371) notes a parallel between this healing miracle and a Hellenistic story about Alcetas of Halice. In this story about Alcetas, the god Asclepios appears to heal the man's sight with the result that the first

Miracles and Tragedy

his massive involvement in the Early Church is to argue from silence instead of from what is said in the text.

The third interpretation, and what I argue here, links Jesus' two-step healing with the covenants made by God with Israel. The first covenant, linked to the giving of the law, has failed. As a result, Jesus is confronting the apparent corruption that such a failure has produced, socially, politically, and religiously. Jesus thus represents the coming of a second covenant, an analogy found in the healed man. This interpretation also fits well within *Collision*. Jesus is making a statement about how the previous paradigm—now represented by the temple and the religious leaders—has only partially revealed who God is to the world. In doing so, he alludes to the obsolete nature of the temple.

The Healing of Blind Bartimaeus (10:46–52)

In 10:46–52, we are told of Jesus' encounter with a blind man named Bartimaeus. While Jesus and his disciples are attempting to leave Jericho, Bartimaeus begins to yell at Jesus, addressing him as the "Son of David" (vv. 47–48) and begs for Jesus to have mercy upon him in the form of healing (v. 51). At once Jesus heals Bartimaeus, and he begins to follow Jesus down the road (v. 52).

We can draw a number of obvious inferences from this story.[69] It is probably not a coincidence that we find a man calling Jesus the "Son of David" just before he enters Jerusalem (11:11).[70] This not only grants Jesus a kingly designation but also equates him with a certain messianic expectation that he discusses further in 12:35.[71] The motif of

---

things he saw "were the trees in the Temple precincts" (371).

69. Marshall ("Jesus as Messiah," 127) suggests that the call for healing has little to do with the fact that Jesus has earned for himself a reputation as a healer and that the title "Son of David" cannot be readily explained by this reputation. Marshall then suggests that Jesus may have earned the title "Son of David" as a result of varied demonic cries that express the authority of Jesus using different idioms. Another possibility is that the title "Son of David" as a healer arose from a tradition that portrays Solomon as a miracle worker. This is also attested by Evans ("Messiah," 241), who points out that Jewish exorcists evoked the name of Solomon in their practices much in the same way that the name of Jesus was being used (9:38).

70. Menken, "Call," 273–90.

71. Jesus' discussion is centered around Ps 110:1, which then becomes a rebuke of the religious leaders (12:38–40). The question of whether the title "Son of David"

kingship is further heightened in the following pericope, in which Jesus commands that his disciples go ahead into Jerusalem and find a donkey for him to ride into the city (11:2). Mark's use of the historic present is overshadowed by his use of the perfect tense to denote the prominence of choosing the donkey. The reason for this may be found in Jesus' paradoxical exhortation that true leadership takes the form of servanthood (10:43), thus making Jesus' kingly assent on a lowly donkey as the Son of David more forceful to the reader. Thus, the healing of Bartimaeus is sandwiched between two important pericopes that denote humility and these periscopes are juxtaposed with certain rulers (10:42).

The healing of Bartimaeus thus plays an important part in illustrating how Jesus continues to assault the temple establishment. The kingdom of God is characterized by humility (10:44), which is the opposite of what characterize the leaders that Jesus refers to (10:42). True kingship—as denoted by the true Son of David—is a kingship that does not cheat the disenfranchised while claiming power for itself (12:40). Therefore, this particular healing story—and the pericopes that surround it—illustrate the ways in which the kingdom of God exemplifies that which the temple and, subsequently, the religious leaders have not exemplified.

---

is intrinsically linked to a healing tradition is debated. According to Robbins ("Blind Bartimaeus," 224–43), first-century Jewish tradition concerning the Son of David did not include healing. As a result, Robbins concludes that the blind Bartimaeus tradition is redacted by Mark in order to create a "link between the authoritative healing activity of Jesus in 1–10 and the Davidic traditions concerning Jesus in Jerusalem" (242). He goes on to conclude that the healing ministries of Jesus in Mark's Gospel mediate Markan Christology, within which Jesus was declared to be the Son of God. Thus, the healing ministries are linked to Jesus' activities in Jerusalem, which include his suffering and death. While I have no reason to disagree with Robbins on this point, I think that his argument could be strengthened by noting the conflict between Jesus and the temple with regard to the use of the title, Son of David. Certainly the christological titles that Mark employs with regard to Jesus are important for establishing his character, but I think they gain *more* importance if we consider them as rhetoric meant to reduce the importance of the temple, thus pointing towards Jesus as that which the temple is incapable of providing. Thus, the title "Son of David" (in addition to "Son of Man") serve as a rhetorical strategy meant to challenge the temple establishment. They also grant Jesus a level of authority—which Robbins argues for—that places him in a position juxtaposed with the temple.

CONCLUSIONS

This chapter has been an overview of each of the healing miracles in Mark's Gospel. What has been shown is that each of the healing miracles fits within the paradigm of *Collision*. In each healing miracle, Jesus illustrates his disregard for several purity laws that are linked to the operations of the temple. In addition, Jesus promotes the idea that God is not accessed through the conventional means of sacrifice that were related to the temple's function. Jesus, as the *spoudean* counterpart to the temple, thus renders the temple obsolete through each of the healing miracles.

6

The Tragic Son of Man

INTRODUCTION

THIS CHAPTER WILL DISCUSS various opinions concerning the title Son of Man as it appears in Mark's Gospel.[1] I will begin by reviewing some of the more prominent studies with regard to the title, offering my critiques throughout. In the section that follows, I will examine

---

1. In addition to the Gospels, the phrase Son of Man appears in a number of other ancient Jewish texts and is used by a number of authors. These include: Pss 8; 80; 1 En. 14; Dan 7; Ezekiel the Tragedian; Dead Sea Scrolls; Similitudes of Enoch; 4 Ezra; Odes of Solomon. These examples contain a variety of usages and meanings for the phrase that span over several centuries. This prompted such thinkers as Paul Ricoeur (*Book of Daniel*, xxii–xxiii), commenting on the text in Dan 7, to suggest that we must leave a bit of play to allow for several concurrent identifications. For example, Dan 7:13 contains a depiction of "one like a Son of Man" who is granted a level of authority, whereas *The Exodus* by Ezekiel the Tragedian depicts God as a human. The appearance of the title in the DSS (4QPseudo-Ezekiel—4Q383–386) depicts the Son of Man as a prophet who is addressed by God, while in other places the title is used to address humanity in general (1QS 11, 20; 1QapGen 13, 21; 11Qtg-Job 9, 26). The Similitudes of Enoch depicts the Son of Man as an earthly being with certain attributes of God, who is considered to be messiah (48:10), the revealer of God (48:6–7), and the righteous one (38:2). 4 Ezra depicts the Son of Man in a way similar to Daniel, while the Odes depicts the Son of Man in a semi-erotic fashion. Psalm 8 depicts the Son of Man as a human being, while Ps 80 could be depicting the Son of Man as a community or as the king of Israel. These examples provide a glimpse at how diversely the title was being used in and around the first century when Mark's Gospel was written. Their diverse applications and meanings make it difficult to determine how it is being used in Mark's Gospel.

The Tragic Son of Man

each of the Son of Man sayings under the paradigm of tragic *Collision* that was established in chapter 3.

RESEARCH CONCERNING THE SON OF MAN SAYINGS

Throughout the Gospel of Mark, Jesus refers to himself as the Son of Man thirteen times (2:10, 28; 8:31, 38; 9:9, 12, 31; 10:33, 45; 13:26; 14:21, 41, 62) but not all of these usages appear in the same manner. This has given rise to a large number of theories that attempt to explain why and how the sayings differ from one another, as well as their overall function within the Markan narrative. This is an extremely difficult problem for Gospel studies, primarily because there is no explanation given—outside of the Son of Man sayings themselves—for why Jesus is using the title in Mark. Even stranger is the fact that no one refers to Jesus as the Son of Man, and so, for some reason, Mark has either reserved or preserved the title only on the lips of Jesus. The major problem—as it appears to me—is the potential allusion to Dan 7:13. This has great implications for eschatology and for Christology because, by identifying with the Son of Man of Dan 7, Jesus adds significant meaning to his messianic status as a future vindicator. However, due to the ambiguous nature of the title, in that it is always used in the third person, one cannot be absolutely sure why Jesus does not simply use a first-person pronoun instead. Another problem is why Jesus *needs* to use the title to establish his character, especially since he is already established as the Messiah and as the Son of God. As we will see, this has led a number of scholars to conclude that an apocalyptic, messianic type character named the "Son of Man" was prominent in Jewish thought in and around the first century. Others have completely rejected the idea that such a character existed in Jewish thought, asserting that there is little or no evidence for it. Still others have suggested that the Son of Man title represents an idiomatic phrase that simply refers to a human being. This option is certainly well attested in the primary literature but is plagued by the fact that the Gospels present Jesus as *the* Son of Man, reducing the generic nature of the idiom. It is then possible that the non-generic, messianic nature of the Son of Man title was placed on the lips of Jesus by the church *ex eventu*, meaning that, while Jesus may have used the title to refer to himself, he did so idiomatically and without any eschatological or messianic coloring.

One of the most prominent scholars in the twentieth century to address the Son of Man problem was Bultmann. Bultmann separated the Son of Man sayings into three categories: (1) the Son of Man as coming; (2) the Son of Man as suffering death and rising again; and (3) the Son of Man as now at work.[2] Of the three categories, Bultmann thought only those sayings within the first were actually spoken by Jesus and that the sayings that make up the other two categories arose within a faith-based community sometime after the resurrection. Conzelmann, taking Bultmann's theory one step further, suggested that none of the Son of Man sayings in the Gospels were original to Jesus, making them all *ex eventu*.[3]

Taylor takes a different position concerning the title in Mark and suggests that, though the title was not messianic before Jesus began to use it, this does not mean that Jesus could not have used the title to refer to himself as the Messiah.[4] The gnomic nature of the title would have been precisely why Jesus chose it to refer to himself in a messianic sense. This makes room for the idea that the term took on messianic coloring during the earliest years of the church precisely because Jesus used it in this way. Taylor comes close to suggesting that the title, especially in Mark 2:10, is used in conflict with the religious leaders to subtly challenge their authority. As a result, Taylor calls Jesus the *mesias absconditus* (the absconded messiah), which means that Jesus uses the term in a way so as to avoid being arrested and tried too early.[5] As the narrative progresses, the meaning of the title begins to become more obvious, sometime around the events at Caesarea Philippi, and Jesus begins to employ it in terms of his messianic suffering. This means that the term begins to take on new meaning as Jesus applies the title more

---

2. Bultmann (*Theology of the New Testament*, 30) understood those sayings from category 3 to be a translation from an Aramaic idiom: "a man" or "I." The second category is primarily *vaticana ex eventu*, while the first category is an older tradition that predates the church.

3. Conzelmann, *Theology of the New Testament*, 135–36. See also Perrin, *Pilgrimage*, 57; Tödt, *Son of Man*.

4. Taylor, *St. Mark*, 200.

5. Taylor, *St. Mark*, 200.

often and in different circumstances. This makes sense in light of there being purpose and function for the Son of Man sayings in Mark's Gospel and it certainly answers the question as to why Jesus refused to use a personal pronoun instead. However, I am not certain that Jesus' use of the title makes him an absconder per se. It appears that his use of the title did not fool anyone with regard to his claims, especially when we consider that the Pharisees were plotting to kill Jesus as early as 3:6 on account of his miracles. In fact, claims about his messianic status do not come into question until Jesus appears before the high priest in 14:61. This means that the Son of Man title must have a different function other than the one Taylor suggests here—as intriguing as his ideas may be.

Vermes responded to the skepticism of Bultmann and Conzelmann by calling it "subjective" and pointed out that, for both of these scholars, an assumption is made concerning the existence of a Son of Man "concept" as well as a corresponding "title."[6] The task for Vermes was then to distinguish the Son of Man sayings that appear to be a generic reference to humanity from those which refer to the eschatological figure of Dan 7:13. Vermes's research yielded extremely interesting results that showed that, of the 66 Son of Man passages found in the Synoptic Gospels, 37 (56 percent) appear to have no link with the Old Testament; 6 (9 percent) of these passages cite Dan 7:13 explicitly; while 21 (32 percent) allude to it indirectly.[7] When we apply these results to the Gospel of Mark alone, 10 (77 percent) Son of Man sayings have no noticeable apocalyptic reference, and only two (15 percent) expressly quote Daniel. The joint Matthew and Luke Son of Man sayings, on the other hand, are roughly split down the middle. The result is that Mark's Son of Man sayings are mainly non-Danielic, while those sayings found in Matthew and Luke are more likely to reference Daniel, either directly or indirectly. What is more, there are times when Matthew or Luke add a Son of Man saying to a tradition where Mark does not. For example, Peter's confession in Matt 16:13 contains Jesus providing a self-reference as the Son of Man, whereas Mark's Jesus uses only a personal pronoun (8:27). This tells us that, at least for Matthew and Mark,

---

6. Vermes, *Jesus the Jew*, 177.
7. Vermes, *Jesus the Jew*, 178. See also the title found on 179.

the Son of Man sayings may function quite differently within the narrative. It could be, if one accepts Mark as the oldest Gospel, that Matthew had time to redact the Markan narrative, applying the title directly to Jesus himself—as in the case of Matt 16:13. It is also possible—though not necessarily exclusively so—that the differences found in Mark and Matthew simply reflect different treatments of the title, perhaps revealing different purposes for the title within their respective narratives. We will return to this idea when we discuss the individual passages themselves.

For Perrin, the function of the title in Mark was to teach early Christians about the true nature of Jesus' messiahship, including suffering and glory, as well as the true nature of Christian discipleship as the way to glory through suffering.[8] This means that Mark's purpose was primarily christological and the different usages of the Son of Man title represent what it means for Jesus to be the Son of God. For example, some usages (9:12; 13:26; 14:21, 41, 62) are sayings that received no redaction from Mark, while other sayings, such as those found in 9:12 and 13:26, are evidence of pre-Markan traditions that Mark inherited and fitted into his narrative. Those sayings in 14:21 and 14:41 are also part of a pre-Markan tradition, more specifically what Perrin calls a *paradidonai* ("betrayed") tradition, in that it recalls Isa 53. The final saying in 14:62 ties each of the sayings together by closely associating the titles Son of God and Son of Man—Perrin identifies this as a Markan compositional technique.[9] In the end, Perrin identifies what he thinks is a threefold purpose for the Son of Man sayings in Mark's Gospel: (1) the necessity for combating a false understanding of Jesus as the Son of God and replacing it with one that emphasizes the necessity of suffering; (2) the necessity of suffering is also extended to the disciples; and (3) the necessity of suffering as the way to the salvation of mankind.[10]

Collins takes up the conversation on several grounds. She first notes that the Son of Man title is not an idiom in Koine Greek, so the

---

8. Perrin, *Pilgrimage*, 78.
9. Perrin, *Pilgrimage*, 87.
10. Perrin, *Pilgrimage*, 92–93.

The Tragic Son of Man

appearance of two articles is rather confusing (ὁ υἱὸς τοῦ ἀνθρώπου).[11] She then points out that the corresponding articular forms of the title in Hebrew and Aramaic rarely appear in material earlier than the Gospels.[12] This leaves us with three options: (1) the Gospel tradition retains an articular form of the title that appeared in either Hebrew or Aramaic; (2) the appearance of the article is new in Mark and reveals a conscious addition to the Aramaic non-articular form; or (3) the appearance of the article is a scribal error and the article was not meant to be present in Mark.

Collins then points out that interpreting the Son of Man title in light of its form and function within a text ought to provide the most satisfactory approach. The "I-sayings," which refer to Jesus' reflections on his coming or his passion, death, and resurrection are most likely to have originated in a post-Easter situation (*ex eventu*) and express interpretations of Jesus' life and work as a whole. Other sayings (Matt 13:27, 41; and Luke 18:8b) belong to secondary interpretations of a similitude or a parable but are late in their composition, thereby not providing a good starting point for determining the origin of the title. Still others (Matt 16:13; Matt 26:64//Mark 14:62//Luke 22:69; Luke 22:48; 24:7) belong to what Collins calls "legendary narratives" and, again, reveal a relatively late composition by an evangelist, earlier editor, or Christian storyteller.[13] With regard to Mark 2:10 and 2:28, examples that Collins terms "legal sayings" or "church rules," it may be possible that these two examples reflect an older form of a saying spoken by Jesus himself.[14] If so, the wording of 2:10 would have been rendered approximately as "human beings have authority on earth to forgive sins." This means that the speaker is not shown, in any way, to be distinctive from other human beings. This will be given further discussion below. As for the way that the apocalyptic Son of Man sayings appear in the Gospels, Collins is hesitant to suggest that any actually came from the lips of Jesus. Instead, she is more comfortable suggesting that, though the Son of Man

---

11. Collins, "Origin of the Designation," 394.

12. Collins, "Origin of the Designation," 394; See also Fitzmyer, "Philologically Considered," 145–53.

13. Collins, "Origin of the Designation," 396–97.

14. Collins, "Origin of the Designation," 397.

tradition originated with Jesus, it is most likely that their appearance in the Gospels is the result of editing that reflects the context of the earliest church.[15]

Kirchhevel separates the Son of Man sayings in Mark into three distinct categories: those found in Mark 1–6 that correspond to Ps 8; those found in 8–14 that correspond to Isa 52:13—53:12; and other usages that correspond to Isa 5:26–30 and which refer to a future parousia.[16] Adams argues, contra R. T. France and N. T. Wright, that the Son of Man sayings in 8:38, 13:24–27, and 14:62 refer to Jesus' parousia and not to his postmortem vindication.[17]

Hay approaches the title by suggesting that understanding the title is dependent upon understanding its Semitic background.[18] Hooker rejects the idea that the Son of Man in Dan 7 refers to an individual and suggests instead that it refers to Israel as a nation. She also rejects the idea that the title was homogeneously messianic,[19] suggesting that in Mark 2:27–28, for example, "there is no evidence in the saying itself

---

15. Collins, "Origin of the Designation," 406.

16. Kirchhevel, "Son of Man," 181.

17. Adams, "The Coming," 39–61; France, *Jesus and the Old Testament*, 139–48; Wright, *Victory of God*, 341, 360–67, 510–19, 632; Wright, *Mark for Everyone*, 111–12, 183–84, 205. In his article, Adams examines the role of "the one like a Son of Man" in Dan 7, 1 En. 37–71, and 4 Ezra 13 and concludes that Mark develops a narrative scheme of coming, going away, and coming *again*.

18. Hay ("Son of Man," 69–75) argues that there are three basic usages of the phrase in Judaism. The first is a completely neutral usage as an expression for a human being. The second is a circumlocution for the pronoun "I." The third, most prominent within Jewish apocalyptic tradition, draws from the figure found in Dan 7:13. At the point when the article was written (1970), Hay notes that most scholars unanimously agree that the title refers only to a circumlocution of the pronoun "I," and outrightly rejects this position (70). Hay rejects what Adams later picks up (see 71n16), and that is, a grouping of the Son of Man sayings into three distinct categories. Hay argues that "this procedure may conceal some tacit assumptions about the relation between the various texts and may obscure the way in which the evangelist himself viewed them" (70).

19. Elsewhere, Hooker ("Insoluble?" 159) outrightly rejects the messianic nature of the title altogether: "The phrase cannot be a messianic title—yet the theory which interprets it as such at least offers a reason for its use; the view that it was an acceptable self-designation offers a plausible explanation as to *how* Jesus could have used it of himself—but it fails to explain *why* he should have employed a colourless phrase which has no particular function."

that 'the Son of Man' was a messianic term."[20] Yet, Hooker accepts the messianic nature of the title in 8:38, suggesting that the title was used in different ways. There is an element of suffering that corresponds both to Jesus' self-designation and to certain Old Testament passages: "the disciples find their lives by losing them, become first by being last, and greatest by being slaves, because the Son of Man himself comes to glory via the path of suffering and humiliation."[21]

Hooker also notes the peculiarity of the pattern of Son of Man sayings in Mark. The apparent isolation of the title found in 2:10 and 28 causes it to appear to "stand aloof" from the remaining Son of Man sayings. Further differences can be found in character and setting.[22] Scholars are often tempted to explain these differences as the result of having been creations of the Early Church—an assertion that Hooker rejects on the basis that positioning within a narrative cannot convincingly explain origin. However, because the sayings in 2:10 and 28 appear in the context of setting up conflict with religious authorities, Hooker notes an apparent pattern: several of the Son of Man sayings in Mark are linked to questions concerning Jesus' authority. She states, "The term Son of Man can appropriately be used when the authority of Jesus is claimed or accepted, and this is why it is used in conversation with those who follow or challenge him."[23] She then states that it is because Jesus is the Son of Man that he acts with authority, and it is for this same reason, because his authority has been rejected by the Jewish authorities, that he must suffer.

---

20. Hooker, *Son of Man*, 102. The parallel with David might suggest a messianic interpretation, but the Son of Man's authority is not dependent upon the implied connection to David, but to Israel, the "man" for whom the Sabbath was made. Jesus is likened to the messianic nature of the Danielic Son of Man, and though no one ever refers to Jesus as the Son of Man, it is likely that Jesus' listeners would have accepted the implications of the term without surprise.

21. Hooker (*Son of Man*, 132–34, 140) rejects the idea that the suffering Son of Man has any reference to the suffering servant songs found in Isa 53. Instead, she sees a correlation between Jesus' suffering as the Son of Man and that of the Son of Man in Dan 7. She also notes a connection between the sufferings of Jesus and Elijah found in Mal 4.

22. Hooker, *Son of Man*, 174.

23. Hooker, *Son of Man*, 179.

Of Conflict and Concealment

This, however, does not fully explain why Jesus chooses to use the term. Once more, if Jesus acts authoritatively, it is because of his authority as the Messiah and Son of God—as established in 1:1—and not as the Son of Man. Jesus performs miracles and exorcisms not because he is the Son of Man, but because he is the Messiah and Son of God. This, again, is why the high priest takes exception to Jesus in 14:63—not because he is the Son of Man, but because he agrees that he is the Son of God (cf. 14:61). This means that a challenge to Jesus' authority—which I agree is actually happening in 2:10 and 28—comes not because Jesus is the Son of Man but because of his other offices.[24]

As for Hooker's treatment of the sayings in 8:38 and 13:26, she suggests that these represent vindication for those who have suffered for Jesus' sake, while those found in 10:45, 14:21, and 14:41 present, according to Hooker, a paradox unto themselves.[25] These are a paradox insofar as they do not seem to present a Jesus who acts with the same type of authority as that with which he acts in 2:10 and 28. And so, Hooker must adopt a pattern of proclamation, denial, and vindication in order to explain how the titles function differently from one another. She is correct in noting that the Son of Man's authority has far-reaching consequences that affect everyone.

The problem with Hooker's final conclusions is that they ultimately fail to explain *why* Jesus chooses to use the term. Certainly, we cannot suggest that the Early Church had some type of "Son of Man" theology, or else we would find mention of it in the New Testament.[26] This creates a number of problems for those who want to suggest that the title was created *ex eventu*—though it is possible, there is very little, if any, evidence for this. The strength of Hooker's argument lies in her observations that the title is used in reference to the authority of Jesus, yet I depart from her with regard to the implications that are drawn. For Hooker, authority is found in the title itself, that is, in Jesus as the Son of Man. However, I think it more plausible to suggest that the title

---

24. See Hooker (*Son of Man*, 180–82) for further discussion.

25. On this, Hooker (*Son of Man*, 181) states, "The remaining 'Son of Man' sayings, Mark 10:45, 14:21, and 41, also contain within themselves the paradox of the Son of Man, for each depicts the Son of Man in a situation in which he does not exercise the authority which is properly his."

26. The possible exception being Heb 2:6, which quotes Ps 144:3.

The Tragic Son of Man

is not meant to create yet another office by which Jesus acts authoritatively. As mentioned, Jesus acts authoritatively precisely because he is the Messiah and Son of God. Instead, the Son of Man title allows Jesus to *avoid* self-designation as the Messiah and Son of God—more will be said on this below.

Caragounis tracks the various appearances of the title throughout Jewish literature such as Daniel, various Jewish and Rabbinic documents, and 4 Ezra. He rejects the idea that the title could be used only as a circumlocutional title because it does not have any Aramaic equivalents that are both contemporary with Jesus and independent of the Gospels.[27] He concludes by suggesting that, although the title was used by Jesus himself, some of the sayings have been "resolved into the personal pronoun or vice versa and the evangelists have given us what Jesus' disciples (in a wider sense) preserved in the tradition on account of the importance that they attached to Jesus' teaching, viz. an authentic picture of his teaching about himself as the Son of Man."[28] He also suggests that Jesus' fight against the powers of darkness, which parallels the fight in Daniel, constitutes the most important area of the Danielic Son of Man legacy to the teachings of Jesus.[29]

Studies like that of Caragounis appear in contrast to ones conducted by Casey, who suggests that Jesus' use of the title is a circumlocution whose origins are found in the Aramaic language.[30] After reconstruct-

---

27. Caragounis, *Son of Man*, 33.
28. Caragounis, *Son of Man*, 242.
29. Caragounis, *Son of Man*, 243. Evans ("Messianic Hopes," 36–37) also argues that Jesus made use of this "curious" title in light of Dan 7 and that this usage leads us to conclude that Jesus was aware of his messianic nature. This is evidenced by his use of the article that lends to the specificity of Danielic Son of Man. He then argues that we can understand such passages as Mark 2:10 and 2:28 in light of Dan 7, both of which promote Jesus as one who has the authority to forgive sins as well as one who is the lord of the Sabbath.
30. An Aramaic background of the title has been argued for on many occasions. One of the earliest advocates of the Aramaic origins of the title was Johannes Coccejus, who suggested that the linguistic background of Matt 8:20 was Aramaic. Julius Wellhausen posited that Jesus' use of the Aramaic title meant "I." Nathaniel Schmidt then argued that the title was purely idiomatic and simply meant "human." Arnold Meyer argued that the use of the article in Greek was a translation of the Aramaic "that Son of Man." Meyer's use of the demonstrative pronoun was mostly rejected, however. Hans Lietzmann later argued that, since the term does not appear among

ing the Aramaic version of several Gospel accounts, Casey argues that Jesus defended himself against his opponents by associating himself with John the Baptist.[31] In doing so, Jesus portrayed his opponents in "an unfavourable image, and retailed their accusations as if to show that they were obviously foolish." As for Jewish tradition, Casey argues that there "was no Son of Man Concept, or *Menschensohnbegriff*, in Second Temple Judaism."[32] He understands the Son of Man figure in Dan 7:13 as a "symbol of the Saints of the Most High," a description of the people of Israel.[33] With regard to 1 Enoch, Casey argues that his careful study of the Aramaic source material leads us to conclude that the Son of Man title is a common term that refers to a human being.[34]

These conclusions are also found in Hare's study, where he concludes that the Aramaic expression *bar enasha* (Son of Man) was "capable of functioning in some contexts as a modesty idiom, whereby the speaker referred to himself exclusively."[35] He openly rejects the idea that the title could sometimes function as a recognizable apocalyptic title: "there is no philological evidence whatsoever, ambiguous or otherwise, for the opposing proposal that *bar enasha* could sometimes function as a recognizable apocalyptic title."[36] As a result, Hare is forced to admit that the apocalyptic Son of Man sayings in Mark did not originate with Jesus, and that these sayings arose in a post-Easter context.[37]

We can conclude from these studies that the Son of Man title in Mark may have originated in a variety of contexts and could be

---

the rabbis, the title must have its origins in 'Hellenistic' Christian theology. For a complete summary of the various arguments, see Lukaszewski, "Issues," 1–27.

31. Casey (*Solution*, 116–43) argues for six authentic Son of Man sayings in the gospel tradition. These include Mark 2:27-28; 9:11-13; 10:45, 14:21; Matt 11:19//Luke 7:34; Matt 12:32//Luke 12:10.

32. Casey, *Solution*, 114.

33. Casey, *Solution*, 114.

34. Casey, *Solution*, 114. For a criticism of Casey's proposal, see Hurtado and Owen, eds., *Who is this Son of Man?*

35. Hare, *Son of Man*, 256.

36. Hare, *Son of Man*, 256.

37. Hare, *Son of Man*, 277. At the end of his book, Hare rejects the idea that the title served as a christological one with a clear theological content. He notes that in Luke and John, as well as in the era of the Apostolic Fathers, the title was used primarily to refer to the humanity of Jesus (280).

understood in variety of ways. It is, therefore, possible that Jesus makes use of the title for this very reason. The problem for interpreters, however, is that Mark never explicitly states why Jesus uses the title, nor do we have ample documents from the first century that make use of the title—unless one adopts a first-century date for Enoch. This means that we must examine how the title functions within the narrative, otherwise, we will continue to play a never-ending guessing game as to which source Mark's Jesus is referring when he uses the title. I will, therefore, avoid discussing the potential origins of the title except to say that, though its origin is uncertain, there is a distinctive way in which Jesus uses the title in Mark's Gospel. It will be argued here that the title in Mark's Gospel functions primarily to obscure Jesus' identity and provides for him a way to continue to conceal his identity, as prescribed by the secrecy motif in chapter 4.

So, what can we say about how the title functions within the context of tragic *Collision*? Before answering this, we must make a number of observations about Jesus' use of the title. The first observation is that Jesus alone uses the title and only in self-reference. Also, there is never a time when anyone else uses the title to describe Jesus, nor do they address Jesus as the Son of Man. This leads to the second observation: Jesus uses the title when he could have just as easily used a first-person pronoun. This, as mentioned, has led scholars to conclude that the title is being used merely as an Aramaic idiom. The third observation is that no one ever reacts to Jesus' use of the term, with a possible exception being in 14:63. However, the high priest's reaction may be due to Jesus' self-designation as "I am," which is understood as a response to the question "Are you the messiah, the son of the Blessed One?"

Since Jesus' use of the title provokes no response from anyone in the narrative, the title could be understood in a number of ways. It is possible that Jesus' use of the title is meant purely as a narrative element, meaning that only the audience has an opportunity to react to it. However, this option does not provide opportunity for reflection on Jesus' historical use of the term. It is also possible that, as suggested above, Jesus' use of the term is meant to be understood as an act of humility that avoids a direct claim of messiahship, especially in Mark

14:61.³⁸ This appears to be counterintuitive, especially in this example, since Jesus positively confirms the high priest's question concerning his relationship to God.

So why does Jesus purposefully avoid self-designation? The answer to this question is similar to the one given in chapter 4 as to why Jesus often demands secrecy. If Jesus is in *Collision* with the temple and his purpose is to subvert the temple and the *ethos* it creates, he cannot openly admit his status as the Son of God . Otherwise, the tragic nature of the plot dissolves³⁹ because it cannot be believed that he is the Son of God. Otherwise, the tragic nature of the plot dissolves because it cannot be believed that that a human or any human institution could withstand conflict with a god. Like Dionysus, who conceals his identity

---

38. Bauckham ("Son of Man," 23–33) notes Matt 26:62//Mark 14:61//Luke 22:67-68 in which Jesus avoids a direct claim to messiahship. He explains the oblique nature of Jesus' reference to Dan 7:13 because it is appropriate to the thought of eschatological vindication (31). It is possible that Jesus' reference to Dan 7:13 here is a situational reference rather than a reference to a character. Since Dan 7 describes a situation of conflict, perhaps Jesus is referring more to the outcome (vindication) rather than the character that brings it about. This would mean that the identity of the character in Dan 7 is somewhat irrelevant.

39. One may be tempted to interpret my solution here as similar to that of those scholars who view the Son of Man sayings as referring to a corporate entity of which Jesus is the head. Such a view was first put forward by Episcopius (*Notae breves*) in 1650. It was later taken up in 1866 by Sytse Hoekstra (*De benaming*, 158), who interpreted the Son of Man in Dan 7:13 not as the Messiah but as a new community of believers. This theory came to its full manifestation in the work of J. Estlin Carpenter and Albert Réville in 1890 and 1897, respectively. For Carpenter (*The First Three Gospels*, 248, 387–88), the Son of Man was not a person, but the kingdom of God that displays the divine forces of Love and Truth. Réville (*Jésus de Nazareth*, 2.194) took the Son of Man sayings in Mark 2:10 and 2:28 to represent humanity conceived in its ideal perfection. Sanday (*Life of Christ*, 129) also argued for a corporate interpretation of the Son of Man sayings and suggested that it was derived not only from Dan 7:13 but also from Ps 8. In 1922, Nils Messel (*Der Menschensohn*) argued for a corporate interpretation of the title in the Similitudes of Enoch. T. W. Manson (*The Teaching of Jesus*, 228), one of the more prominent advocates of this position in the twentieth century, suggested that the Son of Man is an ideal figure who represents the kingdom of God, but when this kingdom fails to succeed among either the people or the disciples, Jesus stands alone as the one who perfectly embodies the correct response to God and his claims. While each of these scholars puts forward thought-provoking ideas, the ideas do not hold up against the fact that most of the Son of Man titles demand a reference to Jesus alone. Therefore, the corporate idea can only be accepted if one assumes that the sayings found in the Gospels have been modified to reflect a more individual reference.

in order to exist in *Collision* with Pentheus, Jesus' identity must remain concealed for the duration of the plot. This explains why Jesus employs the ambiguous Son of Man title during times of conflict with the religious leaders and why the title appears in accounts of suffering and eschatological sayings. Therefore, the Son of Man title has less to do with a particular character that Jesus is alluding to, or identifying with, and everything to do with its function within the narrative. The meaning then, or purpose, of the Son of Man title in Mark is derived from its function within the narrative and not from an outside source. This can be demonstrated, I believe, by a careful analysis of the occasions on which Jesus employs the Son of Man title.

JESUS AS THE SON OF MAN IN MARK

As noted above, the Son of Man title is used thirteen times by Jesus throughout his ministry. Each of these usages is meant to refer to Jesus himself, though the nature of the sayings suggests far-reaching implications for others. Curiously, however, Jesus uses the title twice during the early period of his ministry (2:10 and 2:28) but not again until 8:31. We then find that the title appears more frequently. As noted, this apparent "gap," in addition to the difference in kind of saying, has prompted scholars to suggest that the first two Son of Man sayings are either authentic or inauthentic, depending on whether one believes the rest of the Son of Man sayings to be a creation of the church or to have originated with Jesus himself. However, deciding on the authenticity of the title based on where it appears in the narrative runs the risk of judging the composition of the Gospel based on how we would have written it, rather than accepting the way Mark wrote it.

In what follows, I will categorize the Son of Man sayings into three groups: group A (2:10, 28); group B (8:31; 9:12; 10:33, 45; 14:21, 41); and group C (8:38; 9:9, 31; 13:26; 14:62). The sayings in each of the groups function in different ways throughout the Gospel, hence the need to categorize them. Their importance to this study is that each illustrates a way in which Jesus is in *Collision* with the temple. My categories come closest to those posited by Hooker, but we differ in our conclusions. Hooker asserts that the common theme that holds the sayings together is the authority of Jesus as the Son of Man: proclaimed authority, denied authority, and vindicated authority.[40] What I posit here, is that the authority that Jesus claims comes by way of his position as the Messiah and Son of God and not the Son of Man. The function of the Son of Man sayings is, therefore, a means by which Jesus publicly rejects any self-designation as either the Messiah, or Son of God.[41] I can say this because Jesus never identifies himself as either the Messiah or Son of God, and demands secrecy when called such things. The Son of Man title then becomes a way that Jesus utilizes the confusion over who he is to remain as an opposite to the temple. Hence, the Son of Man title functions within the tragic paradigm of *Collision*.

---

40. Hooker, *Son of Man*, 181.

41. Similar conclusions can be found in a study conducted by Malbon ("The Christology of Mark's Gospel"), in which she suggests that the Son of Man title in Mark is used to illustrate a "deflected Christology." She follows closely behind Kingsbury (*Christology*), who suggests that the gnomic use of the title suggests a "progressive disclosure of Jesus' identity" (90). Malbon argues that the messianic secret—as was first coined by Wrede—is theologically motivated: "The Markan Jesus consistently deflects honour away from himself and toward God" (41). She also notes that Jesus never self-identifies with the titles found in 1:1 and that there is a constant tension between the narrator, who only wants to talk about Jesus, and Jesus, who only wants to talk about God (43). She explains this perceived tension as a creation of the "implied author," whom she distinguishes from the "narrator." I do not think this is a particularly helpful method for discerning what is happening in Mark. Distinguishing what an "implied author" is thinking with regard to the story, especially when distinguished from the narrator, seems very much like a method by which a scholar can interpret Mark in any way they see fit; the "implied author" thus becomes the scholar. Instead, it is more appropriate to allow Mark to be the author and narrator in order to discern why Jesus employs secrecy as well as the Son of Man title. Malbon is correct, I think, with regard to her observations of deflection—Jesus certainly does deflect attention and titles. But little is made of exactly *why* he does so, except Malbon's attempt to create a form of subjective interpretation that she calls "theology." For a Jesus who constantly wants to deflect honor towards God, little is made of God throughout the narrative and hardly any explanation is given by Mark as to *how* God is receiving glory especially since it is Jesus who gets most, if not all, of the attention. In a way, Malbon's interpretation reduces Jesus to a mere pawn, which is ironic considering her goal is to establish a Christology. Instead, it is more plausible to suggest that the secrecy motif as well as the Son of Man title function merely as ways that Jesus can avoid self-designation, and we need not derive a theology based on it.

The Tragic Son of Man

Group A: Mark 2:10 and 2:28

Working with our tragic paradigm, Jesus' usage of the title Son of Man is a way for him to obscure his identity. This is important because it allows Jesus to remain concealed and for the motif of secrecy to continue. If the motif of secrecy dissolves, then Jesus is no longer in a position to be in *Collision* to the temple and the plot ceases to be tragic. Jesus must, at all times, continue in opposition to the temple in order to complete the criteria of tragedy outlined in chapter 3.

With regard to Mark 2:10, Jesus' use of the title here represents its first occurrence in the narrative. I agree with Bauckham that the title appears here as a direct reference to the accusations found in v. 7, which indicates that Jesus' actions and words are meant to be understood in opposition to the beliefs of the religious leaders.[42] However, I depart from Bauckham's treatment of the passage in that, if Jesus wanted people to recognize him for themselves, they would have done so.[43] Instead, we find quite the opposite: there is no evidence in the Gospel of Mark that Jesus' hearers ever really conceive of Jesus as the Messiah or Son of God. While they are certainly amazed by what they see and hear (2:12), we are not told that they ever become fully convinced. This is certainly true of the religious leaders, and mainly true of

---

42. Bauckham, "Son of Man," 31.

43. Bauckham ("Son of Man," 31) writes, "The point is not that Jesus did not wish his God-given role and authority to be recognized, but that he wanted people to recognize for themselves." When Bauckham later comments on the passage in question, he says, "Jesus neither denies nor asserts that others have such authority, but points to his healing as evidence that at any rate one man, himself, does have it. Thus he claims no more than his deed demonstrates, and the obliqueness of the self-reference serves to make his authority not so much a claim as an inference which his hearers may draw for themselves from what they see" (31). This is certainly an attractive hypothesis for why Jesus chooses to refer to himself as the Son of Man here, but it fails to convince. The most obvious reason why it fails is because we have no idea what conclusions the onlookers make because we see no evidence of anyone actually arriving at the right conclusion about Jesus as the Son of Man, Son of God, nor as the Messiah—nor any other title, with the exception of Peter in 8:29 and various demons upon their exorcism. Indeed, the crowds are impressed by what they see (2:12), but we are not told exactly why they are impressed except that they "have not seen anything like this before." This lack of admission appears to me to be indicative of the fact that Jesus is never supposed to be recognized by the titles I have listed—this must only occur after the resurrection if the plot is to remain tragic. Instead, Jesus avoids becoming the very thing that the temple is.

the disciples and other followers—the possible exception being Peter's confession in 8:29. I do not think that Jesus failed in his mission to convince everyone of his message, but I do think this very conspicuous absence of conviction within his audience leads us to conclude that Jesus convincing his audience is not a main focus of Mark's narrative. Instead, it appears that the conflict that is continually made prominent *is* the main focus. This, of course, fits within the tragic paradigm of *Collision* and it helps to explain what is happening in 2:10. According to our paradigm, Jesus must always occupy a position contrary to that of the temple without becoming like the temple, or else the narrative ceases to be tragic. And so, his use of the title in 2:10 has a twofold purpose: (1) to challenge the temple and its practices; and (2) to avoid self-designation, thus avoiding contravening the tragic pattern of two forces pitted against one another.

With regard to the first purpose, Jesus openly challenges a particular belief concerning forgiveness of sins which is represented in 2:7. We have seen above that what the religious leaders are saying is not necessarily wrong—there is ample evidence within Old Testament tradition that only God is able to forgive sins. There is also evidence, as found in 1 Sam 2:25 and Num 15:25, that humans are also at times able forgive one another of sin, though with God as an intercessor. This means that, because humans are able to forgive sin, what Jesus is saying in 2:10 is not necessarily unique. The question remains, however, as to why Jesus chooses to represent himself as the Son of Man since it was not entirely out of the question for humans to forgive one another of sin. It is possible that Jesus' use of the title here represents an idiom that simply means "a human"—this seems to fit the evidence found in Old Testament tradition. But why is Jesus *the* human?[44] We could suggest

---

44. One might note here, as Collins ("Origin of the Designation," 398–99) does, that despite the number of occasions within the Old Testament that explicitly state that only God can forgive sins, Num 15:25 does suggest that, at times, a human can forgive sins—albeit a priest. Collins also points out the idea of sins committed against other humans being forgivable is well represented in Jewish literature. However, there are places within the Old Testament (1 Sam 2:25) in which a sin against God is not forgivable. This reduces the idiosyncratic nature of the saying in Mark 2:10 but the question still remains for Collins as to why Mark altered the idiom to make Jesus *the* Son of Man. She suggests that the issue may be due to a mistranslation at some point in transmission, or perhaps because some oral performer or scribe did

that, since there is no evidence within the Greek language of the title being idiomatic, the appearance of the article represents some type of error in transmission or in translation. This particular conclusion is rejected by Collins, who says that, though it is conceivable, it is more "desperate" and "tendentious."[45] It is possible that the appearance of the article with the Son of Man title is meant to add a level of grammatical prominence, thereby differentiating Jesus from any other person who may be forgiving sins. At this point it is possible to add theological significance to Jesus as being the most prominent human being but, according to the evidence, this does not conclude the issue insofar as other human beings are able to forgive sins.

It appears that the reason for Jesus using the title in 2:10 must have significance beyond the theological categories of Jesus being both Messiah and the Son of God, since both humans and God can forgive sins according to the Old Testament. Since this instance of the title occurs within the context of conflict with the religious leaders, I propose that we can only really define what it means according to the conflict itself. This means that both the meaning of the title and its purpose are derived from the context of the discussion in 2:1–12 and its overall place within the tragic *Collision*. Thus, I conclude that Jesus' use of the title here is the means by which Jesus eludes overstepping his position in the *Collision*, thereby remaining in a position that allows him to continue to challenge his opponent—the temple.

Mark 2:28

The second occurrence of the Son of Man title appears at the end of an argument between Jesus and the religious leaders concerning Sabbath rules (2:23–28). The heart of the issue lies in the fact that Jesus and his disciples appear to be breaking the Sabbath law by harvesting grain, an action that violates the law given in Exod 31:14: "You must keep the Sabbath day, for it is a holy day for you. Anyone who desecrates it must be put to death; anyone who works on that day will be cut off from the community." There are also several traditions in which it was believed

---

not know the language very well. Yet these solutions do not convince Collins, and though they appear conceivable, they are "tedious" and seemingly "desperate" (399).

45. Collins, "Origin of the Designation," 399.

that the Sabbath was created primarily for Israel and not for any other nation, as stated in Jub. 2:31: "And the Creator of all things blessed it, but he did not sanctify all peoples and nations to keep Sabbath thereon, but Israel alone: them alone he permitted to eat and drink and to keep Sabbath thereon on the earth." 4 Ezra 6:55 states that God created the world for "our sakes" (i.e., for humanity), a position that was later advocated by Simeon b. Menasya (c. 180 CE) in his commentary on Exod 31:14, who said that "the Sabbath is delivered over for your sake, but you are not delivered over to the Sabbath."[46]

It is odd that the Pharisees' concern for Jesus' actions are expressed in the form of a question (v. 24) since they presumably knew the law very well. This leads me to conclude that the question is meant as a type of introductory question formula by which the Pharisees can engage and test Jesus. I say this because of the absence of either μή or οὔ, which usually denote that the speaker is leading the listener to an expected response—which would indicate the Pharisees' position in the argument. Instead, it appears that the Pharisees mean to leave the question open ended—indicated by the interrogative pronoun τί—thereby providing an opportunity for Jesus to respond sincerely. Jesus responds in turn with a question, which draws attention to the fact that even David violated the Sabbath at times. I do not think that Jesus' response here is meant to implicate David, but rather to connect Jesus with a messianic motif concerning Israel's anointed king, which would then lend credibility to the idea that Jesus is using the Son of Man title as a means to conceal his messianic identity. This is not a unique interpretation, as shown by the evidence given above, but it is a necessary one within the context of tragic *Collision*. Despite the fact that there are several less dramatic interpretations of Sabbath violation available, Jesus must occupy a position contrary to that of the Pharisees.

I agree with Taylor who suggests that the dialogue ends naturally at v. 26 and that the introduction of a Son of Man saying in v. 27 appears rather awkward.[47] However, the phrase καὶ ἔλεγεν αὐτοῖς ("and he was speaking to them") is used somewhat frequently in Mark (4:13, 21; 6:10; 7:9; 9:1) and always functions as a connecting link. This could

---

46. *Mek. Šabb.* to Exod 31:14.
47. Taylor, *St. Mark*, 218–19.

suggest that the Son of Man saying in v. 27 is actually meant to naturally follow v. 26 even though both Matthew and Luke choose to omit it.[48]

The usual question, despite the apparent textual issues, is why Jesus chooses to use the title in the context of this particular legal debate with the Pharisees. Collins argues that this controversy was composed in a post-Easter situation in which followers of Jesus claimed his authority to settle matters over the observance of the Sabbath.[49] The actual Son of Man saying is then to be understood as simply a means of settling a dispute between Jewish converts to Christianity, though Collins does admit to the possibility that the saying which includes the title could have been original to Jesus.

There is also some concern over whether Jesus meant the title to refer to humanity in general, or whether he was referring to himself as an idealized human who, unlike any other human, has authority over the Sabbath. This, according to Collins, recalls the divine command in Gen 1:28 that humanity should rule over the earth, and leads her to accept Jesus' use of the title as a generic one. If Jesus actually used the title in an instance like this, he could only mean it generically. This presents a problem for Collins since not all of the Son of Man sayings can be taken generically, a problem she admits cannot be adequately explained on linguistic grounds alone.[50]

However, I think the problem can be solved if viewed from the vantage of tragic *Collision*. This is the second occurrence in which Jesus employs the title, and the second occurrence in which the title appears in the context of a conflict with the religious leaders. Since this is so, the solution may actually reside in how the title functions within that conflict. If we consider again how tragedy works, we have two approaches that occupy equally justified positions. By challenging the temple's position—represented here by the Pharisees—Jesus advocates a viewpoint that challenges the social *ethos* put forth by the temple establishment. By saying that the Sabbath was created for the Son of Man and not vice

---

48. See Taylor (*St. Mark*, 218) for a list of the textual variants that surround this use of the title. Though v. 27 may not appear in some manuscripts, it does appear in Sinaiticus—our earliest complete manuscript of the New Testament.

49. Collins, "Origin of the Designation," 400. Collins does not, however, provide any additional information as to what that might be or look like.

50. Collins, "Origin of the Designation," 400.

versa, Jesus is deconstructing social barriers. I say social barriers since, as the evidence suggests, several Jewish traditions promote the Sabbath as a primarily Jewish event. Thus, by challenging how the Sabbath is understood, Jesus is essentially challenging the idea that the Sabbath is a closed event and suggests, instead, that all people are to benefit from it. I take his usage of the Son of Man title here as a means for avoiding self-designation, thereby not violating the tragic paradigm of *Collision* similar to how the title functions in Mark 2:10.

Group B: Mark 8:31; 9:12; 10:33, 45; 14:21, 41

Group B differs from group A in that the sayings found in it are primarily concerned with Jesus' suffering. As mentioned above, the sayings in this section appear somewhat paradoxical: Jesus, who has authority to do the things exercised in the sayings found in group A, chooses not to exercise any authority or preventative measures with regard to his suffering and death. This leads to the logical conclusion that suffering and death, things that are intrinsically linked to tragedy (as discussed in chapter 2), are essential to Jesus' ministry. It could be, and is suggested by Hooker, that the sayings that make up group B are related to Jesus' denial of his own authority.[51] However, since Jesus himself knows what is to happen—and goes to great efforts to make it happen—we cannot say that the sayings in this group really have to do with the denial of Jesus' authority. Instead, it is more plausible to suggest that Jesus is actively working towards his own death, which, of course, he knows will be vindicated by his resurrection. This also fits my proposed paradigm of tragic *Collision*, in which two valued positions are pitted against one another until one inevitably destroys the other. This group of sayings represents—albeit differently from group A—the ways in which Jesus challenges the contrary position, which is occupied by the temple.

The first saying in group B is found in 8:31, in which Jesus announces to his disciples that the Son of Man must suffer many terrible things and be rejected by the religious leaders. There is a considerable gap between this saying and the one previous and, as I discussed above, this gap has little bearing on the authenticity of either of the groups of

---

51. Hooker, *Son of Man*, 181.

sayings. Instead, we must understand these two groups as representing different ways that Jesus challenges the temple. The sayings in group A have more to do with challenging various interpretive issues with regard to Scripture, while group B represents the sayings in which Jesus will be willingly overcome by the position that he opposes.

Two examples from group B feature Jesus referring to his suffering and death as fulfillment of Scripture. On the surface, this tells us that Jesus' suffering and death were foretold (9:12; 14:21) and it is clear that Jesus is aware that this will happen. However, we can also suggest that this, too, fits the tragic paradigm of *Collision*. If we recall what was said in chapter 2 concerning *Collision*, each position in the tragic *Collision* represents a god or high ethical position. Sometimes the god appears in the story, as in the case of the *Bacchae*, but often the god appears as a *deus ex machina*. The tragic nature of a narrative occurs when one position is destroyed by the other only to later be destroyed. The destruction of both positions is necessary so that harmony can be restored. In a way, we can suggest that a position rises up, so to speak, in order to challenge the one-sidedness of the other position. Using the example of the *Antigone*, Antigone must be destroyed in order for the story to appear as tragic. Creon later suffers because he destroyed Antigone—which is itself tragic—and any one-sidedness is dissolved. Thus, the gods that both Antigone and Creon represent are placed in equal order again and all is well.

The polytheistic nature of Greek tragedy easily allows for two positions, each of which represents a god, to act contrarily to one another in *Collision*. However, within a monotheistic culture like Judaism, only one God is represented. This, in my humble opinion, makes Mark even more tragic—God is represented by two forces that are unequivocally opposed to one another. For a Jewish person living in the first century, this must have been extremely tragic. All that they had known and lived for was in relation to the temple—or the God who dwelled within the temple. Now, Jesus appears as the Son of God and stands in opposition to the thing that they had, for their entire lives, striven to uphold. This form of *Collision* is one of the most genuine expressions of tragedy.

With regard to Jesus being preordained to suffer and die according to the Scriptures, it becomes clear following the above explanation, that the outcome of a tragedy occurs as the result of a god(s) attempting to restore harmony. If Jesus rises up to challenge the temple, he *must* die; likewise, the temple must be destroyed. I will talk more about the temple's destruction in relation to group C of the Son of Man sayings, each having to do with future vindication. It is not surprising then to find Jesus appealing to Scripture with regard to his suffering and death as a preordained thing. I think that he knows that his ministry must end in death in order for harmony to be restored. This point is stated perhaps most emphatically in 10:45: "For the Son of Man came not to be served, but to serve others and to give his life as a ransom for many." Jesus' death and the subsequent invalidation of the temple are both common factors in tragedy and are meant to bring about the tragic harmony that occurs when *Collison* is dissolved.

Group C: Mark 8:38; 9:9, 31; 13:26; 14:62

The Son of Man sayings that make up group C differ in appearance and function from those found in groups A and B. As illustrated above, the sayings found in group A function in terms of Jesus challenging current interpretations of Scripture, while those found in group B illustrate the suffering and death of Jesus as a necessary function of tragic *Collision*. The Son of Man sayings found in group C function in close connection to those found in group B because they promise the harmony that is produced by the end of tragic *Collision*. In other words, when Jesus promises his resurrection, this is meant to signal the end of the temple as a social and religious institution.[52]

Having said this, the Son of Man sayings that make up group C function primarily as signals that the temple will not have the ultimate victory in the *Collision* and that harmony will be achieved. We know

---

52. This may seem troubling to those who want to understand what I am saying as a reduction of the resurrection to a mere narrative device meant to conclude a tragedy. This is simply not the case. One must keep in mind as they read this section that I am not at all attempting to debate the historicity of the resurrection—quite the opposite. Instead, I am arguing that each of the Son of Man sayings as they relate to the resurrection serve a purpose and have a function within the tragic narrative of Mark. I am in no way suggesting that the vindication of Jesus and his future return are fictitious, rather, I am suggesting that Mark's telling of the story fits within the tragic paradigm.

The Tragic Son of Man

this for two reasons. The first is that Jesus' death signals the tearing of the curtain that separates the holy of holies from the rest of the temple in 15:38. The second is that we have little narrative concerning the resurrection and post-resurrection events. The reason why Mark chooses to end the narrative in 16:8—I accept the shorter ending—is because there is no need for any more information. This is troubling to many because it is expected that Jesus appear to his disciples much like he does in Matthew, Luke, and John. Mark, however, does not need a longer ending because the major purpose of the story has already been fulfilled.

The Son of Man sayings that make up Group C begin in 8:38 with a warning, for anyone who is ashamed of the Son of Man in the current context, that the Son of Man will be ashamed of him or her during a time of future vindication. The sayings found in 9:9 and 9:31 are concerned with Jesus' actual resurrection, while 13:26 and 14:62 are concerned with Jesus being imbued with power and glory—presumably after the resurrection. The obvious question, again, is why Jesus needs to make use of the title here instead of simply using a personal pronoun. This question has plagued theologians and historians alike, even leading some to question whether Jesus is referring to himself or to another figure instead.

I think that Jesus is referring to himself in these situations, and, according to our tragic paradigm, he has to be. I have thus far understood the Son of Man sayings in Mark's Gospel to be Jesus' attempt at avoiding self-designation, in the attempt to keep his position separate from the temple's in tragic *Collision*. As argued, he must continue to do this in order to dissolve the position that the temple occupies. This is signified not only by Jesus' gnomic use of the title Son of Man, but also by the many times when Jesus demands secrecy from those who might recognize his true self as the Son of God and the Messiah. The sayings in group C are an extension of this and, quite apart from their historicity, function as narrative elements that foretell the end of the tragic *Collision*. Yet, they continue to function within their guise as an avoidance of self-designation, and Jesus is careful to never yield to the temptation of crossing over into the position that the temple occupies. Instead, he signals the end of the temple's regime while at the same time warning anyone else who attempts to occupy a similar position that their violations will be judged. We can then most likely interpret Jesus' words in 14:62 as precisely that: a warning. Not only does Jesus corroborate his prior statements concerning the temple's coming invalidation, but he finally admits who he really is in such a way as to seal his own death (14:64). In addition, Jesus' use of the title here indicates that the temple and religious leaders do not judge him, but that he transcends their judgment. Thus, in one simple and concluding statement, Jesus brings to an end the *Collision* that he had so eagerly engaged in throughout the entire Gospel.

CONCLUSIONS

This chapter has had three goals. The first was to provide a survey—albeit a rather brief survey considering the vast number of writings that are concerned with the Son of Man sayings—of the various positions concerning the Son of Man "problem" in New Testament studies.

The second goal of this chapter has been to examine the Son of Man sayings in Mark's Gospel under the paradigm of tragic *Collision*. As defined in chapter 3, tragic *Collision* dictates that two equally justified powers come into conflict with one another, thus making the story essentially tragic. The result of such conflict is the "cancelling out" of both parties, but not before one destroys the other. This means that Jesus is pitted against his opponent—argued in an earlier chapter to be the temple—and he acts in such a way as to subvert its existence and purpose. The Son of Man sayings, as an avoidance of self-designation, serve as a guise by which Jesus can challenge the temple on a variety of issues without crossing over into the position that the temple occupies. If Jesus self-identifies as the Son of God or the Messiah, the story ceases to be tragic and it then becomes a story of justice or sadness.

The third endeavor of this chapter has been to categorize the Son of Man sayings into three categories which I labelled simply as groups A, B, and C. The sayings found in each respective group appear equally as Son of Man sayings, yet they function quite differently from one another within the narrative. Group A signals occasions when Jesus challenges a number of interpretive issues concerning the law and engages with the religious leaders concerning those interpretations. Group B emphasizes Jesus' suffering, something that must take place within the tragic paradigm. Group C emphasizes those sayings that involve future vindication and serve to signal the end of the tragic *Collision*.

7

Final Conclusions Concerning Mark's Genre
The Tragic Christ

THE QUESTION OF GENRE is important for Synoptic Gospel studies, and this monograph has attempted to answer this question by suggesting that Mark's Gospel was written in the form of Greek tragedy. This thesis runs contrary to the argument of many scholars who suggest that the Synoptic Gospels were written as biographies of Jesus' life. With regard to Mark, this simply cannot explain the number of historical anomalies that appear. The appropriate step forward is to recognize that historical approaches to the Gospel of Mark can only be buttressed by arguments from silence.

One such example of an anomaly that became a prominent feature of this study, was the motif of secrecy that occurs at several points throughout Mark's narrative. This motif, termed "the Messianic Secret" by Wrede in 1901, sought to explain Mark's attempt to account for a lack of messianic claims during Jesus' ministry. It is alleged that Mark created a secrecy motif out of an attempt, on his part, to center the resurrection as the most prominent proclamation of Jesus' identity as Messiah. As was noted in chapter 4, this is problematic for two reasons. The first, is that it assumes a historical motive for Mark's secrecy motif. Wrede's argument that Mark had to create a secrecy motif in order explain the lack of messianic self-identification in Jesus' ministry is an argument from silence, since Wrede cannot know what the Gospel

Final Conclusions Concerning Mark's Genre

writer was thinking with regard to this motive. In other words, we have no way of testing whether there is a discrepancy between Mark and the historical Jesus' potential use of a secrecy motif—all we have, for better or worse, is Mark's Gospel as it appears. To go outside of the text in order to account for motives is to make a case on the basis of evidence to which no one has access.

A second problem concerns the title that Wrede chose for the secrecy motif. Labelling the motif "the Messianic Secret" is a misnomer since the secrecy motif does not always allude to Jesus' messianic status. I noted that Wrede is correct, insofar as he identified a secrecy motif, but the commands for secrecy, as they pertain to parables and healing miracles, may lead scholars to make false assumptions regarding the purpose of said parables and healing miracles.

For more than a century, Wrede's attention to a secrecy motif has been accepted and rejected with fleeting moments of agreement amongst scholars concerning what Mark—or perhaps Jesus—intended. This study has attempted to address this discussion from the point of view that Mark's Gospel was written as a Greek tragedy and, as a Greek tragedy, the motif of secrecy is readily explained by way of tragic plot. By suggesting that Mark's Gospel fits the genre of Greek tragedy, I have separated the Gospel from the traditional historical methods of interpretation. Instead, by interpreting Mark from a literary standpoint, I have concluded that the historical anomalies may not be anomalies after all.

By removing Mark from the constraints of historical methodologies, questions concerning plot, Jesus' use of the title "Son of Man," healing miracles, gnomic parables, and constant conflict can be more readily explained. If we suggest that the features of Mark's Gospel are historical, we are often faced with more problems than solutions. This is, perhaps, the primary argument against Mark's Gospel being a biography: if Mark were writing a biography, surely, he would have portrayed Jesus in a much less ambiguous manner. Likewise, it seems unlikely that a biography would contain a story about a Son of God and Messiah who failed to convince anyone of his person and his mission—save, perhaps, the demons and a centurion. Reading Mark as a

Greek tragedy makes these features of Mark much less ambiguous, and offers a reason for why certain things, like a secrecy motif, are needed.

Throughout this study, I have identified three major elements, or characteristics, of tragedy that are prevalent within most, if not all, works of this genre. The first, is that the protagonist must be of elevated character. This is what Aristotle called a *spoudean* protagonist: a character who is better, in every respect, than we are. The second, is that tragedy always involves some type of suffering and death and these can, at times, also be paired with claims of resurrection and immortality. The third is what Hegel called tragic *Collision*: a conflict between two independently justified positions. Being independently justified creates the tragic *pathos* that the audience member experiences while viewing or reading the narrative. This is illustrated by Jesus' continual conflict with the religious authorities who represent Jesus' main opponent: the temple and its social and religious *ethos*.

In order to fully explain how each of these three tragic elements function within Mark's Gospel, I divided this study into six chapters. The first chapter was an attempt to summarize and evaluate the major scholarly works that have already compared Mark's Gospel with the genre of tragedy. What was found is that most previous studies have hinged their discussion of Mark as tragedy on Aristotle's *Poetics*, a position from which I wish to separate myself.

A second chapter built upon the first by surveying a large number of theories concerning how tragedy works. I began with Plato and Aristotle, who wrote in the fourth century BCE, and concluded with twentieth-century theorists. At a minimum, this survey reveals how important tragedy has been throughout two thousand years of literary analysis. It also reveals a common misconception concerning tragedy: Aristotle's theory of tragedy found in his *Poetics* was simply a description of tragedy and this description was not the major theory of tragedy that was being utilized when Mark's Gospel was composed. This means that most New Testament scholarship that attempts to compare Mark and tragedy, by way of Aristotle, is misled with regard to the starting point of their argumentation.

My third chapter was an attempt to elucidate the elements of tragedy found in Mark's Gospel. What was found is that Mark's

Final Conclusions Concerning Mark's Genre

Gospel contains three major elements that are prevalent to all tragedy: a *spoudean* protagonist, suffering and death, and tragic conflict or *Collision*. This chapter also made an observation as to the function of tragedy within society. Tragedies are usually written at a time of great social and political turmoil, and the *spoudean* protagonist serves as an expression of a cure for that turmoil. Mark's Gospel then fits well within this observation, especially when one considers the continual conflict between Christianity and the empire as well as between Christianity and Judaism.

A fourth chapter dealt primarily with the motif of secrecy within tragic plot, doing so in three steps. The first step was to explain how secrecy works and here I examined a number of tragedies in which this motif is clearly illustrated. The most prominent was, perhaps, the *Bacchae*, in which Dionysus purposefully conceals his identity as the son of god in order to bring about proper worship of himself in Thebes. Dionysus then reveals his identity through a number of miracles and actions. Another example was found in the *Seven Against Thebes*, in which hiddenness and recognition are used to further the plot and create a sense of *pathos*. The second step to elucidating how the motif of secrecy works within tragic plot was to discuss and summarize Wrede's "Messianic Secret," as well as a number of scholarly opinions concerning it. It was shown that a historical approach to interpreting the Gospels is, and has been, wrought with false assumptions as well as misleading observations concerning the plot of Mark's Gospel. Instead, I suggested that Mark, and especially his motif of secrecy, should be interpreted in light of tragic secrecy and recognition. The third step to elucidating how the motif of secrecy works within tragic plot was to explain how parables, exorcisms, and various recognition scenes validate my theory that Mark was written as a tragedy. Each of these things is meant to conceal Jesus' identity as the Son of God until his crucifixion and resurrection. This is not a historical phenomenon, but rather a tragic one according to which Jesus must remain concealed in message and deed, in order for the plot to remain tragic. If Jesus is revealed too quickly, the plot no longer has force and its sense of meaning is lost.

The fifth chapter of this study explains how Jesus' healing miracles fit within the paradigm of tragic *Collision*. Jesus heals many people as a *spoudean* protagonist, but he does so in tension with the temple and its traditions. When Jesus heals, he often places himself into a compromising position with regard to the temple's purity laws. Jesus seems unaffected by the continual persecution that he receives from the religious leaders for his perceived impurity, which reveals his discontent with the current religious *ethos* of the temple and its practitioners. By becoming impure, Jesus poses a direct challenge to this *ethos*, even totally rendering the temple and its laws obsolete in the process.

The sixth, and final chapter of this study, discusses Jesus' gnomic use of the title "Son of Man" in Mark's Gospel. It analyzes each of the usages of the "Son of Man" title and identifies the role of conflict within each. What was found is that Jesus often uses the title to avoid self-designation as Messiah or some other powerful figure. In doing so, Jesus is able to retain his hiddenness and continue the plot. In other words, if Jesus is revealed too early as the Son of God or Messiah, he would not be crucified because, presumably, everyone would hail him as such and the crucifixion and resurrection would not follow. Instead, the clever use of a title that helped Jesus avoid a divine self-designation serves to propel the plot towards its climactic end, which is the crucifixion and resurrection.

In sum, reading Mark's Gospel as a tragedy is an important step forward in the discussion of the Gospel genre. Not only does it offer explanations for several anomalies which have caused great confusion for hundreds of years, it also intervenes into the discussion of genre in such a way that we can no longer assume that Mark was written as an ancient biography. Mark's Gospel is not an account of Jesus' life. It is, instead, interested in illustrating the ways in which a religious paradigm shift occurred in first-century Israel. No longer the dominating facet of religion and culture for the Jews, the temple was rendered obsolete by Jesus' actions. In doing so, Jesus released God from the confines of a sacred space in the temple into a fluid relationship with humanity that encompasses all people regardless of status, sex, or race. This is an extremely important lesson that Mark wants to teach, and the genre of tragedy affords him the capacity to do so.

Bibliography

Achtemeier, Paul J. "Miracles and the Historical Jesus: Mark 9:14-29." *CBQ* 37 (1975) 471-91.
Adams, Edward. "The Coming of the Son of Man in Mark's Gospel." *TynBul* 56.2 (2005) 39-61.
Ahl, Frederick. *Seneca: Three Tragedies.* Ithaca: Cornell University Press, 1986.
Albertz, Martin. *Die synoptischen Streitgesprache.* Berlin: Trowitzsch und Sohn, 1919.
Alexander, Joseph Addison. *The Gospel According to Mark.* Grand Rapids: Baker, 1980.
Arnim, Hans Friedrich August von. *Leben und Werke des Dio von Prusa: mit einer Einleitung: Sophistik, Rhetorik, Philosophie in ihrem Kampf um die Jugendbildung.* Hildesheim: Georg Olms, 2004.
Aune, David E. "The Problem of the Messianic Secret." *NovT* 11 (1970) 1-31.
Barth, Fritz. *Die Hauptprobleme des Lebens Jesu.* Gütersloh: C. Bertelsmann, 1907.
Bauckham, Richard. "The Son of Man: 'A Man in my Position' or 'Someone'?" *JSNT* 23 (1985) 23-33.
Beach, Curtis. *The Gospel of Mark: Its Making and Meaning.* New York: Harper & Row, 1959.
Beasley-Murray, G. R. *Jesus and the Future: An Examination of the Criticism of The Eschatological Discourse, Mark 13, with Special Reference to the Little Apocalypse Theory.* London: MacMillian, 1954.
———. *Jesus and the Kingdom of God.* Grand Rapids: Eerdmans, 1986.
Beavis, Mary Ann. *Mark.* Grand Rapids: Baker, 2011.
Beck, Robert R. *Nonviolent Story: Narrative Conflict Resolution in the Gospel of Mark.* Maryknoll, NY: Orbis, 1996.
Bekker, Immanuel. *Anecdota Graeca II.* Berlin: Apud G. C. Nauckium, 1816.
Best, Ernest. *The Temptation and the Passion: The Markan Soteriology.* SNTSMS 2. Cambridge: Cambridge University Press, 1965.

Bibliography

Betz, Hans Dieter. "Jesus as Divine Man." In *Jesus and the Historian*, edited by F. T. Trotter, 114–33. Philadelphia: Westminster, 1968.

Bieber, Margarete. *The History of the Greek and Roman Theater*. Princeton: Princeton University Press, 1939.

Bilezikian, Gilbert. *The Liberated Gospel: A Comparison of the Gospel of Mark and Greek Tragedy*. Eugene, OR: Wipf & Stock, 1977.

Blackburn Sr., Barry L. "Jesus' Healing of a Paralyzed Man (Mark 2.1–12): A Quadrigal Reading." *Leaven* 19 (2011) 43–48.

Blevins, James L. "The Messianic Secret in Markan Research, 1901–1976." ThD diss., Southern Baptist Theological Seminary, 1965.

———. "Seventy-Two Years of the Messianic Secret: A Review Article." *PRSt* 2 (1975) 192–200.

Blomberg, Craig L. *Interpreting the Parables*. 2nd ed. Downers Grove, IL: InterVarsity, 2012.

Boring, M. Eugene. *Mark: A Commentary*. London: Westminster John Knox, 2006.

Bowie, E. L. "Apollonius of Tyana: Tradition and Reality." *ANRW* 2.16.2 (1978) 1652–99.

Boyle, A. J. *Octavia: Attributed to Seneca*. Oxford: Oxford University Press, 2008.

———. *Roman Tragedy*. London: Routledge, 2006.

Bradley, Andrew Cecil. "Hegel's Theory of Tragedy." In *Criticism: The Foundations of Modern Literary Judgment*, edited by Mark Schorer et al., 55–65. New York: Harcourt, Brace & World Inc., 1948.

Brant, Jo-Ann. *Dialogue and Drama: Elements of Greek Tragedy in the Fourth Gospel*. Peabody, MA: Hendrickson, 2004.

———. *John*. Paideia Commentaries on the New Testament. Grand Rapids: Baker, 2011.

Brink, C. O. *Horace on Poetry*. 3 Vols. Cambridge: Cambridge University Press, 1971.

Broadhead, Edwin K. *Prophet, Son, Messiah: Narrative Form and Function of Mark 14–16*. JSNTSup 97. Sheffield: Sheffield Academic Press, 1994.

———. *Teaching with Authority: Miracles and Christology in the Gospel of Mark*. JSNTSup 74. Sheffield: Sheffield Academic Press, 1992.

Brown, Colin. "Synoptic Miracle Stories: A Jewish Religious and Social Setting." *Foundations and Facets Forum* 2.4 (1986) 55–76.

Bultmann, Rudolf. *The History of the Synoptic Tradition*. Oxford: Blackwell, 1968.

———. *Theology of the New Testament*. Translated by Kendrick Grobel. New York: Charles Scribner's Sons, 1951.

Burch, Ernest W. "Tragic Action in the Second Gospel: A Study in the Narrative of Mark." *JR* 11 (1931) 346–58.

Bibliography

Burkill, T. A. *Mysterious Revelation: An Examination of the Philosophy of St. Mark's Gospel.* Ithica: Cornell University Press, 1963.

Burridge, Richard. *What are the Gospels? A Comparison with Greco-Roman Biography.* 2nd ed. Grand Rapids: Eerdmans, 2004.

Cairns, D. S. *The Faith that Rebels: A Re-examination of the Miracles of Jesus.* London: SCM, 1933.

Campbell, Joseph. *The Hero with a Thousand Faces.* Novato, CA: New World Library, 2008.

Caragounis, Chrys C. *The Son of Man: Vision and Interpretation.* Eugene, OR: Wipf & Stock, 2011.

Carpenter, J. Estlin. *The First Three Gospels: Their Origin and Relations.* London: Sunday School Association, 1890.

Cartledge, Paul. "'Deep Plays': Theatre as Process in Greek Civic Life." In *Greek Tragedy*, edited by P. E. Easterling, 3–35. Cambridge: Cambridge University Press, 1997.

Casey, Maurice. *The Solution to the 'Son of Man' Problem.* LNTS 343. London: T. & T. Clark, 2009.

Cherbonnier, Edmond. "Biblical Faith and the Idea of tragedy." In *The Tragic Vision and the Christian Faith*, edited by Nathan A. Scott Jr., 23–55. New York: Association, 1957.

Cole, R. Alan. *The Gospel According to St. Mark: An Introduction and Commentary.* Leicester: InterVarsity, 1961.

Collins, Adela Yarbro. *Mark.* Hermeneia. Minneapolis: Fortress, 2007.

———. "The Origin of the Designation of Jesus as the 'Son of Man.'" *HTR* 80 (1987) 391–401.

Conybeare, F. C. *Philostratus: The Life of Apollonius of Tyana.* 2 vols. LCL 16–17. Cambridge: Harvard University Press, 1912.

Conzelmann, Hans. "Gegenwart und Zukunft in der synoptischen Tradition." *ZTK* 54 (1957) 277–96.

———. *An Outline of the Theology of the New Testament.* Translated by John Bowden. London: SCM, 1969.

Cook, Michael J. *Mark's Treatment of the Jewish Leaders.* NovTSup 51. Leiden: Brill, 1978.

Crossan, John Dominic. *In Parables: The Challenge of the Historical Jesus.* New York: Harper & Row, 1973.

Danker, Frederick W. "The Demonic Secret in Mark: A Re-examination of the Cry of Dereliction (15.34)." *ZNW* 61 (1970) 48–69.

Davies, W. D., and Dale C. Allison. *Matthew: A Shorter Commentary.* London: T. & T. Clark, 2004.

Dawson, Audrey. *Healing, Weakness and Power: Perspectives on Healing in the Writings of Mark, Luke and Paul.* Milton Keynes: Paternoster, 2008.

Bibliography

Dewey, Joanna. "The Literary Structure of the Controversy Stories in Mark 2:1—3:6." *JBL* 92 (1973) 394–401.

Dibelius, Martin. *From Tradition to Gospel*. London: James Clarke, 1971.

———. *Gospel Criticism and Christology*. London: Ivor, Nicholson & Watson, 1935.

Dodd, C. H. *The Parables of the Kingdom*. New York: Charles Scribner's Sons, 1936.

Dostal, Robert J. "Introduction." In *A Cambridge Companion to Gadamer*, edited by Robert J. Dostal, 1–12. Cambridge: Cambridge University Press, 2002.

Duff, John Wright. *A Literary History of Rome*. London: Bern, 1953.

Dunn, J. D. G. "The Messianic Secret in Mark." *TynBul* 21 (1970) 92–117.

Edwards, James R. "Markan Sandwiches: The Significance of Interpolations in Markan Narratives." *NovT* 31 (1989) 193–216.

Else, Gerald. *Aristotle's Poetics: The Argument*. Cambridge: Harvard University Press, 1963.

English, Donald. *The Message of Mark: The Mystery of Faith*. Downers Grove, IL: InterVarsity, 1992.

Episcopius. *Notae breves in xxiv. priora captia Matthaei*. In vol. 2 of *Opera theologica* (Amsterdam: Blaev, 1650).

Evans, Craig A. *Jesus and His Contemporaries: Comparative Studies*. Leiden: Brill, 2001.

———. *Mark 8:27—16:20*. WBC 34a. Nashville: Thomas Nelson, 2001.

———. "Mark's Incipit and the Priene Calendar Inscription: From Jewish Gospel to Greco-Roman Gospel." *JGRChJ* 1 (2000) 67–81.

———. "The Messiah in the Old and New Testaments: A Response." In *The messiah in the Old and New Testaments*, edited by Stanley E. Porter, 230–48. Grand Rapids: Eerdmans, 2007.

———. "Messianic Hopes and Messianic Figures in Late Antiquity." *JGRChJ* 3 (2006) 9–40.

Eve, Eric. *The Jewish Context of Jesus' Miracles*. JSNTSup 231. New York: Sheffield Academic, 2002.

Fieberg, Paul. *Jüdische Wundergeschichten des neutestamentlichen Zeitalters*. Tübingen: Mohr Siebeck, 1911.

Fitzmyer, Joseph. "The New Testament Title 'Son of Man' Philologically Considered." In *A Wandering Aramean: Collected Aramaic Essays*, 143–61. SBLMS 25. Missoula, MT: Scholars Press, 1979.

Fowler, Robert M. *Let the Reader Understand: Reader-Response Criticism and the Gospel of Mark*. Harrisburg, PA: Trinity, 2001.

France, R. T. *Jesus and the Old Testament: His Application of the Old Testament Passages to Himself and His Mission*. Vancouver: Regent College Publishing, 1998.

Bibliography

Frickenschmidt, Dirk. *Evangelium als Biographie: Die vier Evangelien im Rahmen antiker Erzählkunst*. Tügingen: Francke, 1997.
Frye, Northrup. *Anatomy of Criticism: Four Essays*. Princeton: Princeton University Press, 1957.
Funaioli, Gino. *Grammaticae Romanae Fragmenta*. Leipzig: Teubner, 1907.
Gadamer, Hans-Georg. *Truth and Method*. Translated by Joel Weinsheimer and Donald G. Marshall. London: Continuum, 1975.
Gaiser, Frederick J. "In Touch with Jesus: Healing in Mark 5:21–43." *WW* 30 (2010) 5–15.
Gallagher, Eugene V. *Divine Man or Magician? Celsus and Origen on Jesus*. SBLDS 64. Chico, CA: Scholars, 1982.
Gellrich, Michelle. *Tragedy and Theory: The Problem and Conflict Since Aristotle*. Princeton: Princeton University Press, 1988.
Gowler, David. *What are They Saying About The Parables?* New York: Paulist, 2000.
Greenspan, Daniel. "Poetics: The Rebirth of Tragedy at the End of Modernity." In *Kierkegaard and the Greek World Tome II: Aristotle and Other Greek Authors*, edited by Jon Stewart and Katalin Nun, 59–80. Surrey: Ashgate, 2010.
Grondin, Jean. "Gadamer's Basic Understanding of Understanding." In *A Cambridge Companion to Gadamer*, edited by Robert J. Dostal, 36–51. Cambridge: Cambridge University Press, 2002.
Guelich, Robert A. *Mark 1—8:26*. WBC 34a. Nashville: Thomas Nelson, 1989.
Gundry, Robert H. *Mark: A Commentary on His Apology for the Cross*. Grand Rapids: Eerdmans, 1993.
Guttmann, Alexander. "The Significance of Miracles for Talmudic Judaism." *HUCA* 20 (1947) 363–406.
Halliwell, Stephen. "Introduction." In *Aristotle XXIII*. LCL 199. Cambridge: Harvard University Press, 1995.
Hare, Douglas R. A. *Mark*. Louisville, KY: Westminster John Knox, 1996.
———. *The Son of Man Tradition*. Minneapolis: Fortress, 1990.
Harris, B. F. "Apollonius of Tyana: Fact or Fiction?" *JRH* 5 (1969) 189–99.
Hay, Lewis S. "Mark's Use of the Messianic Secret." *JAAR* 35 (1967) 16–27.
———. "The Son of Man in Mark 2:10 and 2:28." *JBL* 89 (1970) 69–75.
Hegel, G. W. F. *Aesthetics: Lectures on Fine Art*. Translated by T. M. Knox. 3 vols. Oxford: Clarendon, 1975.
———. *Early Theological Writings*. Translated by T. M. Knox. Philadelphia: University of Pennsylvania Press, 1971.
———. *Lectures on the History of Philosophy*. Translated by E. S. Haldane and Frances H. Simson. 3 vols. London: Rutledge and Keegan Paul, 1892.

———. *Lectures on the Philosophy of History*. Translated by J. Sibree. London: Henry G. Bohn, 1857.

———. *The Philosophy of Fine Art*. Translated by F. P. B. Osmaston. 4 vols. New York: Hacker Art Books, 1975.

Hendrick, Charles W. "The Role of 'Summary Statements' in the Composition of the Gospel of Mark: A Dialogue with Karl Schmidt and Norman Perrin." *NovT* 26 (1984) 289–311.

Hendriksen, William. *New Testament Commentary: Exposition of the Gospel According to Mark*. Grand Rapids: Baker, 1975.

Herzog, William R., II. *Parables as Subversive Speech: Jesus as Pedagogue of the Oppressed*. Louisville, KY: Westminster John Knox, 1994.

Hiebert, D. Edmond. *Mark: A Portrait of the Servant*. Chicago: Moody, 1974.

Hobbes, Thomas. *Leviathan*, edited by Richard Tuck. Cambridge: Cambridge University Press, 1996.

Hoekstra, Sytse. *De benaming "De Zoon des Menschen": Een historisch-Kritisch onderzoek*. Amsterdam: P. N. Van Kampen, 1866.

Hofius, Otfried. "Jesu Zuspruch der Sündenvergebung: Exegetische Erwägungen zu Mk 2,5b." In *Neutestamentliche Studien*, 38–56. WUNT 132. Tübingen: Mohr Siebeck, 2000.

Holladay, Carl H. *Theios Aner in Hellenistic Judaism: A Critique of the Use of This Category in New Testament Christology*. SBLDS 40. Atlanta: Society of Biblical Literature, 1977.

Hooker, Morna D. *The Gospel According to Saint Mark*. London: Continuum, 2001.

———. "Is the Son of Man Problem Really Insoluble?" In *Text and Interpretation: Studies in the New Testament Presented to Matthew Black*, edited by Ernest Best, 155–68. Cambridge: Cambridge University Press, 1979.

———. "Mark's Parables of the Kingdom." In *The Challenge of Jesus' Parables*, edited by Richard N. Longenecker, 79–101. Grand Rapids: Eerdmans, 2000.

———. *The Son of Man in Mark*. Montreal: McGill University Press, 1967.

Hunter, Archibald M. *The Gospel According to Saint Mark*. London: SCM, 1948.

———. *The Works and the Words of Jesus*. London: SCM, 1973.

Hunter, Richard, and Donald Russell. *Plutarch: How to Study Poetry—De Audiendis Poetis*. Cambridge: Cambridge University Press, 2011.

Hurtado, Larry W. *Mark*. Grand Rapids: Baker, 1989.

Hurtado, Larry W., and Paul I. Owen, eds. *Who is this Son of Man? The Latest Scholarship on a Puzzling Expression of the Historical Jesus*. LNTS 390. London: T. & T. Clark, 2011.

Bibliography

Janko, Richard. *Aristotle on Comedy: Towards a Reconstruction of Poetics II.* London: Duckworth, 1984.
Jaspers, Karl. *Tragedy is Not Enough.* Translated by H. A. T. Reiche et al. Boston: Beacon, 1952.
Jay, Jeff. *The Tragic in Mark.* HUT 66. Tübingen: Mohr Siebeck, 2014.
Jeremias, Joachim. *The Parables of Jesus.* 2nd ed. New York: Charles Scribner's Sons, 1972.
Johansson, Daniel. "Jesus and God in the Gospel of Mark: Unity and Distinction." PhD diss., University of Edinburgh, 2011.
Jones, John. *On Aristotle and Greek Tragedy.* New York: Oxford University Press, 1962.
Jones, Peter Rhea. *The Teaching of the Parables.* Nashville: Broadman, 1982.
Juel, Donald H. *A Master of Surprise: Mark Interpreted.* Minneapolis, MN: Augsburg Fortress, 1994.
Jülicher, Adolf. *Die Gleichnisreden Jesu.* Freiburg: J. C. B. Mohr, 1888.
Kallas, James. *The Significance of the Synoptic Miracles.* London: SPCK, 1961.
Kaufmann, Walter, ed. *Basic Writings of Nietzsche.* New York: The Modern Library, 2000.
Kee, Howard Clark. *Community of the New Age: Studies in Mark's Gospel.* Philadelphia: Westminster, 1977.
Keener, Craig S. "*Otho*: A Targeted Comparison of Suetonius's Biography and Tactius's *History*, with Implications for the Gospels' Historical Reliability." *BBR* 21 (2011) 331–56.
Keil, H. *Grammatici Latini.* 3 Vols. Hildesheim: Georg Olms, 1961.
Kelly, H. A. "Aristotle—Averroes—Alemannus on Tragedy: The Influence of the *Poetics* on the Latin Middle Ages." *Via* 10 (1979) 161–209.
———. *Ideas and Forms of Tragedy from Aristotle to the Middle Ages.* Cambridge: Cambridge University Press, 1993.
Kennedy, George A. "Classical and Christian Source Criticism." In *The Relationships Among the Gospels: An Interdisciplinary Dialogue*, edited by William O. Walker Jr., 125–55. San Antonio: Trinity University Press, 1978.
Kierkegaard, Søren. *Either/Or, A Fragment of Life.* Translated by Victor Eremita. London: Penguin, 1992.
———. *Fear and Trembling/The Sickness Unto Death.* Translated by Walter Lowrie. Princeton: Princeton University Press, 2013.
Kim, Tae Hun. "The Anarthrous *huios theou* in Mark 15.39 and the Roman Imperial Cult." *Bib* 79 (1998) 221–41.
Kingsbury, Jack Dean. *The Christology of Mark's Gospel.* Philadelphia: Fortress, 1983.
———. "The 'Divine Man' as the Key to Mark's Christology—The End of an Era?" *Int* 35 (1981) 243–57.

Bibliography

Kirchhevel, Gordon D. "The 'Son of Man' Passages in Mark." *BBR* 9 (1999) 181–87.

Kistemaker, Simon. *The Parables: Understanding the Stories Jesus Told*. Grand Rapids: Baker, 1980.

Krook, Dorothea. *The Elements of Tragedy*. New Haven: Yale University Press, 1969.

Lane, William L. *The Gospel According to Mark*. Grand Rapids: Eerdmans, 1974.

Lang, Friedrich Gustav. "Kompositionsanalyse des Markusevangeliums." *ZTK* 74 (1977) 1–24.

Lattimore, Richmond. *Story Patterns in Greek Tragedy*. Ann Arbor, MI: University of Michigan Press, 1969.

Lausberg, Heinrich. *Handbuch der literarischen Rhetorik*. Band I. Munchen: Hueber, 1960.

Licona, Michael R. *Why Are there Differences in the Gospels? What We Can Learn from Ancient Biography*. Oxford: Oxford University Press, 2017.

Lightfoot, R. H. *The Gospel Message of Mark*. Oxford: Oxford University Press, 1962.

Linnemann, Eta. *Parables of Jesus: Introduction and Exposition*. London: SPCK, 1966.

Lohse, Eduard. *Mark's Witness to Jesus Christ*. WCB 3. London: Lutterworth, 1955.

Lucas, Frank L. *Tragedy: Serious Drama in Relation to Aristotle's "Poetics."* New York: MacMillan, 1958.

Lukaszewski, Albert A. "Issues Concerning the Aramaic behind ὁ υἱὸς τοῦ ἀνθρώπου: A Critical Review of Scholarship." In *Who is this 'Son of Man?' The Latest Scholarship on the Puzzling Expression of the Historical Jesus*, edited by Larry Hurtado and Paul L. Owen, 13–27. LNTS 390. London: T. & T. Clark, 2011.

MacDonald, Dennis R. *The Homeric Epics and the Gospel of Mark*. New Haven: Yale University Press, 2000.

Malbon, Elizabeth Struthers. "The Christology of Mark's Gospel: Narrative Christology and the Markan Jesus." In *Who Do You Say That I Am? Essays on Christology*, edited by Mark Allen Powell and David R. Bauer, 33–48. Westminster: John Knox Press, 1999.

Mann, C. S. *Mark*. AB 27. New York: Doubleday, 1986.

Manson, T. W. *The Teaching of Jesus: Studies in Form and Content*. Cambridge: Cambridge University Press, 1959.

Marcus, Joel. "Blanks and Gaps in the Markan Parable of the Sower." *BibInt* 5 (1997) 247–62.

Marrou, H. I. *A History of Education in Antiquity*. Translated by George Lamb. New York: Sheed and Ward, 1956.

Bibliography

Marshall, I. Howard. "Jesus as Messiah in Mark and Matthew." In *The Messiah in the Old and New Testaments*, edited by Stanley E. Porter, 117-43. Grand Rapids: Eerdmans, 2007.

Marxsen, Willi. *The Beginnings of Christology, Together with the Lord's Supper as a Christological Problem*. Translated by P. Achtemeier and L. Nieting. 1960. Philadelphia: Fortress, 1979.

———. *Mark the Evangelist*. Translated by J. Boyce et al. New York: Abingdon, 1969.

McMahon, Philip A. "On the Second Book of Aristotle's Poetics and the Source of Theophrastus' Definition of Tragedy." *HSCP* 28 (1917) 1-46.

———. "Seven Questions on Aristotelian Definitions of Tragedy and Comedy." *HSCP* 40 (1929) 97-198.

Menken, J. J. Maarten. "The Call of Blind Bartimaeus (Mark 19:46-52)." *HvTSt* 61 (2005) 273-90.

Messel, Nils. *Der Menschensohn in den Bilderreden des Henoch*. BZAW 35. Giessen: Töpelmann, 1922.

Michel, Laurence. "The Possibility of a Christian Tragedy." In *Tragedy: Modern Essays in Criticism*, edited by Laurence Michel and Richard B. Sewall, 210-33. Englewood Cliffs: Prentice-Hall, 1963.

Moloney, Francis J. *The Gospel of Mark: A Commentary*. Grand Rapids: Baker, 2002.

Moser, T. "Mark's Gospel—A Drama?" *TBT* 80 (1975) 528-33.

Murray, George G. "Greek Drama." In *EB* 7:582. Chicago: Benton, 1953.

Nadich, Judah. *Jewish Legends of the Second Commonwealth*. Philadelphia: Jewish Publication Society of America, 1983.

Nagy, Gregory. *The Ancient Greek Hero in 24 Hours*. Cambridge: The Belknap Press of Harvard University Press, 2013.

Neusner, Jacob. *A Life of Yoḥanan ben Zakkai (ca. 1-80 C. E.)*. StPB 6. Leiden: Brill, 1970.

Nietzsche, Friedrich. *The Birth of Tragedy*. In *Basic Writings of Nietzsche*, edited and translated by Walter Kaufmann, 15-144. New York: The Modern Library, 2000.

Oates, Whitney J., and Eugene O'Neill. *The Complete Greek Drama: All the Extant Tragedies of Aeschylus, Sophocles and Euripides, and the Comedies of Aristophanes and Menander, in a Variety of Translations*. 2 Vols. New York: Random House, 1938.

Paolucci, Anne. *Hegel On Tragedy*. Smynra, DE: Griffon, 2001.

Parris, David. "Metaphors, Cognitive Theory, and Jesus' Shortest Parable." In *Horizons in Hermeneutics: A Festschrift in Honor of Anthony C. Thiselton*, edited by Stanley E. Porter and Matthew R. Malcolm, 148-174. Grand Rapids: Eerdmans, 2013.

Bibliography

Pelling, Christopher. *Greek Tragedy and the Historian*. Oxford: Clarendon, 1997.

Pentecost, J. Dwight. *The Parables of Jesus*. Grand Rapids: Zondervan, 1982.

Perrin, Norman. *Christology and a Modern Pilgrimage: A Discussion with Norman Perrin*, edited by H. D. Betz. Claremont: Society of Biblical Literature, 1971.

———. *What is Redaction Criticism?* London: SPCK, 1970.

Polhill, John B. "Perspectives on the Miracle Stories." *RevExp* 74 (1977) 389–99.

Porter, Stanley E. "Jesus and Resurrection." In *Jesus in Continuum*, edited by Tom Holmén, 323–54. WUNT 289. Tübingen: Mohr Siebeck, 2012.

———. "Paul Confronts Caesar with the Good News." In *Empire in the New Testament*, edited by Stanley E. Porter and Cynthia Long Westfall, 164–97. McMaster New Testament Studies Series 10. Eugene, OR: Pickwick, 2011.

Radford, Robert T. *Cicero: A Study in the Origins of Republican Philosophy*. New York: Rodopi, 2002.

Räisänen, Heikki. *The 'Messianic Secret' in Mark*. Translated by Christopher Tuckett. Edinburgh: T. & T. Clark, 1990.

Reitzenstein, Richard. *Hellenistic Mystery-Religions: Their Basic Ideas and Significance*. Translated by John E. Steeley. Pittsburgh: Pickwick, 1978.

Reville, Albert. *Jésus De Nazareth: Études Critiques sur les Antécédents de L'Histoire Évangélique et la Vie de Jésus*. Paris: Libraire Fischbacher, 1897.

Rhoads, David, et al. *Mark as Story: An Introduction to the Narrative of a Gospel*. Minneapolis: Fortress, 1999.

Ricoeur, Paul. "Forward." In *The Book of Daniel*, by André Lacocque, xv–xxiii. Montreal: McGill University Press, 1967.

Robbins, Vernon K. "The Healing of Blind Bartimaeus (10:46–52) in the Marcan Theology." *JBL* 92 (1973) 224–43.

———. *New Boundaries in Old Territory: Form and Social Rhetoric in Mark*. Emory Studies in Early Christianity 3. New York: Peter Lang, 1994.

———. Review of *The Liberated Gospel: A Comparison of the Gospel of Mark and Greek Tragedy*, by Gilbert Bilezikian. *CBQ* 41 (1979) 480–81.

Robinson, James M. "On the *Gattung* of Mark (and John)." In *Jesus and Man's Hope*, edited by David G. Buttrick, 1:99–129. 2 vols. Pittsburgh: Pittsburgh Theological Seminary, 1970.

———. *The Problem of History in Mark*. SBT 21. London: SCM, 1957.

Rose, Valentinus. *Aristotelis qui Ferebantur Liborum*. BSGRT. Lipsae: Aedibus B.G. Teubneri, 1886.

Rosenmeyer, Thomas G. *The Masks of Tragedy: Essays on Six Greek Dramas*. Austin: University of Texas Press, 1963.

Ross, W. D. *Aristotelis Fragmenta Selecta*. Oxford: Clarendon, 1955.

Bibliography

Ruprecht Jr., Louis A. "Mark's Tragic Vision: Gethsemane." *RL* (1992) 1–25.
Russell, D. A., and Michael Winterbottom, eds. *Classical Literary Criticism*. Oxford: Oxford University Press, 1972.
Rutherford, R. B. *Greek Tragic Style: Form, Language and Interpretation*. Cambridge: Cambridge University Press, 2012.
Safrai, Shmuel. "The Teaching of the Pietists in Mishnaic Literature." *JJS* 16 (1965) 15–33.
Sanday, William. *The Life of Christ in Recent Research*. Oxford: Clarendon, 1907.
Sandys, John Edwin. *A History of Classical Scholarship: From the Sixth Century B. C. to the End of the Middle Ages*. 2 vols. Cambridge: Cambridge University Press, 1906.
Schanz, Martin. *Geschichte der Römischen Literatur*. München: Beck'sche, 1927.
Schmiedel, Otto. *Die Hauptprobleme der Leben-Jesu-Forschung*. Tübingen: J. C. B. Mohr, 1906.
Schwartz, Elias. "The Possibilities of Christian Tragedy." *College English* (1960) 208–13.
Schweitzer, Albert. *The Quest of the Historical Jesus*. Translated by William Montgomery. New York: MacMillan, 1961.
Scourer, Emil. *Das messianische Selbstbewusstsein Jesu Christ*. Göttingen: Vandenhoeck & Ruprecht, 1903.
Segal, Charles. *Dionysiac Poetics and Euripides' Bacchae*. Princeton: Princeton University Press, 1982.
Selvidge, Maria J. "Mark 5:25–34 and Leviticus 15:19–20: A Reaction to Restrictive Purity Regulations." *JBL* 103 (1984) 619–23.
Shuler, Philip L. *A Genre for the Gospel: The Biographical Character of Matthew*. Philadelphia: Fortress, 1982.
Slusser, Dorothy M. "The Healing Narratives in Mark." *ChrCent* (1970) 597–99.
Smith, Morton. "Prolegomena to a Discussion of Aretalogies, Divine Men, the Gospels and Jesus." *JBL* 90 (1971) 174–99.
Smith, Stephen H. "A Divine Tragedy: Some Observations on the Dramatic Structure of Mark's Gospel." *NovT* 37 (1995) 209–31.
Soden, Hermann von. *Die wichtigsten Fragen im Leben Jesu*. Leipzig: J. C. Hinrichs'sche, 1904.
Sorrentino, Paul. "God's Cosmic Drama: Christian Tragedy in the Puritan Vision of Life." *Sound* 63 (1980) 432–50.
Standaert, B. *L'Evangile selon Marc: Composition et genre littéraire*. Nijmegen: Stichting Studentenpers, 1978.

Bibliography

Steele, Greg. "The Theology of Hiddenness in the Gospel of Mark: An Exploration of the Messianic Secret and Corollaries." *ResQ* 3 (2012) 169–85.

Stein, Robert H. *An Introduction to the Parables of Jesus*. Philadelphia: Westminster, 1981.

Stendahl, Brita K. *Søren Kierkegaard*. Boston: Twayne, 1976.

Stern, David. *Parables in Midrash: Narrative Exegesis in Rabbinic Literature*. Cambridge: Harvard University Press, 1991.

Sternberg, Meir. *The Poetics of Biblical Narrative*. Bloomington: Indiana University Press, 1985.

Sticca, Sandro. "Christian Drama and Christian Liturgy." *Lat* 26 (1967) 1025–34.

Stone, Jerry H. "The Gospel of Mark and Oedipus the King: Two Tragic Visions." *Soundings* 67 (1984) 55–69.

Talbert, Charles H. *What is a Gospel? The Genre of the Canonical Gospels*. Philadelphia: Fortress, 1977.

Tarrant, R. J. *Seneca's Thyestes*. APATS 11. Atlanta: Scholars, 1985.

Taylor, Vincent. *The Gospel According to St. Mark*. 2nd ed. London: MacMillan, 1966.

Tennant, Frederick Robert. *Miracle and its Philosophical Presuppositions*. Cambridge: Cambridge University Press, 1925.

Thiselton, Anthony C. *Hermeneutics: An Introduction*. Grand Rapids: Eerdmans, 2009.

Tödt, H. E. *The Son of Man in the Synoptic Tradition*. Translated by Dorothea M. Barton. London: SCM, 1965.

Twelftree, Graham H. *Jesus The Miracle Worker: A Historical and Theological Study*. Downers Grove, IL: InterVarsity, 1999.

Van der Loos, Hendrik. *The Miracles of Jesus*. NovTSup 9. Leiden: Brill, 1965.

Vermes, Geza. "Ḥanina ben Dosa." In *Post-Biblical Jewish Studies*, edited by G. Vermes, 127–214. SJLA 8. Leiden: Brill, 1975.

———. *Jesus the Jew: A Historian's Reading of the Gospels*. London: Collins, 1973.

Vernant, Jean-Pierre. "The Masked Dionysus." In *Myth and Tragedy in Ancient Greece*, edited by Jean-Pierre Vernant and Pierre Vidal-Naquet, 381–412. New York: Zone, 1988.

Via, Dan O. *The Ethics of Mark's Gospel—In the Middle of Time*. Philadelphia: Fortress, 1985.

———. *Kerygma and Comedy in the New Testament*. Philadelphia: Fortress, 1975.

Wake, Peter. *Tragedy in Hegel's Early Theological Writings*. Bloomington: Indiana University Press, 2014.

Bibliography

Watling, E. F. *Seneca: Four Tragedies and Octavia*. Harmondsworth: Penguin, 1966.
Weeden, Theodore J. *Mark—Traditions in Conflict*. Philadelphia: Fortress, 1971.
Weiss, Bernhard. *Die Geschichtlichkeit des Markusevangeliums*. Berlin: Edwin Runge, 1905.
Weiss, Johannes. *Der älteste Evangelium*. Göttingen: Vandenhoeck & Ruprecht, 1903.
Wenham, David. *The Parables of Jesus*. Downers Grove, IL: InterVarsity, 1989.
Wire, Antoinette Clark. *The Case for Mark Composed in Performance*. Biblical Performance Criticism 3. Eugene, OR: Wipf & Stock, 2011.
Wrede, William. *Das Messiasgeheimnis in den Evangelien*. Göttingen: Vandenhoeck & Ruprecht, 1901.
Wright, N. T. *Jesus and the Victory of God*. London: SPCK, 2012.
———. *Mark for Everyone*. Louisville: Westminster John Knox Press, 2004.
Zerba, Michelle. *Tragedy and Theory: The Problem of Conflict since Aristotle*. Princeton Legacy Library. Princeton: Princeton University Press, 1988.

Index of Modern Authors

Achtemeier, P. J., 155
Adams, E., 186
Ahl, F., 37
Albertz, M., 166
Alexander, J. A., 142
Allison, D. C., 134
Aquinas, T., 152
Arnim, H. F. A. von, 59
Aune, D. E., 128, 130–32

Barth, F., 123
Bauckham, R., 192, 195
Beach, C., 12, 34, 35
Beasley-Murray, G. R., 86, 133
Beavis, M. A., 104, 146, 169, 171, 172, 176
Beck, R. R., 105
Bekker, I., 52
Best, E., 34
Betz, H. D., 93, 158
Bieber, M., 62
Bilezikian, G., 12, 16–22, 35, 40, 41, 140–43
Blackburn Sr., B. L., 166
Blevins, J. L., 123, 124
Bloomberg, C. L., 135, 138
Boring, E., 144
Bowie, E. L., 153
Boyle, A. J., 52–54, 58
Bradley, A. C., 65
Brant, J., 104, 149
Brink, C. O., 57
Broadhead, E. K., 77, 157, 158
Brontë, C., 1
Brown, C., 152

Bultmann, R., 153, 157, 182, 183
Burch, E. W., 12–16, 19, 32, 34
Burkill, T. A., 140, 155
Burridge, R., 3, 38

Cairns, D. S., 152
Calvin, J., 152
Campbell, J., 3, 5, 7
Caragounis, C. C., 189
Carpenter, J. E., 192
Cartledge, P., 115
Casey, M., 189, 190
Cherbonnier, E., 12, 25
Cole, R. A., 175
Collins, A. Y., 38, 144, 184–86, 196, 197, 199
Conybeare, F. C., 153
Conzelmann, H., 127, 128, 182, 183
Cook, M. J., 88
Crossan, J. D., 138

Danker, F. W., 34
Davies, W. D., 134
Dawson, A., 155
Dewey, J., 166
Dibelius, M., 153, 157, 166
Dodd, C. H., 134
Dostal, R. J., 71
Dostoyevsky, F., 1
Duff, J. W., 17
Dunn, J. D. G., 124, 128–32

Edwards, J. R., 155
Else, G., 64
English, D., 143

Index of Modern Authors

Episcopius, 192
Evans, C. A., 143, 145, 153, 161, 177, 189
Eve, E., 160, 163

Fieberg, P., 152
Fitzmyer, J., 185
Fowler, R. M., 129
France, R. T., 186
Freud, S., 1
Frickenschmidt, D., 3
Frye, N., 1, 72, 73
Funaioli, G., 55

Gadamer, H. G., 1, 70-72
Gaiser, F. J., 171
Gallagher, E. V., 158
Gellrich, M., 43-46, 63, 64, 66
Goethe, J. W., 1
Gowler, D., 134
Greenspan, D., 67, 68
Grondin, J., 70
Guelich, R. A., 169, 171, 175
Gundry, R. H., 164, 176
Guttmann, A., 152

Halliwell, S., 47
Hare, D. R. A., 144, 190
Harris, B. F., 153
Hay, L. S., 127, 128, 186
Hegel, G. W. F., 1, 27, 64-67, 74, 78-82, 86, 112, 120, 208
Heidegger, M., 1, 70
Hendrick, C. W., 36
Hendrikson, W., 169
Herzog, W. R., 136
Hiebert, D. E., 164
Hobbes, T., 11
Hoekstra, S., 192
Hofius, O., 167
Holladay, C. H., 158
Hooker, M., 135, 136, 138, 143, 173-75, 186-88, 193, 194, 200
Hunter, A., 152, 167
Hunter, R., 59, 60
Hurtado, L. W., 144, 165, 167, 170, 171, 175, 176, 190

Janko, R., 47
Jaspers, K., 25, 26
Jay, J., 12, 38-41
Jeremias, J., 134
Johansson, D., 167, 168
Jones, J., 64
Juel, D. H., 138
Jülicher, A., 134, 135
Jung, C., 1

Kallas, J., 152
Kaufmann, W., 69
Kee, H. C., 159, 160
Keener, C. S., 3
Keil, H., 51, 112
Kelly, H. A., 48-50, 56, 57, 60-63
Kennedy, G. A., 3
Kierkegaard, S., 1, 66-68
Kim, T. H., 145
Kingsbury, J. D., 158, 194
Kirchhevel, G. D., 186
Kistemaker, S., 138
Krook, D., 160

Lane, W. L., 164, 165, 171
Lang, F. G., 12, 35, 38
Lattimore, R., 90, 93, 95, 107, 108, 118-20
Lausberg, H., 35
Licona, M. R., 3
Lietzmann, H., 189
Lightfoot, R. H., 166
Linnemann, E., 138
Locke, J., 152
Lohse, E., 167
Lowrie, W., 68
Lucas, F. L., 17
Lukaszewski, A. A., 190

MacDonald, D. R., 146
Malbon, E. S., 194
Mann, C. S., 169
Manson, T. W., 192
Marcus, J., 135, 138
Marrou, H. I., 36
Marshall, D. G., 70
Marshall, I. H., 94, 177

Index of Modern Authors

Marxsen, W., 93, 157
McMahon, P. A., 45, 47, 48, 50–52, 55, 56, 62, 63
Menken, J. J. M., 177
Messel, N., 192
Michel, L., 22
Millar, A., 1
Moloney, F. J., 145, 169, 171, 176
Moser, T., 12
Murray, G. G., 18

Nabokov, V., 1
Nadich, J., 152
Nagy, G., 98–101, 105, 118
Neusner, J., 152
Nietzsche, F., 1, 27, 69, 70

Oates, W. J., 18, 22
O'Neill, E., 18, 22
Owen, P. I., 190

Paolucci, A., 64, 65
Parris, D., 135
Pelling, C., 115
Pentecost, J. D., 138
Perrin, N., 36, 92, 182, 184
Polhill, J. B., 158
Porter, S. E., 145, 173

Radford, R. T., 55
Räisänen, H., 123, 132, 133
Reitzenstein, R., 158
Réville, A., 192
Rhodes, D., 84
Ricoeur, P., 180
Robbins, V. K., 21, 93, 178
Robinson, J. M., 34, 86, 93
Rose, V., 47
Rosenmeyer, T. G., 116, 117
Ross, W. D., 47
Ruprecht, L. A., 27, 28, 29, 30
Russell, D. A., 59, 60, 118
Rutherford, R. B., 93

Safrai, S., 152
Sanday, W., 130, 192
Sandys, J. E., 45, 46, 50–52, 55, 57, 59, 60
Schanz, M., 55

Schmiedel, O., 123
Schwartz, E., 12, 25
Schweitzer, A., 123, 130, 136
Scourer, E., 123
Segal, C., 115
Selvidge, M. J., 171
Shakespeare, W., 1, 22
Shuler, P. L., 3
Sluser, D. M., 164, 165
Smith, M., 93
Smith, S. H., 12, 19, 30–38, 40, 41
Soden, H., 123
Sorrentino, P., 12, 26
Standaert, B., 12, 30–32, 35
Steele, G., 128
Stein, R. H., 134
Stendahl, B. K., 67
Stern, D., 135
Sternberg, M., 135
Sticca, S., 26, 27
Stone, J. H., 12, 22–26, 28

Talbert, C. H., 3
Tarrant, R. J., 37
Taylor, V., 126, 127, 166, 169, 176, 182, 183, 198, 199
Tennant, F. R., 152
Thiselton, A. C., 135
Tödt, H. E., 182
Tolstoy, L., 1
Twelftree, G. H., 154, 156

Van der Loos, H., 151–55
Vermes, G., 152, 169, 183
Vernant, J., 113–15
Via, D. O., 35, 37

Wake, P., 86
Watling, E. F., 37
Weeden, T. J., 136
Weiss, J., 93, 123
Wellhausen, J., 189
Wenham, D., 138
Wire, A. C., 138
Wrede, W., 122–27, 129–32, 146, 157, 194, 207, 209
Wright, N. T., 186

Zerba, M., 66

Index of Ancient Sources

OLD TESTAMENT

Genesis

1:28	199
20:17	167

Exodus

15:26	167
31:12–17	170
31:14	150, 170, 197, 198
34:5–7	167
34:7	167
35:2	170

Leviticus

14	164
14:2–32	164
14:8	164
15	171
15:26–27	171
15:29	171
15:30	171

Numbers

12	167
15:25	196
15:32–36	170
16:41–50	167
19:11–13	173

Deuteronomy

28:15	167
28:22	167
28:27–28	167
28:35	167
28:59–61	167
32:39	167

1 Samuel

2:25	196

2 Samuel

7:12–14	131
12:15	167
24:16	167

1 Kings

17:17–24	172

2 Kings

1:8	34
4:18–37	172
5	167
20:5	167

1 Chronicles

21:1	167

Index of Ancient Sources

2 Chronicles
16:12	167

Job
1:6–12	167
2:1–6	167

Psalms
2:7	34
6:2	167
8	186, 192
22	24
30:2	167
103:3	167
110:1	177
144:3	188

Isaiah
5:26–30	186
6:9–10	133, 134
19:22	167
29:13	89
30:26	167
35:5–6	175
43:25	167
44:22	167
52:7	131
52:13—53:12	186
53	184, 187
56:7	85

Jeremiah
7:11	85

Ezekiel
34:16	131

Daniel
7	180, 181, 186, 187, 189, 192
7:13	181, 183, 186, 190, 192

Zechariah
13	131

Malachi
4	187

APOCRYPHA

Sirach
38:1–15	160

Epistle of Jeremiah
6:37	160

PSEUDEPIGRAPHA

2 Baruch
73:2	160

1 Enoch
14	180
37–71	186
38:2	180
48:6–7	180
48:10	180

4 Ezra
6:55	198
13	186

Jubilees
2:31	198

NEW TESTAMENT

Matthew
8:20	189
8:28–34	142
9:18	172

Index of Ancient Sources

11:19	190
12:9–14	169
12:16	152
12:32	190
13:27	185
13:41	185
16:13	183–85
26:54	29
26:62	192
26:64	185

Mark

1–10	178
1–6	186
1–5	154
1	9, 121, 140
1:1—8:30	14
1:1—8:26	19, 33, 140
1:1—3:7a	157
1:1—3:6	35, 36
1:1–15	9
1:1–13	33, 35, 36, 40, 93
1:1	9, 10, 143, 149, 188, 194
1:2–8	34
1:7	94
1:11	9, 34, 83, 94, 109
1:12	173
1:13	34, 87
1:14	33, 36
1:15	9, 36, 77, 131
1:16—3:6	36
1:21–28	141–43
1:21	141
1:22	19, 88, 150
1:23–26	34
1:24	141
1:25–28	130
1:25	124
1:27–28	32
1:27	14, 19, 36
1:30–31	163
1:34	34, 124, 142, 156, 163
1:35	95
1:38	145
1:39	34, 164, 173
1:40–45	163, 172
1:40–41	152, 156
1:42	165
1:43–45	130
1:44	124, 153, 158, 164, 168, 174
1:45	95
2	150, 166
2:1–3:6	16, 165, 166, 169
2:1–12	163, 166, 197
2:1	164
2:5	88, 167
2:6–10	88
2:6	165
2:7	195, 196
2:10	181, 182, 185, 187–89, 192, 193, 195–97, 200
2:11	165
2:12	36, 149, 195
2:12b	14
2:16	88
2:18–22	139
2:18	33, 88
2:23–28	197
2:23–27	169
2:24	88, 198
2:26	199
2:27–28	186, 190
2:27	198, 199
2:28	181, 185, 187–89, 192, 193, 195, 197
3	150
3:1–6	89, 168
3:1–5	156, 163
3:2	88, 168, 169
3:4	89
3:5–6	89
3:5	165
3:6	31, 88, 89, 106, 150, 170, 183
3:7—8:26	35
3:7—6:6	157
3:11–12	142
3:11	34
3:12	124
3:13—6:6	36
3:15	34
3:20–30	137, 141
3:22–27	34
3:31–35	137
4:1–20	133
4:3	138

Mark (continued)

4:10	134
4:11–12	132, 133, 134
4:13–20	133
4:13	24, 198
4:14	137
4:20	137
4:21–23	139
4:21	198
4:22	139
4:40–41	136
4:40	24
4:41	14, 36
5–9	150
5:1–20	34, 142, 143
5:7	41, 142
5:13	142
5:15	40
5:21–43	172
5:24–34	170, 172
5:24	170
5:25–26	171
5:28	171
5:29	171
5:30–44	176
5:34	136
5:36	152
5:37	173
5:39–40	173
5:39	172
5:40	173
5:42	173
5:43	124, 173, 174
6:1–6	143, 156
6:6–13	104
6:6b—8:27a	157
6:7–13	36
6:10	198
6:12–13	25
6:13	34, 158
6:14—8:26	36
6:14–29	33
6:37	136
6:49–52	136
7	167
7:1–20	175
7:1–7	89
7:1	88
7:5	88
7:9	198
7:10–11	89
7:14–16	175
7:17–18	175
7:18–23	89
7:18	136
7:24–30	34
7:29	136
7:31–37	172, 174
7:33	172, 175
7:36–37	103
7:36	124, 130, 172, 174, 175
7:37	14, 36
8–14	186
8:4	136
8:14–21	136, 176
8:22—10:52	144
8:22–26	32, 143, 172, 175
8:23	172
8:26	124, 172, 174
8:27—10:52	34, 35, 157
8:27—10:45	144
8:27–33	176
8:27–31	40
8:27–30	14, 19, 21, 30, 32, 36, 37, 144
8:27–28	32
8:27	183
8:28	33
8:29	103, 176, 195, 196
8:30	124, 144
8:31—16:8	14, 19, 33, 140
8:31—10:45	36
8:31–33	34
8:31	14, 20, 23, 24, 33, 103–5, 108, 109, 144, 181, 193, 200
8:32–34	136
8:33	87, 103
8:34–38	104
8:38	181, 186–88, 193, 202, 203
9:1	198
9:5–7	14
9:7	34, 109
9:9	20, 122, 124, 181, 193, 202, 203
9:11–13	33, 34, 190
9:12	105, 181, 184, 193, 200, 201
9:14–29	34, 143

Index of Ancient Sources

9:24	136, 143	13:5–36	87
9:25	143	13:5–6	87
9:31	20, 105, 181, 193, 202, 203	13:9	87
9:32–34	136	13:10	87
9:38–39	34	13:12	108
9:38	177	13:14	108
10:13–16	136	13:19	108
10:32	136	13:24–27	186
10:33–34	105	13:26–27	108
10:33	181, 193, 200	13:26	181, 184, 188, 193, 202, 203
10:34	20	14	27
10:35–41	136	14:1—16:8	35, 157
10:35–36	25	14:1	36
10:37	104	14:2	36, 106
10:42	178	14:3—15:47	36
10:43	178	14:3–9	136
10:44	178	14:21	105, 181, 184, 188, 190, 193, 200, 201
10:45	108, 181, 188, 190, 193, 200, 202	14:28	20
10:46–52	36, 177	14:32–42	136
10:47–48	152, 177	14:36	23, 95, 105, 109
10:48	136	14:41	181, 184, 188, 193, 200
10:51	177	14:47	136
10:52	177	14:49	106
11	85, 150	14:50	136
11:1—13:37	35, 157	14:61	143, 183, 188, 192
11:1—12:44	36	14:62	104, 181, 184–86, 193, 202–4
11:2	178	14:63	188, 191
11:11	85, 106, 177	14:64	204
11:15–19	20	14:66–72	104, 136
11:15–18	106	15:2	20
11:18	20, 85, 106	15:9	20
11:27–33	16, 20, 34	15:12	20
11:27	106	15:18	20
12:1–12	20	15:26	20
12:12	106	15:29	145
12:13–40	16	15:32	20, 143
12:13	20, 106	15:34	23
12:18–27	20	15:37–38	84
12:18	106	15:37	145
12:28	106	15:38	137, 145, 203
12:35	106, 177	15:39	20, 41, 136, 144, 146
12:38–40	177	15:43	141
12:40	178	16:1–8	34, 36
13	86, 108	16:5–7	34
13:1	36, 87	16:6	35
13:2	36, 87	16:7	105
13:3–37	36		

Mark (continued)

16:8	203

Luke

6:6–11	169
7:34	190
8:26–34	142
8:49–50	172
12:10	190
18:8b	185
22:48	185
22:67–68	192
22:69	185
24:7	185

Acts

2:22	149
5:1–11	167
12:21–23	167

Romans

1:4	131

1 Corinthians

11:29–30	167

2 Corinthians

12:7–8	167

Hebrews

2:6	188

DEAD SEA SCROLLS

1QS

11	180
20	180

1QapGen

13	180
21	180

11QtgJob

9	180
26	180

RABBINIC WRITINGS

m. Šabb.

18	169

m. Yoma

8:6	169

Mek. Šabb.

to Exod 31:14	198

GRECO-ROMAN WRITINGS

Aelius Donatus

De. Com.

6.1	54

Aeschylus

Ag.

176–83	95

Choe.

33	164–263

Seven

43	116
71	116
170	116
644	117

Index of Ancient Sources

Aristotle

Poet.

1382a 21–25	119
1385b 12–16	119
1448b	4
1447a 14–19	48
1448a 1–20	48
1449b	81
1449b–1450a	19
1449b 23–28	4, 46
1449b 27–28	48
1450a 6.9–14.	18
1450b 7.26.	31
1452a 10–11	21
1452a 22–23	119
1452a 29–32	118
1452b 11.1	32
1452b 12.14–20	33
1453b 26–43	49
1454b–c	118
1459b 3–5	49
1459b 6–8	49
6.6	14
8	15

Cicero

Brut.

2.1.69–75	53
60	55

Div.

2.28	151

Fin.

1	50
2	50
6	50

Diodorus

Bib. hist.

4.26.1	100

Diogenes Laertius

Lives

5	50
36	50

Diomedes of Halicarnassus

Ars. Gramm.

3	54
427	60
465	60
483–84	60

Comp.

16	50

Dem.

3	50

GL

1.489	54

Isocr.

5	50

Lys.

14	50

Donatus

Comm. Ter.

1.5	62
4.2	62

Euripides

Bacc.

1–6	9
449	115
496–506	162

Index of Ancient Sources

Bacc. (continued)

500	114
596–603	162
672–774	162
924	114

Homer

Il.

218–28	99
410–16	98

Horace

Ars.

180–82	54
285–8	54

Livy

29.20.11	54

Ovid

Am.

3.1.39–42	57

Med.

2.553–54	57

Trist.

2.381	57

Philo

Legat.

148	145
149	145

Flacc.

74	145

Plato

Gorg.

502b	43

Leg.

7.816b–817	43, 45
48a	45

Phileb.

104–5	43

Resp.

394a–395	44
435c–442d	44
606b	45
606e	43

Pliny the Younger

Ep.

7.17	37

Plutarch

Alex.

1.2	10

Caes.

3.1–4	7, 8

Mor.

14–37	60

Thes.

1.3	8, 9

Index of Ancient Sources

Quintilian

Inst.

x.1	55

Seneca the Younger

Ep.

24.25	59

Sophocles

Ant.

2.278	14
1348–53	90

Oed. tyr.

31–39	91
41	91
43–44	91
46	91
1223–1530	33

Suetonius

Dom.

7	37

Gram.

1.2	52

Tactitus

Dial.

2.1–3.3	37

Virgil

Aeneid

6.791–793	145

Volcacius Sedigitus

Gellius

15.24	53

Xenophon of Ephesus

Eph.

3.1–3	39

EARLY CHRISTIAN WRITINGS

Augustine

Civ.

vi.2	55

Jerome

Jov.

1.47	50

Origen

Cels.

2.52	152

www.ingramcontent.com/pod-product-compliance
Lightning Source LLC
Chambersburg PA
CBHW051055230426
43667CB00013B/2303